Reservation Representation and Social Justice

Reservation Representation and Social Justice

Prof. Naidu Ashok
&
Dr. Rajesh Kota

KALPAZ

ISBN: 9789353242763

First Published, 2020

Published by

Kalpaz Publications
C-30, Satyawati Nagar,
Delhi – 110052
Ph.: 011-47034999, 9811692060
www.kalpazpublications.com
E-mail: kalpaz@hotmail.com

Printed at: G. Print Process, Delhi

Contents

Foreword ... 7
Preface ... 11
Acknowledgements ... 13
List of contributers ... 15

1. Nationalism of Social Justice and the Reservations ... 17
   — *Inukonda Thirumali*
2. Revisiting Reservation Policy in India ... 31
   — *Prof. K. Nageshwar*
3. Philosophy of Reservation and Public Opinion in Contemporary India ... 43
   — *Narender Kumar*
4. The Republic of Reservations and the Roster Struggle ... 53
   — *N. Sukumar*
5. Reservation and Social Justice: Historical Perspective ... 65
   — *Prof. Adapa Satyanarayana*
6. Trends in Reservation Policy of India: An Analysis from Social Justice to Economic Justice ... 81
   — *Dr. E. Venkatesu*
7. History of Reservations Policy in India: An Overview ... 95
   — *Dr. Panthukala Srinivas, Dr. Sareen Chatla*
8. Religion, Representation and the Politics of Reservation: Critical Reflections ... 109
   — *Prashant Kumar Kain*
9. A Case of MRPS Movement in Andhra Pradesh and Telangana ... 135
   — *Dr. Chandraiah Gopani*
10. Secularism in India and Dalits ... 153
   — *Dr. B. Balaswamy & Dr. K. Rajesh*

11. Nomadic, Semi-Nomadic and Denotified Tribe Reservations in Telangana State: Prospects and Possibilities 163
— Dr. Bheenaveni Ram Shepherd

12. Affirmative Action: Reservations and Quotas in India: Other Backward Classes (OBCs) 179
— Dr. Chalamalla Venkateshwarlu

13. Governmentality towards the Implementation of the Reservations the Dynamics of Caste & Politics in Indian Democracy: A Reference to OBCs in Telangana 193
— Dr. Y. Prabhanjan Kumar Yadav

14. Right to Equality in India: Relevance of Reservations in Favour of Backward Classes 203
— Dr. Someshwar Bonakurthy

15. Theme: Introductions 10% Reservation for Ews 215
— Dr. Elisha Kolluri

16. Representation of Muslim Women in Urban Local Politics: A study of Greater Hyderabad Municipal Corporation................. 231
— Dr. Pallavi Kabde

17. Historical specificities of Reservation and 'Social Justice': A Hermeneutic Reading. 237
— Reshma R.N

18. Reservations in India: Mapping the Caste, Class Debates 261
Prof. Naidu Ashok & Dr. Rajesh Kota

Index 273

Foreword

For a complex and critical understanding of India, we need to grapple with the historical specificity of Indian society which is the caste system. Its centrality is visible in the social totality that includes the economic, social, and cultural dimensions. This generalization has to be appreciated in the context of continuously evolving social reality of India.

The process of development and modernity, India has witnessed since the colonial period and vigorously after independence must be a critical reference point to understand the changing character of caste in its internality and in relation to the other aspects of society. One of the most visible shifts in caste system being initiated during the colonial period and got increasing pursued and hastened after Independence is the disruption in the caste – occupation nexus. This has not led to any effect on the rituality of caste – in fact we see an even enhanced ritual aspect of caste. It is a case of heightened caste *sans* economic standing.

With the decline of caste occupations as a result of the political economy of modernity we see the economic marginalization, displacement and exclusion in a concrete substantive way of large productive communities of society. Its rapidity and expanse in the post-Independence period has pushed large sections of the occupational artisan, service and labouring castes into the informal unorganized sectors thereby into a state of uncertainty, insecurity and marginality.

Paradoxically, modernity has also aroused interest among the subaltern castes towards the opportunities visible in the modern structures of state, market and related institutions. It is in the processes and resultant anxieties associated with this transition to modernity we need to locate the importance of the policy of reservations.

Thus we need to ask: what have these marginalized communities got in return for their marginalization in the process of modernization? One visible policy initiative that promised to accommodate the otherwise displaced and marginalized is reservations. It is a different question whether is it in any way compensation proximate to the quantum of loss. The reservations in India have been in three sectors of education, employment and politics.

The history of reservations in India can be divided into three phases: (1) Pre-Independence period; (2) post-independence period; and (3) Post-Liberalization period. This broad periodisation both captures the complexity and nuances in the history of reservations.

Reservation issue has to be appreciated in the context of the politics of electoral democracy in India. Given the compulsions of electoral democracy no political party can afford to displease the electoral constituencies that matter in arithmetic terms. Thus reservations continue to enjoy vocal support of political parties cutting across the ideological spectrum.

In the history of any nation it is instructive to undertake a periodic review of its progress in terms of direction, pace and path. It is the prime responsibility of social scientists – historians, political scientists, economists and sociologists – to critically assess, examine and update the registers of social and political progress - movement of society on the path of progress– aspectually and comprehensively.

The reservation issue deserves such a critical review. It has seen hiccups, controversies, charges of impropriety, misuse and inadequacies and lackadaisical even disinterested implementation. Reservation being an important question has seen complex discursive provenance – apart from the political one, the judicial discourse evaluating its constitutionality has been a fairly detailed. This goes to highlight the centrality of it to post-independent India's political life.

As a criterion of evaluation it may be instructive to distinguish between reservation as policy and reservation as ideology. In other words, on which side of social policy auditing reservations have weighed –as an effective policy instrument or to service the political purpose of the regimes in power? An evaluation on this axis would be instructive to appreciate the continual relevance even feasibility or otherwise of it.

With the Indian economy taking a neo-liberal policy turn since the early 1990s vowing less government and promising market privatization, there arises a serious question on the relevance and fate of reservations as a positive policy measure in the changing context. This as we know has given rise to the demand for reservations in the ever expanding private sector. This paved the way for a debate on the rationality, logistics and feasibility apart from the desirability of reservations in a market economy that is supposed to privilege merit, strive for efficiency and generate profit.

Thus the context is set for the renewal of old polarities, stereotypes in new forms suitable and appealing to the neo-liberal context.

The present volume *Reservations, Representation and Social Justice,* which is an outcome of a seminar conducted in the century old Osmania University, Hyderabad assumes importance as it is an important step in the direction of a collective collaborative reflection on both the history and contemporaneity, the constitutional-legal and political, the promise and practice, policy and implementation of the reservations in India. The volume comprising of papers by scholars young and eminent would be appreciated for the detail and comprehensiveness at stock-taking, diagnosis and prognosis of India's journey on the path of democracy and attempt at the creation of a just society.

Prof. K Srinivasulu
(Retired Professor, Department of Political Science)
Former Dean, Faculty of Social Sciences, O.U
Senior Fellow at ICSSR

Preface

The reservation in India is often a debatable issue, not only in legislations but also in academics and public sphere. Reservations were originally perceived as a national campaign of establishing social equalities by correcting past wrongs as part of affirmative action. They are aimed to facilitate the educational and economic upliftment among the pitiful and socially discarded sections living in miserable conditions throughout the history. Of late, this feeling of harnessing the society gradually believed sabotaging with a penchant and nefarious suspicion that is working against the interests of majority upper castes. New and old points of debate emerged against the policy such as merit basis, basis of considering reservation, creamy-layer reservation in private sector, and reservations for economic weaker sections. There are lot of misunderstandings prevailing on these terms such that, reservations are anti-meritorious, reservations are hogged away by creamy-layer of the reserved categories, reservation in private sector means dooming of private sector and so on. In this tone and lines, a plethora of arguments commonly advocated are presented with intrinsic realities, that are pro or against the continuation of reservations, and are discussed elaborately in this project.

Reservation Policy has been discussed with its judicial articulation and emerging trends. This book extensively covers the philosophical foundations of the reservations and examines the transformation in the idea of reservations. It also observed that, how reservation policy has been discussed with its judicial articulation and emerging trends, more particularly, it assumes that the 10% quota for the Economically Weaker Sections (EWS) completely overturns the original logic of the reservations.

We hope, this book will bring some clarity and order on this issue to help not only students and academicians in sustaining interest in contentious issues but also policy makers in developing an appropriate policy for safeguarding the reservations in India. The findings of this volume will raise and bring forth divergent questions as to the relevance and possible impact of the proposed policy.

This book is the culmination of seminar presentations containing 18 research papers, which covered majorly reservations and legal perspectives, trajectory and philosophical background of the reservations, reservations and religion, roster system and contemporary movements at the university level, Mandal movement and OBC reservations, caste and class perspectives of the reservations, reservations and paradigm shifts and so forth.

Acknowledgements

This book is manifestation of seminar presentations, which was organised by the Dean, Faculty of Social Sciences, Osmania University, Hyderabad, and sponsored by ICSSR-SRC and Telangana State Council of Higher Education, Government of Telangana State. The seminar was on "Reservations, Representation and Social Justice" heldin April, 2019. We owe a lot to the sponsor institutions for having supported to conduct the seminar of contemporary relevance.

Our heartfelt thanks to all the paper contributors; despite of taking time, we have received potential papers from them. No doubt that each paper is unique in its own way and offer new insights to deliberate the theme and relevance of reservations in India in order to attain the dream of social justice in long-run. Our sincere thanks to Prof. K. Srinivasulu, former Dean, Faculty of Social Science, Osmania University, Hyderabad for having accepted to write a foreword for this book.

Finally, we extent our thanks to Amit Garg of Gyan Publications, New Delhi for considering these scripts for publication.

List of contributers

Sl. No.	*Name of the contributor*	*Paper titled*
1.	**Prof. Inukonda Thirumali** Historian, Teaches at Sri Venkateswara College, University of Delhi Mail Id: ithirumali@yahoo.co.in Contact No:9391386814	Nationalism of Social Justice and the Reservations
2.	**Prof. K. Nagewshar** Department of Mass and Communications Osmania University, Hyderabad- Email.Idprof.knageshwar@gmail.com Contact No:9618068910	Revisiting Reservation Policy In India
3.	**Prof. Narender Kumar** Professor at Centre for Political Studies, School of Social Science, Jawaharlal Nehru University, New Delhi. Mail Id:kumarr.narender@gmail.com Contact No: 9810114467	Philosophy of Reservation and Public Opinion in Contemporary India
4.	**Prof. N. Sukumar** Faculty in school of Political science, Delhi University. Mail Id: skn70@yahoo.com Contact No: 7032165860	The Republic of Reservations and the Roster Struggle
5.	**Prof. Adapa Satyanarayana** Department of History, Osmania University, Hyderabad Mail Id: adapa_satyam@yahoo.com Contact No: 9573405551	Reservation and social justice: A historical Perspective
6.	**Dr. E. Venkatesu** Department of Political Science, Hyderabad Central University, Hyderabad Mail Id: evs103@gmail.com Contact No: 9441482535	Trends in Reservation Policy in India: Analysis from Social Justice to Economic Justice
7.	**Dr. Panthukala Srinivas & Dr. Sareen Chatla** Department of Cultural Studies, English and Foreign Language University (EFLU), Hyderabad. Mail.Id:seenanna@gmail.com Contact No. 8332951975	History of Reservations Policy in India: An Overview
8.	**Dr. Prashant Kumar Kain** Department of Cultural Studies, English and Foreign Language University (EFLU), Hyderabad Mail.Id:prashant.kain@gmail.com Contact No: 7416257562	Religion, Representation and the politics of Reservation: Critical Reflection

9.	**Dr. Chandraiah Gopani** Assistant Professor, G.B Pant Social Science Institute, Allahabad Central University Mail.Id:gchandraiah2007@gmail.com Contact No: 9956377352	Struggles for Sub-Categorization of Scheduled Castes (SC) Reservations: A Case of MRPS Movement in Andhra Pradesh and Telangana
10.	**Dr. B. Balaswamy** Department of Mass communication, Osmania University, Hyderabad. & **Dr. K. Rajesh,** Guest faculty, department of political science, Osmania University, Hyderabad, Mail Id: baalaswamy@gmail.com Contact No: 9849578445	Secularism in India and Dalits
11.	**Dr. Bheenaveni Ram Shepherd** Assistant Professor, Department of Sociology, Osmania University, Hyderabad, Mail Id: bheenaveni@gmail.com Contact No: 9492574081	Nomadic, Semi-Nomadic and Denitrified Tribes Reservations in Telangana State: Prospects and Possibilities
12.	**Dr. Chalamalla Venkateshwarlu** Assistant Professor, Dept. of Political Science, Osmania University, Hyderabad Mail.Id:chalamallavenkateshwarlu@gmail.com Contact No: 9346311388	Affirmative Action: Reservations and Quotas In India: Other Backward Classes (OBCs)
13.	**Dr. Y. Prabhanjan Kumar Yadav** Asst. Professor Dept. of Mass Communication Telangana University Nizamabad, Telangana State Mail.Id:prof.prabhanjan.yadav@gmail.com Contact No: 9394243344	Governmentality towards the Implementation of the Reservations The Dynamics of Caste & Politics in Indian Democracy: A Reference to OBCs in Telangana
14.	**Dr. Someshwar Bonakurthy** Guest Faculty, Department of Sociology Osmania University, Mail.Id:ousomeshwar@gmail.com Contact No: 9293762498	Right to Equality in India: Relevance of Reservations in Favour of Backward Classes
15.	**Dr. Elisha Kolluri** Senior Faculty, N.S.R College of Education V.V. Campus, Jambagh, Hyderabad Mial.Id:elishakolluri.hyd@gmail.com Contact No:	Introduction of 10% Reservation for EWS
16.	**Dr. Pallavi Kabde** Head, Dept of Public Administration Dr. B.R. Ambedkar Open University, Hyderabad Mail Id: pallavikabde@gmail.com Contact No: 7093320885	Representation of Muslim Women in Urban Local Politics: A study of Greater Hyderabad Municipal Corporation
17.	**Reshma R.N** Ph.D Scholar, University of Hyderabad, Department of Political Science, School of Social Science. Mail.Id: rnreshmarn@gmail.com	Historical specificities of Reservation and 'Social Justice': A Hermeneutic Reading.
18.	**Prof. Naidu Ashok** Dean faculty of Social Sciences, Osmania University, Hyderabad, Mail.Id:naiduashok88@gmail.com Contact No: 9441059440 **Dr. Rajesh Kota** Department of Political Science, Osmania University, Hyderabad, Mail.Id:rajeshkotaou@gmail.com Contact No: 9666345099	Reservations In India: Caste, Class perspectives

Chapter - 1

Nationalism of Social Justice and the Reservations

—*Inukonda Thirumali*[1]

Abstract

This article demonstrates that the social justice emanated from the last stage of the nationalist movement. The lower classes therefore gained provisions for reservations in jobs and legislatures. Reservations and notion of social justice were thus part of nationalism. To make India a nation the nationalist movement had to recognize the existences of different social groups with varied social status and their sectional needs and rights. Their wellbeing, respective rights and upping on par with others was thus became central objective of the constitution.

Introduction

The constitution out of this fortitude emerges as an historical agreement for eradication of untouchability, and to give them their due share in services and legislatures. It agrees to continue the British implemented reservations to the "tribes" of the excluded, partially excluded areas. The constitutional document also agrees, in principle, to give modern education to regain their place in the society for the Other Backward Classes, an omnibus legal category. This composite category was created by the Independent India to do away the "communal representations". The "minorities" rights were made legal, but women issue was decided to resolve within the family fold without specific guarantees other than the fundamental rights. Therefore the constitution was not simply "a lawyer's document, for the lawyers, by the lawyers"[2]. The above constitutional propositions constitute itself into a philosophical vision of equity and equality of opportunities to different strata. Further it was declared that "we the people of India" supposedly entire nation had agreed to give equal opportunities to all. Nandalal Bose, well known painter of the time, had drawn the paintings expressing the spirit of the nationhood from the history of common heritage on the original constitution[3].

The Background

On the eve of Independence various social perceptive movements had arisen and asserted their social existences and political interests. And such political expressions took organizational forms to effectively place their case before the British rulers independent of the Congress. The Congress' general notion of representing every ones needs linking to freedom struggle was challenged and the Congress as movement of undifferentiated "Indians" was in defense before the colonial rulers[4]. With the rise of such political challenges from below the Congress had exhausted its multi-community Indian representative character became one among the representative parties[5]. Religious nationalism also on the other hand challenged the Congress leadership. The Congress was however a major force but transformed as centrist political structure between the religio-political parties and the social justice forces[6]. The British was well aware of diversity within Indian society and nationalism and rise of diverse movements. Therefore when transfer of power was decided the SCs and STs were still in the constitutional frame of 1935 Act arguing for their place in the Constituent Assembly and the forth coming Constitution.

Dr. B.R. Ambedkar at this juncture came to centre stage as representative of cultural diversity and social heterogeneity and political polarity. The Hindu Mahasabha, Muslim League and non-Brahmin politicians started mediation with him. Dr. Ambedkar used the opportunity to promote more caste's rights and talking about India as amalgam of castes. Thus reservation as mode of participation in services and political representation for various communities has come before the nation. It was agreed that through the reservations only India would become an inclusive and integrative country thus a nation. Entire political leadership of the country came to agreement that all castes and communities particularly Scheduled Castes and Scheduled Tribes shall continue to get equal partnership in running the country as provided in 1935 act. The Constituent Assembly thus became the arena of ideological and political discourse to make India a democracy. Democracy means at this hour was an inclusiveness of alienated social groups into the constitutional frames and politics[7]. The Constitution thus becomes the agreement of the people for upgrading the lower castes on par with others.

Social Justice Turn 1942-1944

There was a turn towards new political aspirations during the last few years of the British rule. It could be called an undercurrent of nationalism from below from the beginning of the 20th century wherein the lower class organizations became parallel to the Congress. Mahars of Maharashtra, Nadars of Tamilnadu, Ezhavas of Kerala and Namasudras of Bengal started organizing as groups parallel to the Congress nationalism. All of them have shown a symbolism of unity in forming Depressed Class forum at Bombay in November 1917 under Justice Sir Narayana Ganesh Chandavarkar. A conference was held in 1918 in Baroda inviting many more. After withdrawal of Non-Cooperation Movement different political streams came open against the Congress nationalism in all parts of the country. Bihar's Goalas and Jats around Delhi and non-Brahmins in South India and Western India emerged a new nationalist trend. The self-respect movement of Ramaswamy Naikar in Tamil Country and Non-Brahmin party of Bhaskar Rao Jadav in Maharastra is well known in the new trend. In this backdrop All India Depressed Class Leaders' Conference was held in 1926 at Nagpore. That was a turning point in the lower class nationalism.

In 1928 Dr. Ambedkar became its President. Ambedkar gave a clear all India parallel political stances to this movement in 1930 at Nagpore. He set a new agenda (construed to be anti-Congress agenda) arguing for separate electorate for the Depressed Classes before the Simon Commission. It has become a national debate and set the agenda of nationalism for empowerment of the DCs.

The Hindu Mahasabha worried that the untouchables may go away from the Hindu fold. Therefore at the behest of Hindu Mahasabha leader B.S. Munje made friendly association with Gandhian outcast leaders. In February 1932 what is known as [M.C.] Rajah-[B.S.] Munje Pact was signed in support of the joint electorate with Hindus. And finally on the pressures of British functionaries including the then Viceroy, Ambedkar signed the Poona Pact with Gandhi in 1932. The Depressed Class issue thus became part of the national agenda and nation's concern. The Depressed Classes became part of nationalist politics. The Congress started therefore to encourage such DC factions within the party. All India Depressed Class League was also formed in 1935 Jagjivan Ram as leader under protégé of Rajendra Prasad. Congress has accepted this political trend from below thus had floated Harijan Sevak Sangh. The DC leaders' agenda came to prominence on the national political agenda. Many more such organizations came into being in different parts of the country in Punjab and Bengal.

The temple entry movements were undertaken and further visiting the untouchable's residential quarters to attract them to their political line of thinking began after Congress Governments were sworn in 1937 in most of the provinces. National politics, in this scenario, was not meant just the independence from the British but integration of the lower orders of the society into nationalist politics.

The Congress Provincial Governments of 1937 disappointed the peasants, DCs and Muslims by not taking up their sectional issues. All the Premiers were Brahmins but Gandhians and earned the name as rightists within the Congress. There was demand for land reform by the peasant organization but the Congress Governments did not bother. Cow protection entered into their agenda causing communal rift in the provinces. Eradication of untouchability and temple entry movement was on the agenda even that was not taken up seriously[8]. The possible character of the congress rule in Independent India was anticipated by the Muslim League and the Scheduled castes.

Ambedkar, in this new spirit started a new party All India Scheduled Caste Federation in 1942. M.C. Rajah who was very close to Gandhi disappointed with the Congress Governments joined the Federation. Same time Ambedkar started a fierce campaign against Gandhi and the Congress and published his attacks as a book *What Congress and Gandhi Have Done to the Untouchables* in 1945[9]. Thus the Scheduled Caste's movement turned the situation in its favour. Sarat Chandra Bose brother of Subhas Chandra Bose made the scheduled caste group known as Calcutta Schedule Caste League to associate with the Congress. When Stafford Cripps mission came to India they invited Ambedkar and Rajah to represent their view on Swaraj along with the Muslim League and Congress. It indicates that the caste question assumed importance thus Ambedkar has become national leader with issue of the Depressed Class/Scheduled Caste. Ambedkar was considered to be a leader of national stature. Ambedkar became the sole representative of Scheduled Castes, and that has become an issue on par with Muslim question. The British Government and its officials had recognized Ambedkar as legitimate representative of the SCs and caste question in India.

In Special Scheduled Caste Political Conference held in Allahabad in December 1942 Ambedkar declared that India was not a nation but constellation of nations warning the British and Congress that the Scheduled Caste would have their specific identity. After Gandhi's stand that "Harijan salvation" lay in their religious integration into Hindu society. The Punjab Depressed League and Punjab Balmiki Depressed Classes League brought in new dimension that the scheduled castes are part of the Hindu society in terms of religion and culture. There was a movement in the country to own Haijans part of the Hindus. Then Dr. Ambedkar, keeping this dimension in view, emphasized that Harijans were a "religious minority". His aim was to put them in parallel to Muslims or Sikhs. Ambedkar thus learnt to communicate with the top dominant nationalist leadership of the country without sacrificing his intended politics.

In this debate in 1943 the Secretary of State for India opined that Ambedkar emerged a national leader and said Ambedkar was "the right and only proper representative of the Depressed Classes". In November 1944 a Non-Party Conference was held under Tej Bahdur Sapru to discuss the basis of future constitution of India. It had invited Ambedkar to send a representative to be on the sub-committee on par with other parties. Ambedkar further put before the Government that Scheduled Castes constituted to have been about 6 to 7% of the whole population of India and they shall have a seat in Central Assembly, a representative in the Indian Civil Service, reservation of 8.5 percent in Central Services and so on. Thus he worked out a strategy of bargain for the Scheduled Castes in political representation and Government service proportionate to their population.

Further in May 1945 Ambedkar came to the dominant nationalist stance saying that Constitution should be "framed by Indians for Indians with voluntary consent of Indians". At the same time he declared that "The Scheduled Castes stand for the freedom of India and not for the Congress-High class Hindu rule". At the same time he categorized the people into "servile classes" and "governing classes"[10]. That means he divided people into social justice forces and the other Indians. He stepped up his battle opening channels with mainstream nationalist politics and emerging only sole leader with powerful backing of various social identities and groups. Independence has become an immediate issue and nation was in mood to attain independence. Dr. Ambedkar too was interacting with the British and national leaders. The social justice and Ambedkar's AISCF suffered a debacle in 1946 elections. He was however recognized as "the only Scheduled Caste man of outstanding ability". Even in this scenario political parties like Muslim League, Hindu Mahasabha had opened dialogue with him. This political turn had impacted the Constitution making.

The Constitution Making

The British rulers under these circumstances agreed to constitute a Constituent Assembly. Elections have come to elect members to CA through indirect elections with limited franchise. The CA was constituted in July 1946 with 296 members from all provinces. The Congress won 208 of 296 allotted to the provinces. Earlier in Provincial elections in December 1945 Congress became victorious. Out of 1, 585 seats in all provincial legislatures congress won 925 seats i.e. about 58 percent of seats capturing about 85 percent of the seats in non-Muslim seats. The Congress in this background clearly expressed its intention to behave like "mirror of the nation" in Nehru's words. Within the Congress the luminaries Jawaharlal Nehru, Sardar Patel, Rajendra Prasad, and Moulana Abdul Kalam Azad emerged prominent leaders of Constitution making. They included Alladi Kuppu Swamy Iyyar, N. Gopalaswamy Iyyengar and B. R. Ambedkar as experts on legal issues. Ambedkar had many advantages he was historian, economist and expert of law and constitutions of prominent countries, apart from this he emerged a social justice ideologue and politician with stature on par with top Congress luminaries. And above all he brought in the social justice turn in to the nationalism. The caste issues that was growing along with the mainstream nationalism but Ambedkar made it part of nationalism. Thus he becomes a most suitable person to head the drafting committee. Therefore the constitution has to focus on social reform and renascence[11]. Dr. Ambedkar was needed despite lost the election, but entered the CA from Bengal and later from Bombay.

The Constituent Assembly, thus was constituted, agreed that it had two objectives first was to attain independence and freedom. The second was social revolution i.e. freedom from all sorts of oppressions. S. Radhakrishnan proposed 3rd objective socio-economic revolution a transition from primitive rural economy to scientific and planned agriculture and industry. This has done away the Sriman Narayana Agarwal's village based Gandhian constitution. Rural handicrafts and peasant economy based economic planning village based election to State legislature and Parliament were discussed but the C.A members agreed upon only modern industry based economy and British type of party based elections parliamentary system[12].

On the whole social justice agenda was accepted by the members. After constituting CA Jawaharlal Nehru moved Objectives Resolution setting nation's agenda for social justice. He stated that primarily objective was - social justice to emancipate the DCs economically and politically. Root cause of this was in Objectives Resolution it was product of 1940s turn in people's movement it was a new dimension of nationalism.

Objectives Resolution: Objectives resolution was the basis to specify the basic character of the constitution. On the basis of discussions Nehru came to the decision about the needs of various existential groups to make India a nation[13].

> Wherein shall be guaranteed and secured to all the people of India justice, social, economic and political; equality of status, of opportunity, and before the law, freedom of thought, expression, belief, faith, worship, vocation, association and action, subject to law and public morality; and wherein adequate safeguards shall be provided for minorities, backward and tribal areas, depressed and other backward classes.

The nationalism turned towards social justice and constitution's basic concern thus becomes justice to all meant equality particularly of the below with others. Equality i.e. caste equality in Indian context became foremost issue before the nation[14]. In the Constitution, thus 1st Part is territory, 2nd part the citizenship. And in 3rd part of the Constitution Fundamental Rights. All these issues definitely sound European notions raised in French revolution. Thus articles 14 talks about Equality before Law, the 15 proposes the Prohibition of discrimination on grounds of religion, race, caste, sex or place of birth. And article 16 enunciates equality of opportunity in matters of public employment article 17 abolished untouchability and 18 abolished titles also. But to some extent equality, prohibition on grounds of religion and caste etc., equality of opportunity and abolition of untouchability brought the issues to Indian reality. That is how the constitution makers with such philosophical considerations and political understanding gave importance to equality and abolition of the practices that would perpetuate the caste. This was what the basic spirit of the constitution designed for India.

However the Depressed Classes became Scheduled Castes in 1935 itself. For the Scheduled Castes about 151 seats were reserved in 1935 elections. Scheduled Tribes issues were basically British proposed "tribes" in excluded or partially excluded areas. The CA accepted as they were in colonial regime. Political reservations apart from reservations in services were continuation of the colonial legacy but a revolutionary measure was they acquired specific right to enter into civil service, legislatures and cabinet also.

The articles 14 to 16 proposed equality, prohibition of discrimination and equality of opportunity. Under article 17, untouchability was abolished. But it does not mean every single communities needs would be met separately. The constitution felt that "It is a society based on hierarchy, caste inequality, and blatant discrimination, equality of opportunity such as existed in Britain and the United States would not be enough to provide the measures to provide the means for enhancing the well-being of the poor". The scholar felt "Instead special measures would be required, such as reservations of places in representative institutions, government agencies, and public institutions for backward and disadvantaged classes and groups"[15].

The Criminal tribes were identified and listed, for example did not come under the constitutional purview or any provisions of article per se. The article 240 was formulated for some left out communities was vague that entangled in the legal and judicial disputes. Some others were suffering "community ostracism, wandering, begging, witchcraft and prostitution endemic characteristics of nomadic tribes shall had been included. They were living in about as "127 groups aggregating 22.268 lakhs in 1949 and 24.64 lakhs in 1951" living outside the civilization. There are a large number of small communities who eke out a precarious existence in the country side. They have no fixed place of residence and they move from place to place in search of food or employment. They often rear pigs and poultry, hunt old animals to satisfy their hunger and collect forest produce to make a living. They live in thatched sheds or gunny tents, and move in groups. They believe in witchcraft. Because of the insecurity of their life, some of these communities are given to crime"[16]. Justice Venkatachaliah commission said in 2002 that "The denotified tribes/communities have been wrongly stigmatized as crime prone and subjected to high handed treatment as well as exploitation by the representatives of law and order as well as by the general society"[17]. On the whole 116 identified criminal tribes living in about 50 settlements known as "open prisons" confined to fenced camps guarded by armed police used to construct, roads, railways and dams never have come to the notice of constitution makers. Therefore about 350 such tribes were to be forsaken into OBC category to come under constitutional frame to receive certain benefits. They did not get any constitutional remedies as specified under articles 32-35, or enjoyed cultural rights under 29-31. The constitution was drafted under influence of Western political thoughts and democratic rights did not come closure to existential reality of India and grassroots living patterns.

Fundamental rights therefore are more oriented towards the untouchables, which was practiced in and around the caste based village structures. Untouchabilty brought bad name to the nationalists, and Ambedkar also made it a political issue. Therefore nationalist intelligentsia adopted the constitution exclusively to eradicate the untouchability and related issues like bonded labour.

Here is the foundation for Indian democracy. For centuries the communities kept aside from the civilized social classes have been legally and constitutionally integrated into social mainstream with special provisions to empower them too through reservations in services as well as in legislative bodies. Some were brought under the provisions of the constitution for educating them. In the words of Kaka Kalelkar with regards to the nomadic tribes "may be distributed in small groups in towns and villages where they come into contact with other people, and get an opportunity for turning a new leaf. This would help in their eventual assimilation in society"[18]. After discussion in the Assembly the experts thus visualized making India a democracy in evolutionary and graded fashion in future.

A nation is emerging as a composition of various existential and interest groups and communities whose rights, security and dignified survival with co-existing with other was the foundation of Indian democracy. It is historical form of government that exists with active support of all living social groups. Their well being, security, work opportunities historically transferred to the State. The State was supposedly made representatives of all people.

Govind Vallabh Panth was however critical of the recognition of the communities as that would cause "the unwholesome, and to some extent a degrading habit of thinking always in terms of communities and never in terms of citizens. But it is, after all citizens that form communities and the individual as such is essentially the core of all mechanisms and means and devices that are adopted for securing progress and advancement. It is the welfare and happiness of the individual citizen which is the object of every sound administrator and statesman"[19].

Yet the communal (social) constituencies created for various social segments were foregone in the 1935 Act. New reservation policy of reserved constituencies for SCs and STs were agreed upon. The non-reserved category voters shall vote the reserved category candidates. This transition to joint electorate did not help, and Dr. Ambedkar himself lost elections. Election based on majority principle would happen in such way for the dominant political players. Reservation had become a technical and nominal that did not produce genuine representatives. The constitution makers thus had done away with communal constituencies. If the communal constitutions continued the peasants, artisans, service castes, nomads, traders, intellectuals would have representations to raise their issues form their sectional point of view.

Indian democracy thus conceived had historical limitations. The territorial constituencies were a shot in the arm for socially dominant that strengthened their social hegemony for furthering the political power during 1937 itself, and even in 1946 that made the constitution. And already Indian nationalism was of Brahminical in core but transformed to some extent on the eve of transfer of power to superior castes' polity. Caste entered into politics that means into the parties dominated the territorial constituencies. Thus caste entered into parities and politics through backdoor in their place in first general election itself in 1952. Caste becomes essential part of politics and parties. The social groups based on profession, the profession based on caste was the existential reality of India ultimately rendered in to passive voters but not sovereigns as expected. The concept of nation had become an impossible desire because of social hegemony and political power. History, the culture of inequality, conventional caste traditions and dominant practices determined the Indian ideologies and politics. This is specific to India. Dr. Ambedkar therefore says in 1949 adopting the constitution, "In politics we will have equality and in social and economic life we will have inequality. In politics we will be recognizing the principle of one man one value. In our social and economic life, we shall, by reason of our social and economic structure, continue to deny the principle of one man one value"[20].

The social domination transformed into political domination through the election in 1937 and 1946. The new power had become absolute itself marginalizing the colonial power. There was no universal franchise but reserved constituencies, the rich voters hegemonised the power. The quantum of power passed into the Indian legislatures passed into the hands our hegemonic castes. The elections held in 1952, more in 1957 under universal franchise the lower communities from below were barred to cast vote. They were subjected to social boycott denying the work. They were denied the services like taking water from common water source; deny grazing rights to their cattle and so on. The India democracy was born in this manner. The national power was created, exercised by only hegemonic but the rights were granted as charity. That was what the nationalism and democracy historically resulted into.

Many life sustaining issues like property right, elimination of poverty, compulsory education, health and equal rights over resources were only listed in Directive Principles of State Policy. They were only ultimate objectives of the state not immediate objectives. They were necessitated to list for the closure integrations with the dominant. The constitution would be implemented by those which have to attain equality.

Conclusion: India, on the basis of constitution, agreed to be a nation of communities and castes. Their representatives elected through limited franchise and indirect election to Constituent Assembly made the constitution in most democratic and amicable fashion. Different social groups depending up on their social standing certain articles are framed. The representatives declared the constitution on behalf of the people. The CA identified the underprivileged social classes and made provisions for their advancement through education. The Constitution also agreed the existence of multiple religious faiths and ways of living with equal right to faiths and worship. The members of CA did not give due consideration to gender rights, family agreed to be the basic cultural norm and women will have their rights within the family. Her property inheritance rights were subject of tradition and family culture. The members declared private property was sacrosanct. Rights on land were respected but to protect peasant rights they agreed to introduce land reform. India would become sovereign democratic republic headed by President who would be indirectly elected. The Government is a parliamentary form the members are directly elected and responsible to the people. Election of representatives was to be done through territorial constituencies that were formed for the advantage of upper caste and patriarchy. The objectives of reservations and social justice were thus not fully met. May be seen the Supreme Court judgment on 10th May 2019 grasped the spirit of the constitution: Reservations are not exception to the rule of equality of opportunity. They are rather the true fulfillment of effective and substantive equality by accounting for the structured conditions into which people are born. Establishing the position of the SCs and STs are worthy participants in the affairs of governance is intrinsic to an equal citizenship[21]

References

B. Shiva Rao (ed) *The Framing of India's Constitution*, Select Documents, Universal Law Publishing House, New Delhi, 2012 (reprint)

B. Shiva Rao ,Ambekar's speech (ed)to CA on 25 1949.

Case in point was II Roundtable Conference in 1932.

Cf. Sudipta Kaviraj, "A critique of the Passive Revolution" in Partha Chatterjee (ed) *State and Politics in India* OUP., 2011.

Constitution of India preserved in Parliament House reprinted under the authority of Government of India, Ministry of Culture, New Delhi 2010.

Dr. Babasaheb Ambedkar Writings and Speeches, Vol.5, Education Department of Government of Maharashtra, Bombay 1990.

Durga Das Basu, *Introduction to the Constitution of India,* Prentice-Hall of India, New Delhi, 1995.

Granville Austin, *The Indian Constitution: Cornerstone of a Nation,* Oxford, New Delhi 2012 (fp 1966.

Justice D.Y.Chandrachud, Supreme Court Judge on 10 May on Karnataka Reservation in Promotion.

Kaka Kalelkar, Report on the Backward Class, paragraph. 135, 2008, (Ministry of Social Justice & Empowerment, Government of India) *Report of the Backward Classes Commission*, Vol. 1.

M.C. Rajah Papers, Pamphlets. No. 2. Nehru Memorial Museum and Library, New Delhi.

M.C. Rajah, *Divide and Quit: An Eyewitness Account of the Partition of India*, in Partition Omnibus, Oxford University Press, New Delhi 2011.

Paul R. Brass, *The Politics of India since Independence*, Foundation Books, 1997 (FP. Cambridge University Press Reprint 1990, New Delhi.

Sekhar Bandyopadhyaya, "Transfer of Power and the Crisis of Dalit Politics in India, 1945-47", *Modern Asian Studies,* 34.4.2000.

S.N.Vohra & Sabysachi Bhattachary (ed.) *Looking Back: India in the Twentieth Century*, National Book Trust in association with India International Center, New Delhi 2002.

The Sapru Committee, Constitutional Proposals of 1945, Appendix. IX.

Notes

1. Historian, taught at Sri Venkateswara College, University of Delhi, presently lives in Hyderabad.
2. Cf. Sudipta Kaviraj, "A critique of the Passive Revolution" in Partha Chatterjee (ed) *State and Politics in India* OUP., 2011 (fp.1(97. p. 50; L.M. Singhvi says it "is a legal, political and cultural document" in S.N. Vohra & Sabysachi Bhattachary (ed.) *Looking Back: India in the Twentieth Century*, National Book Trust in association with India International Center, New Delhi 2002. p. 16.
3. Constitution of India preserved in Parliament House reprinted under the authority of Government of India, Ministry of Culture, New Delhi 2010.
4. Case in point was II Roundtable Conference in 1932.
5. May be seen the various offers, plans proposed by the British to bring about unity within warring groups, Part 1 of *The Documents of India's Constitution: Select Documents*, (ed.) by B. Shiva Rao, Universal Law Publishing House, New Delhi, 2012 (FP 1996.
6. The Communists emerged into a massive political movement but did not aspire to come center stage rather challenged every one thus in rural and in certain working class areas despite strong but no specific role in the transfer of power. But the social justice dimension of politics from below was ignored by the historians.
7. Democracy meant later elections, political assertions and formation of governments etc.
8. M.C. Rajah, ".... the Congress party men in Madras representing the Caste Hindus deviated from the [Poona] Pact...our community in the Legislative Assembly have to follow the caste Hindus blindly...." In a letter to Gandhi dated August 25, 1938, Gandhi's reply 1 Oct, 1938, M.C. Rajah Papers, Pamphlets. No. 2. Nehru Memorial Museum and Library, New Delhi. Penderel Moon, as Chief Secretary of Punjab explored that performance of the Congress Governments was a factor for communal turn in 1940s. See his *Divide and Quit:*

An Eyewitness Account of the Partition of India, in Partition Omnibus, Oxford University Press, New Delhi 2011.

9. *Dr. Babasaheb Ambedkar Writings and Speeches*, Vol. 5, Education Department of Government of Maharashtra, Bombay 1990.
10. Sekhar Bandyopadhyaya, "Transfer of Power and the Crisis of Dalit Politics in India, 1945-47", *Modern Asian Studies,* 34.4.2000, pp. 893-942.
11. The social background of the most influential members of the drafting committee, CA was like this: 9. Brahmins, 7 High Caste Hindus, 2 Muslims, 1 Christian and 1 Scheduled caste person. Granville Austin, *The Indian Constitution: Cornerstone of a Nation,* Oxford, New Delhi 2012 (fp 1966) p. 24.
12. B. Shiva Rao (ed.), Op. Cit.
13. Ibid; Durga Das Basu, *Introduction to the Constitution of India,* Prentice-Hall of India, New Delhi, 1995, p. 20.
14. Constitutional Proposals of The Sapru Committee, 1945, Appendix. IX.
15. Paul R. Brass, *The Politics of India since Independence*, Foundation Books, 1997 (FP. Cambridge University Press Reprint 1990, New Delhi, p. 3.
16. Kaka Kalelkar, Report on the Backward Class, paragraph 135. Quoted in Balkrishna Renake, Report of National Commission for Denotified, Nomadic and Semi-Nomadic Tribes, 2008, (Ministry of Social Justice & Empowerment, Government of India), p. 4.
17. Quoted in Report of The National Commission for Denotified, Nomadic and Semi-Nomadic Tribes, 2008, p. 6.
18. *Report of the Backward Classes Commission*, Vol. 1. p. 36.
19. B. Shiva Rao et.el. (ed) *The Framing of India's Constitution*, Select Documents, Universal Law Publishing House, New Delhi, 2012 (reprint), VII, 63.
20. Ambekar's speech to CA on 25 1949, B. Shiva Rao (ed.) op.cit., p. 944.
21. Justice D.Y. Chandrachud, Supreme Court Judge on 10 May on Karnataka Reservation in Promotion.

Chapter - 2

Revisiting Reservation Policy in India

— Prof. K. Nageshwar

Abstract

Reservations as a policy of affirmative action is perhaps the most politically controversial, socially polarising aspect of constitutional scheme and public policy measure in contemporary Indian political history. At a time when scars of historical injustice still haunt our society, inequalities galore, deprivation and skill deficit is rampant and opportunities are skewed, the reservations however, controversial still remains the relevant theme . However, much water has flown since the adoption of the policy and therefore as assessment of the same is of a paramount importance.

Indian jurisprudence gives as an exciting reading of the judicial discourse that has gone into the theme in question. Certain aspects can be delineated for the purpose of arriving at clarity on reservations and social justice.

1. *Does modern India still need reservations? Does the right to affirmative action go contrary to the principle of equality enshrined in the constitution?*
2. *What should be the basis for extending these positive discriminations? Does the caste outlive its utility as the basis for reservation or still it holds relevant.*
3. *How should we balance between the competing constitutional provisions and objectives? Should this act of balancing need to impose a quantitative limit on the extent of quotas? Are there any exceptions to this?*
4. *Should the policy on reservations remain static even after seven decades of its implementation? If not, what changes are needed to realise that its core objectives are effectively fulfilled.*

Introduction

Constitution, reservations and Economic Criteria

The law enacting the reservations for economically weaker sections has to pass the judicial test.

The constitutional amendment faces three specific judicial vulnerabilities.

Firstly, the Apex court in Indira Sawhney case said, solely the economic criteria does not fit into the 'doctrine of reasonable' classification for providing reservations. The Supreme Court in this historical verdict considered as the Magna Carta of the reservations jurisprudence clearly stated in Para 689 ,"... any reservation or affirmative action on economic criteria or wealth discrimination cannot be upheld under doctrine of reasonable classification. Reservation for backward class seeks to achieve the social purpose of sharing in services which had been monopolised by few of the forward classes. To bridge the gap, thus, created the affirmative action's have been upheld as the social and educational difference between the two classes furnished reasonable basis for classification. Same cannot be said for rich and poor. A classification based on economic conditions for purposes of Article 16(1) would be violative of equality doctrine". Thus the apex court has drawn a clear distinction between social and economic backwardness. Thus, the reading of Indian jurisprudence gives an impression that the highest court of the land has been stating that economic backwardness can be a ground for exclusion, but not for inclusion as far as affirmative action like reservations is concerned.

Secondly, the apex court in the same verdict observed that reservations being an extreme form of protective affirmative action, should be within the minority and quotas in any manner should be within fifty percent. This principle of balancing equality has been upheld in several of the judgments during the course of five decades of India's jurisprudence. The Supreme Court in Indira Sawhney said that the principle of balancing equality ordains reservation, of any manner, not to exceed 50%. Still it is being argued that the 50 percent limit enforced by the apex court is valid only to caste based reservations. The Supreme Court in MR Balaji, Indira Sawhney, Ram Singh etc., has been stating that the 50 percent limit is not a quantitative restriction but integral to the concept of right to equality which again form the basic structure of the constitution. Even the Parliament cannot amend the basic structure as per the Kesavananda Bharati case.

Thirdly, the reservations under article 16(4) of the constitution should qualify the test of not 'adequately represented'.

The exercise of power to reserve is coupled with duty to determine backward class of citizens and if they were adequately represented. If the Government failed to discharge its duty then the exercise of power stands vitiated. This is what the Supreme Court stated in the Indira Sawhney case

(Para 695). Thus it is a constitutional obligation on the part of the State to first ascertain that a group of people in this case what the new law calls economically weaker sections are not adequately represented in educational and employment before reserving 10 percent seats.

Economic criteria for quotas: Implementation challenges

The Centre's decision to introduce ten percent reservation for economically backward sections of society is fraught with several implementation challenges too, which may lead to its misuse and abuse.

Income limit for availing the quota would be around Rs eight lakh per year. A family with a monthly income of Rs 65,000 to Rs 70,000 cannot be construed as poor and economically weak by Indian standards.

Considering that over 90 percent of the Indian economy is informal and unorganised, an income-based reservation policy is highly vulnerable to gross misuse, at the cost of those who are actually marginalised.

Barring salaried people in the government and corporate sector, the rich and upper middle-class sections of society can easily appropriate these quotas, given the corrupt nature of the Indian public administration that has to certify incomes.

Besides, several sectors of the economy, such as agriculture and business ventures, do not yield stable incomes. The incomes of these families tend to be volatile. A person may be classified as "poor" in one year and may avail the benefit of the quota, and may be classified as "not poor" in the following years. While incomes may change from year to year, the educational and employment benefits that a person receives due to such a classification are of a permanent nature.

Caste and Reservation: Constitutional Perspective

Reservations for any community cannot be accorded at the sweet will of any particular government. Nor it can be done due to political pressure by any politically organised community.

The judiciary has struck down the decision taken by the UPA government on extending reservations to Jats in nine States.

Courts have set aside many administrative decisions made in ignorance of relevant material, or is based upon patently irrelevant material or for that matter is made mala fide. The assessment of a statutory Backward Classes Commission can constitute relevant material.

In Ram Singh vs. Union of India popularly called Jats reservations case, the apex court said, "Though caste may be a prominent and distinguishing factor for easy determination of backwardness of a social group, this Court has been routinely discouraging the identification of a group as backward solely on the basis of caste.

Article 16(4) as also Article 15(4) lays the foundation for affirmative action by the State to reach out to the most deserving. Social groups who would be most deserving must necessarily be a matter of continuous evolution. New practices, methods and yardsticks have to be continuously evolved moving away from caste-centric definition of backwardness."

The affirmative action for weaker sections in the form of reservations is for backward classes but not backward castes. The constitution deliberately uses class in the relevant provisions quoted above.

In M R Balaji vs. State of Mysore in 1963, the Supreme Court held that a purely caste-based policy of reservations would violate the Constitution.

While this blanket position was undermined in NM Thomas and Indra Sawhney, the position remains that while castes, which are generally "socially and occupationally homogenous classes" (Indra Sawhney, para 84), can constitute a convenient starting point for a reservations, the ultimate criterion is class backwardness.

This means that caste groupings do not exhaust the scope of reservations under the constitutional scheme; and conversely, to the extent that a caste wishes to claim the benefits of the reservation scheme, it must demonstrate that qua class, it suffers from the social backwardness that Article 16 envisages.

The Supreme Court in Ramsingh case further said, "An affirmative action policy that keeps in mind only historical injustice would certainly result in under-protection of the most deserving backward class of citizens, which is constitutionally mandate."

In National Legal Services Authority vs. Union of India, the apex court observed, "New practices, methods and yardsticks have to be continuously evolved moving away from caste-centric definition of backwardness. This alone can enable recognition of newly emerging groups in society which would require palliative action..."

The Apex Court in Ram Singh case further stated,"[the] inclusion of the politically organized classes (such as Jats) in the list of backward classes mainly, if not solely, on the basis that on same parameters other groups who have fared better have been so included cannot be affirmed."

The judiciary seems to be holding the view that politically powerful castes can leverage upon their political clout and might appropriate affirmative action like reservations. If so, the courts would obviously step in as the judiciary in a constitutional democracy is endowed with the responsibility of preventing brute majoritarianism taking the political process hostage to the detriment of discrete and insular minorities.

Stating that backwardness is a manifestation caused by the presence of several independent circumstances which may be social, cultural, economic, educational or even political, Supreme Court in the Ram Singh case said, "The perception of a self-proclaimed socially backward class of citizens or even the perception of the "advanced classes" as to the social status of the "less fortunate's" cannot continue to be a constitutionally permissible yardstick for determination of backwardness, both in the context of Articles 15(4) and 16(4) of the Constitution.

Neither can any longer backwardness be a matter of determination on the basis of mathematical formulae evolved by taking into account social, economic and educational indicators. Determination of backwardness must also cease to be relative; possible wrong inclusions cannot be the basis for further inclusions but the gates would be opened only to permit entry of the most distressed. Any other inclusion would be a serious abdication of the constitutional duty of the State."

The Constitution and Reservations: The fifty percent limit

The judiciary interpreted that the Constitution stipulates that reservations should not exceed 50 per cent.

The rationale for imposing 50 per cent rule is based on the relationship between affirmative action in the form of protective discrimination and the equality provisions of Indian Constitution. Vinay Sitapati in the section on reservation in The Oxford Handbook of The Indian Constitution (edited by Sujit Choudhary et al, 2016) terms this as one of balance between competing Constitutional principles of formal equality, social justice and efficiency.

Article 16(4) permits reservations as being an exception to the Constitutional principle of right to equality enshrined in Article 16(1). Since the exception cannot be greater than the rule, the reservations cannot exceed 50 per cent. H M Seervai in Constitutional Law of India (vol 1, Universal Book Traders) and Anirudh Prasad in Reservation Policy and Practice in

India: A Means to an End (South Asia Books) describe this as Ambedkar constitutional vision.

Constitution enunciates a right to equality. It is the cornerstone of Indian Constitution. Article 16(4) calling for reservations is in fact a continuation of Article 16(1) that guarantees equality. The logic behind Article 16(4) is that unequals cannot be treated equally and, therefore, deserve affirmative action in favour of them. Therefore, it is wrong to read the reservations provisions of the Constitution as independent of or superior to equality provisions. Thus reservations provisions cannot limit the equality provisions, but can only be an extension of it.

In a majority judgement, the Supreme Court in the famous Indra Sawhney Case articulated that balancing various provisions of the Constitution meant that total quotas could not cross 50 per cent in any given year.

The apex court limits reservations to 50 per cent through Indra Sawhney Case verdict. But, Tamil Nadu has 69 per cent reservations. The Indra Sawhney Case posed a threat to the Tamil Nadu reservation formula. To protect these reservations, Parliament placed Tamil Nadu quota legislation in the Ninth Schedule of the Constitution. Laws placed in the Ninth Schedule were considered to be immune from judicial review till the later day Constitutional interpretation by the Supreme Court.

However, a recent verdict by the apex court held that even the laws in the Ninth Schedule are subject to judicial review if they violate the basic structure of the Constitution.

The Constitutional principles of equality, social justice and efficiency in public administration should be balanced. The Constitution clearly articulates equality. The provisions related to reservations are aimed at promoting social justice without detriment to the concept of equality.

Article 335 of the Constitution balances its vision of social justice in the form of reservations with the objective of maintaining efficiency of public administration. The limit of 50 per cent on the total reservations is placed to ensure this balance between what seems to be mutually contradictory yet complementary Constitutional provisions.

Article 335 states: "The claims of the members of the Scheduled Castes and the Scheduled Tribes shall be taken into consideration, consistently with the maintenance of efficiency of administration, in the making of appointments to services and posts in connection with the affairs of the Union or of a State."

Any form of protective discrimination in the form of reservations may promote social justice but would have an adverse impact on merit and efficiency which is also a Constitutional vision. Therefore, it is imperative to ensure that one Constitutional provision does not dominate the other.

Reservations cannot be opposed on the ground of merit or efficiency as Constitution itself allows such positive discrimination in favour of unequals. However, it is equally erroneous to frame a policy of affirmative action through protective discrimination completely undermining the principles of merit and efficiency. Thus, the 50 per cent limit is socially justified and constitutionally valid.

Caste and class overlap in India to a significant extent. The marginalised castes are marginalised classes. Reservations address the caste-based inequalities. Yet, caste and class are not synonymous. There are other forms of inequalities too. For instance, there are economically backward sections among upper castes even as compared to some of the marginalised caste families.

While accepting the greater similarity between caste and class to justify the reservations despite Constitutional vision of equality, the exception to the principle of caste-class similarity cannot also be ignored that too after the seven decades of social and economic development and decades of implementation of reservations.

Reservations policy fails to address other forms of inequalities that transcend caste. Therefore, limiting reservations to 50 per cent would prevent further accentuation of other forms of inequalities that transcend caste.

The Articles 15(4) and 16(4) of the Constitution that enable the state to provide reservations for certain classes are special provisions as enunciated in the said articles itself. In M R Balaji verdict, the Constitutional bench of the Supreme Court held that special provision must be within reasonable limits.

A special provision is not a provision which is exhaustive in character, so that in looking after the advancement of those classes, the state would be justified in ignoring altogether the advancement of the rest of the society. It is because the interests of the society at large would be served by promoting the advancement of the weaker elements in the society.

If a provision which is in the nature of an exception completely excludes the rest of the society that clearly is outside the scope of such a provision of the Constitution, it would be extremely unreasonable to assume that in enacting Articles the Parliament intended to provide that where the advancement of the Backward Classes or the Scheduled Castes and Tribes was concerned, the fundamental rights of the citizens constituting the rest of the society were to be completely and absolutely ignored. A Special provision must be within reasonable limits. The interests of weaker sections of society which are a first charge on the state and the Center have to be adjusted with the interests of the community as a whole. Special provision should be less than 50per cent.

The apex court in Indra Sawhney case stated that the special provisions contemplating reservations only "speaks of adequate representation and not proportionate representation." The court further observed: "Adequate representation cannot be read as proportionate representation."

The Indra Sawhney Judgment held that the provision conceived in the interest of certain sections of society should be balanced against the guarantee of equality which is a guarantee held out to every citizen and to the entire society. It is relevant to point out that Dr Ambedkar himself contemplated reservation being "confined to a minority of seats." No other member of the Constituent Assembly suggested otherwise. It is thus clear that reservation of a majority of seats was never envisaged by the founding fathers.

The implementation of reservations in India is beset with many inadequacies and anomalies. Despite judiciary pronouncing creamy layer to exclude the forward among the backward from the purview of reservations, the policy is hardly implemented given the character of Indian economy and society. Political populism and compulsions of electoral democracy make it almost impossible to review the policy of reservation for a possible exclusion of any caste.

The manner in which the policy of reservations was actually executed makes the balancing act much more essential. However, there can be exceptions to this rule of 50 per cent limit. The apex court in Indra Sawhney case itself appreciated such extraordinary circumstances that make limit unwarranted.

The court said, "While 50 per cent shall be the rule, it is necessary not to put out of consideration certain extraordinary situations inherent in the great diversity of this country and the people. It might happen that in far-flung and remote areas the population inhabiting those areas might, on account of their being out of the main stream of national life and in view of conditions peculiar to and characteristical to them, need to be treated in a different way, some relaxation in this strict rule may become imperative. In doing so, extreme caution is to be exercised and a special case made out."

Reservation and sub-classification/sub-categorisation

The process of development or implementation of reservations effected class formation within a class, thus creating an impermeable membrane to block the percolation of benefits of reservations to the most deprived.

The Article 16(4) of the Constitution says, "Nothing in this article shall prevent the State from making any provision for the reservation of appointments or posts in favour of any Backward Class of citizens which, in the opinion of the State, is not adequately represented in the services under the State." It is beyond controversy in Indian jurisprudence that Scheduled Castes and Scheduled Tribes are also included in the expression "Backward Class of citizens".

This reveals that the constitutional scheme of reservations as a positive discrimination mechanism is based on the philosophy of providing equal justice by correcting the imbalances in education and employment. Therefore, if a section of a class enjoys disproportionate benefits to the detriment of the others, sub-categorisation of the class is justified in accordance with the spirit of the constitution itself.

Such a sub-categorisation does not take away the benefit of reservations from anyone by sub-grouping. The categorisation is not an act of exclusion through application of creamy layer. Instead, it is only sought to be a remedy to deprivation of reservation for one group as the other disproportionately enjoys. Allotting a separate percentage of reservation for a subgroup from amongst the total reservation allotted to that group does not amount to depriving one class of the benefits of reservations.

The judicial objection to sub-categorisation of SCs can be on the ground that Scheduled castes are homogeneous and should be considered as a class in themselves for the Constitutional scheme of reservations.

But Justice VR Krishna Iyer said in State of Kerala vs N M Thomas, that a plain reading of Articles 341 and 342 of the Constitution (provisions related to SC and ST reservations) brings out the quintessential concept that they (Scheduled Castes and Scheduled Tribes) are an amalgam of castes, races, groups, tribes, communities thereof found on investigation to be the lowliest and in need of massive State aid and notified as such by the President.

The reservation policy cannot be oblivious to the difference in degree of backwardness within a class of citizens as the philosophy of affirmative action is aimed at uplifting the most depressed and the most deprived. Therefore, having found a class of persons within the OBCs or SCs OR STs as having been deprived of such benefits the State has the exclusive legislative power to make such grouping for reservation under Articles 15(4) and 16(4) of the Constitution.

If a scientific study of social and economic conditions and the pattern of reservations empirically establishes that some particular groups within a group have cornered all the benefits at the cost of others in the said List, with a view to see that the benefit of reservation percolates to the weaker of the weakest it is necessary to enact sub-categorisation.

Further, sub-classification of the reserved classes is permissible in view of the judgment of the Supreme Court in the case of Indra Sawhney v. Union of India and Ors. 1992.

The Apex court in Indra Sawhney said," We are of the opinion that there is no constitutional or legal bar to a State categorising the Backward Classes as backward and more backward..."

If all of them are grouped together and reservation provided, the inevitably result would be that the less backward would take away all the reserved posts leaving none for more backward.

In Indra Sawhney, the court further observed "if the connecting link is the social backwardness, it should broadly be the same in a given class. If some of the members are far too advanced socially (which in the context, necessarily means economically and, may also mean, educationally) the connecting thread between them and the remaining class snaps. They would be misfits in the class.

Alter excluding them alone, would the class be a compact class. In fact, such exclusion benefits the truly backward. Difficulty, however, really lies in drawing the line - how and where to draw the line? For, while drawing the line, it should be ensured that it does not result in taking away with one hand what is given by the other. The basis of exclusion should not merely be economic, unless, of course, the economic advancement is so high that it necessarily means social advancement".

Chinnappa Reddy, J. in Vasant Kumar, said: "We do not see why on principle there cannot be a classification into Backward Classes and More Backward Classes, if both classes are not merely a little behind, but far behind the most advanced classes. In fact, such a classification would be necessary to help the more backward classes; otherwise those of the Backward Classes who might be a little more advanced than the more backward classes might walk away with all the seats".

In the state of Jammu and Kashmir v. Triloki Nath Khosa and Ors., Supreme Court held, "Classification, however, is fraught with the danger that it may produce artificial inequalities and therefore, the right to classify is hedged in with salient restraints; or else, the guarantee of equality will be submerged in class legislation masquerading as laws meant to govern well marked classes characterised by different and distinct attainments. Classification, therefore, must be truly founded on substantial differences which distinguish persons grouped together from those left out of the group and such differential attributes must bear a just and rational relation to the object sought to be achieved".

References

Ambedkar, B.R.: States and Minorities in B.R. Ambedkar: Writings and Speeches, Bombay: Maharashtra Government: Volume 1, 1947.

Ambedkar, S.N.: Reservation Policy, Issues and Implementation, A.B.D., Publishers, Jaipur, India, 1st ed. 2008.

Bains, Ravinder Singh: Reservation Policy and Anti-Reservationists, New Delhi, 1994.

Bakshi, P.M.: The Constitution of India; Universal Law Publication Co. Pvt. Ltd., 2004.

Bakshi, R.K.: Dalit Movement Role of Dr. B.R. Ambedkar, Adhyan Publishers, New Delhi, 2010. Barker, Earnest: Principles of Social and Political Theory (London: 1967).

Chatterjee, Sarajit Kumar: The Scheduled Castes in India, Vol. 4, Gyan Publishing House, Delhi, 1996. Desai, I.P.: Caste, Caste-Conflict and Reservation, Ajanta Publications, Delhi, 1985.

Devi, Savita: Dr. B.R. Ambedkar Massiah of the Dalits, Krantikal Prakashan on behalf of A.D.P. College, Publication Cell, Nagaon, 2011.

Dhavan, Rajeev: The Supreme Court of India: A Socio-Legal Critique of its Juristic Techniques, N.M. Tripathi, Bombay, 1975.

Galanter Marc: Competing Equalities; Law and the Backward Classes in India, New Delhi, Oxford University Press, 1984.

Gandhi, Mohandas K.: Collected Works of Mahatma Gandhi, Vol. 40, New Delhi, Publication Division, Government of India, 1968.

Ghurye, G.S., Caste and Class in India, Popular Book Depot, Bombay, 1957. Ghurye: Caste and Race in India, Bombay Popular Prakashan, 1979.

Goldman: Justice and Reverse Discrimination (Princeton University Press), 1979

Hasan, Zoya: Politics of Inclusion, Cases, Minorities, and Affirmative Action, 1st published 2009, Oxford University, New Delhi.

Iyer, Krishna, V.R.: Dr. Ambedkar and the Dalit Future, published in 2010, B.R. Publishing Corporations, Delhi.

Kothari, C.R.: Research Methodology Methods and Techniques, 2nd Ed. 2003, Wishwa Prakashan, New Delhi.

Maheshwari, S.R.: The Mandal Commission and Mandalisation, New Delhi: Concept, 1991.

Mathew, Thomas: Caste and Class, Dynamics-Radical Ambedkarite Praxis, New Delhi, 1992.

Mathur, Gautam: The Rectification of Positive Discrimination, Institute of Applied Manpower Research, New Delhi, 1982.

M.N. Sreenivas (ed): Caste: Its Twentieth Century Avatar, New Delhi, Viking, 1996.

Sharma, Arvind: Reservation and Affirmative Action, Modes of Social Integration in India and the United States, 1st published in 2005, Sage Publications India Pvt. Ltd., New Delhi.

Thorat, Sukhadeo, Aryama Negi, Prashant: Reservation and Private Sector, Published in 2005 (I.I.D.S., New Delhi), Rawat Publications, Jaipur.

Chapter - 3

Philosophy of Reservation and Public Opinion in Contemporary India

— *Narender Kumar*[1]

Abstract

The idea of Reservation remains contested. The contestation comes from different quarters. Even those who are the beneficiaries of the policy sometimes become critical and those supposedly victims are seen to favour the idea. This paper tries to look at the philosophy behind the conception of Reservation by discussing about the origin, evolution and the objectives of the idea. And then looks at the public opinion on Reservation especially from those who have been considered the victims of the caste system in Indian society namely the Scheduled Castes and Other Backward Classes. The case of Scheduled Tribes is limitation of the study due to they not being the beneficiaries on account of consideration of caste. The philosophy part of the paper is based on the secondary literature and the public opinion part is based on a survey that was conducted in five different major cities and their surrounding rural areas for another study[2]*. The paper argues that the philosophy of Reservation is rooted in addressing the inequality among the social groups but the beneficiaries remain apparently the individuals or families showing some kind of contradiction in the philosophy and the outcome of the idea. Secondly, it argues that based on the quantitative data collected, it cannot be concluded that only the beneficiaries remain the supporters of reservation and the victims oppose it revealing further the complexity of the issue.*

Introduction

Evolution of Reservation Policy

The reservation policy primarily evolved as a form of representation to those who either had no representation or insufficient representation in the public institutions. For the first time it was Princely State of Mysore during 1874-1885 that 20 percent middle and lower range jobs in Police department were reserved for Brahmins and rest of the all for Muslims, Hindus and Indian Christians (Thimmaiah1997:108). It is interesting to note that one of the communitiesi.e. Brahmins who areconsidered to be most opposed to reservations is primarily responsible for the origination of the policy. This is also true for the socalled upper castes who demanded special treatment to Indians for ICS services during the British rule in India. In another case, the Maharaja of Mysore in 1918 appointed a committee under the chairmanship of the then Chief Justice of the Chief court Sir. Leslie. C. Miller to examine the conditions and suggest measures to provide adequate representation to depressed classes in the province. Interestingly now barring Brahmins all other communities were termed as backward and several recommendations were put forth for the betterment of the Backward Classes including exemption from qualifying educational tests, relaxation of severity of prescribed tests, enhancement of scholarships to students and above all that preference should also be given to BC students while admitting them to educational institutions. Now, it was to be in reverse order first to the depressed classes and then for the classes such as Hindus, Muslims and Indian Christians, and finally to the Brahmins (Kuppuswamy 1978:60).

In case of Tamilnadu, after the Justice Party was elected to power and quotas were reserved for five specific groups in 1924. Various communities were given distinctive quotas viz. the Non Brahmins(present day OBCs) who were estimated to be 72 percent in the population were given a quota of 41.67 per cent; Anglo Indians with Christians had four per cent population and were given a quota of 16.67percent quota; Mohammedans though only seven percent in population were also given a quota of 16.67 per cent, and; Depressed classes constituted 14 percent of population were given a quota of only 8.33 percent. However, these quotas did not remain stagnant. As the time passed the well-off non-Brahmin Hindu groups cornered all the benefits arising out of this policy. Accordingly a separate reservation policy was imagined and applied in 1947, which enhanced the share of non-Brahmin Hindus to 42.86 percent. Another category of backward Communities was introduced with a quota of 14.29 percent. However, the quota for SC was significantly upgraded to 14.29 percent. However, the quota for Anglo Indians Christians and Mohammedans put together was condensed to a merely of 7.14 percent (Guhan 1991:48).

In Western India, Sahuji Maharaj of Kolhapur who took reign of the province in 1894 initiated "loosening the stranglehold of Brahmins on the administration and society" and on 26 July 1902 took a decision of implementing 50 per cent reservations for depressed classes and the Backward castes in educational institutions and in government jobs. This was the first instance of purely caste-based reservation in modern India and it earnedhim as the father of modern-day reservations that confined to these castes in the 20th century.[3]

The role of Dr. Ambedkar in concretizing the policy is well known. He represented the case of Untouchables in1919 before the Southborough Committee that was appointed by the British to look into the question of representation in the legislature. He argued that the real social divisions of India then are: Touchable Hindus; Untouchable Hindus; Mohammedans; Christians; Parsees, and; Jews (Ambedkar 1979:250).

Distinguishing Untouchables from the non-Untouchables, he argued that from the point of view of communication the Hindus, in spite of castes, divide themselves into two significant groups—the touchables and the untouchables. The touchables have enough communication between them to enable us to say that the conflict of like-mindedness so far as they are concerned is not much to be dreaded. But there is a real difference and consequent conflict between the like-mindedness of the touchables and the untouchables. Untouchability is the strongest ban on the endosmosis between them. And that is why they needed special and their own representation (Ambedkar 1979:249).

Finally Ambedkar convinced the British and later the members in the Constituent Assembly of India to make special provisions for the deprived sections of the society. This was due to the unrelenting efforts of Ambedkar that the provisions were made part of the fundamental rights itself which include various Articles under Right to Equality.

Delineating Philosophy of Reservation

- Group Deprivation as a Foundation for consideration of Reservation
- Though victims are groups but beneficiaries are individuals for being the members of the group
- Complexity due to the presence of Graded inequality in Indian society
- Foundation of philosophy of Reservation is Social and Educational inequality and not Economic Inequality
- Economic inequality is part of evolution and changing circumstances
- Complexity is not merely in its foundation but extended due to the Evolution as well

Post Colonial Period

The post colonial period witnessed continuation of the reservation policy but in a different format. The case of SC and ST was clear and got consent from the Constituent Assembly but the case of Backward Castes/Classes was put in the Constitution to be decided for the future governments after studying their position and it was in this context that for the first time Kaka Kalelkar Commission was appointed during Nehru's premiership. However, before that a case was filed in the Madras High Court against the special provisions and the court found the merit in the case and ruled against the constitutional mandate for reservations. But to make the verdict null and void, the First Constitutional Amendment was passed by the Parliament under the leadership of Dr. Ambedkar as the law minister. He gave a very interesting statement on the floor of the House regarding the judicial intervention and said "......I have often in the course of my practice told the presiding judge in emphatic terms that I am bound to obey his judgment but I am not bound to respect it" (Ambedkar 1997:334). And I would like to argue.

Looking at the conditions of the Backward classes Kaka Kalelkar Commission was appointed by Nehru and the Commission made the following major findings:

- On thc basis of criteria evolved by it, the commission listed 2339 castes as socially and educationally backward.
- In all science. engineering. medicine, agriculture, veterinary and other technical institutions reservation of 70 percent of seats should be made for qualified students of BCs till such time as accommodation is provided for all the students eligible fix admission. The remaining 30 percent and also all seats unavailed of by BC should go to rest of the students.
- In making selection to the reserved quota of seats., qualified candidates from extremely BC should be taken into consideration first, and in making distribution, the principle of flavoring the lower of the two claimants among the candidates from the various communities should be followed
- The circumstances and the social conditions prevailing in the country necessitate greater consideration for the most backward and unrepresented communities in the group.

Nevertheless the recommendations of the Kaka Kalelkar Commission were not implemented due to the absence of mutual consent among the members of the Commission about its own findings and the Janta Party government in 1978 constituted another body popularly known as Mandal Commission under the chairmanship of B.P. Mandal. Some of the major recommendations included:

- It recommended two separate criteria for identifying the backward section of the Hindu community and of other communities where caste system is non- existent.
- An employee was considered to be socially hackward if he does not belong to any of the three- twice born (Dwij) Varnas i.e. he is neither a Brahmin or Kshatriya nor a Vaishya.
- He was deemed to be educationally backward if neither his father had studied beyond primary level.
- As regards the non-Hindu communities, an employee was considered to be socially backward if (i) he was a convert from those Hindu communities or if he is not convert from his parental income is below poverty line;(ii) he was deemed to be educationally backward if neither his father nor his grand father had studied beyond the primary level.
- The government decided that candidates belonging to socially and educationally backward castes recruited on the basis of merit in an open competition on merit same standards prescribed for the general candidates shall not be adjusted against the reservation of 27 percent.

There has been a major contention of making reservation above 50 percent and in one of such cases following the recommendations of A.N. Sathanathan committee, the Tamil Nadu government revised the quota of reservation to 18 percent for SC/ST, 31 percent for BCs and 51 percent was kept open. In 1980 the M.G. Ramachandran government enhanced the share of BCs to 50 and correspondingly reduced the selection for open positions to 31 percent, thus making the reservation 69 percent (Guhan : 1991:48).

Public Opinion about the Reservation Policy

The reservation policy is being implemented in various forms since long and there have been individuals opinion; legislators opinion; experts opinion but there probably is a lack of systematic study on the opinion of the shareholders whether against or in favour. Public opinion plays an important role in democracy for the continuation or discontinuation of a public policy. Britannica encyclopedia[4] defines public opinion is 'an aggregate of the individual views, attitudes, and beliefs about a particular topic, expressed by a significant proportion of a community.' There remain differences among the social scientists as a section looks it as a fusion of the views of all or a certain segment of society, whereas another section as assemblage of many contradictory or conflicting views on a subject matter. Nevertheless the developments in quantitative methods have led to an understanding that public opinion is collective view of a specific and definite population or of even of an ethnic group at times.

In this section, partial results of a survey conducted in five major cities(Delhi, Lucknow, Calcutta, Bhopal, Bengluru and Mumbai) of the country have been presented to ascertain the public opinion of the people across three social groups viz. General, OBCs and SCs. This probably is rare survey that was conducted to empirically test the opinion of the people about the reservation policy. Generally we come across individual opinions or experts' opinion on the issue but not a systematic survey about the policy itself. The respondents for the survey come not only from diverse social backgrounds but also from amongst the Students, Employees and Common Masses. The issue of reservation is little technical, as it needs somekind of awareness among the respondents about the basics of reservation policy. Thereforethe respondents were intentionally chosen from relatively educated background who had some idea about the reservation policy.

Table 3.1: Level of Popular Support for Reservation

Type of Support	*Reservation Policy for SC*	*Reservation Policy for OBCs*
Strong Support	34.7	29.3
Weak Support	21.5	27.5
Neither	13.8	15.7
Weak Disapproval	12.0	10.0
Strong Disapproval	18.0	17.4

Source: Opinion Survey on Reservation Issues 2017.

Table 3.1 shows that there is a Strong Support for the reservations for the SC as compared to the OBCs and similar is the case when it comes to weak support where OBC reservation is given weak support by more as compared to the SCs. However, the data on weak disapproval and strong disapproval is almost same having very less difference on the opinion about the reservations for these two groups. IF we combine Strong and Weak Support, there is no difference for the reservation for the SCs as well for the OBCs. However, there is little difference when disapproval of both kinds i.e. Weak and Strong are combined together. However, this is also a negligible difference. The only viable interpretation in this regard is that the category of OBC has been a fluid category where sometimes even relatively well off sections of the society have got the status of OBC, probably this is the reason for the Weak disapproval and Strong disapproval for this section compared with the SCs. Even if we compare Strong support and Strong disapproval then the results finds 16 percent or almost double favour for SC and 12 percent more Strong support for the OBCs that might lead to a conclusion of a major support for the policy against its opposition.

Table 3.2: Support for Longitudinal Extension of Reservation Policy

Type of Support	*Reservation Policy for SC*	*Reservation Policy for OBCs*
For Longer Period	37.2	32.9
For a While	35.9	37.1
No Longer	26.9	30.0

Source: Opinion Survey on Reservation Issues 2017.

Table 3.2 depicts that combined together For Longer Period and For a While have a majority support of about 73 percent and thus the reservations still are considered relevant by majority of the people whether they come from the beneficiaries classes or from the non-beneficiaries one as the sample size had half of those who were not beneficiaries of the policy. When looked carefully then there is more support for the reservation policy to be continued for a longer period for the SCs than for the OBCs. The different is of around 5 percent. This different gets reduced when it comes to the continuation of reservation for the SC and the OBCs. Now a little higher number wanted for the OBCs than the SCs. One of the interpretation in this regard could be that reservation for OBCs started after 42 years when compared with the SCs. Though when the opinion is expressed for no need of reservation any longer, again the more are against reservation for the OBCs. This somehow reflects some contradiction. However when the percentages of first two and the last one are compared then the support for longitudinal reservation is more for the SCs than the OBCs. Nevertheless this difference is not of great significance.

When looked at on the statistics of both the tables, one may conclude that the Weak disapproval and Strong Disapproval combined together in the table 3.1 and No longer in the Table 3.2 show a consistency with minor difference for continuation of reservation policy in the longer run and the disapproval for both the SC and the OBCs. However, a majority of the respondents i.e. more than 50 percent support the existing reservation system for both the communities as per Table 3.1 and a significant number of 70 percent want its continuation as per Table 3.2.

Interlinking Philosophy of Reservation and the Public Opinion

Philosophy of reservation is primarily and fundamentally linked to group deprivation. Even after the introduction of Economically Weaker Section category to the reservations, the basic unit of benefit remains social group, as those getting the reservation are members of the non-reserved social groups. Secondly though the reservation is given to the group but the beneficiaries are the individuals but as members of that group under which they have been placed. So far as public opinion is concerned, there clearly is a majority support for the policy, though there has been some difference between the SC and OBC beneficiaries but that is due to the presence of graded inequality in the Indian society that places individuals at a certain level and they remain at that level without experiencing any kind of strict social mobility. And that difference may explain the difference in opinion for the SC and OBC reservation policy.

Though the Constitution of India embeds the philosophy of reservation in the social and educational deprivation but after the 1992 judgment of the Supreme Court, the conception of creamy layer had been added to the reservation process brining the economic factor in. And probably this is due to that the National Democratic Government in 2018 passed a bill to grant reservation to the economically deprived sections of the General society, who are not part of SC/ST/OBC groups, though they may not be socially and educationally backward.

Thus one may argue that the foundation for bringing the economic backwardness in the reservation policy was initiated with the court verdict on the creamy layer in Mandal case that culminated in the granting of quota to those who have may be socially and educationally better off but economically deprived. This could be termed as having changed the philosophy of reservation that continued primarily on the basis of social and educational deprivation. It needs to be observed how the issue of economic deprivation is handled in case of SC and also the Scheduled Tribes who have the constitutional sanction to be beneficiaries for being socially and educationally at disadvantage and not economically deprived that was the basic philosophy of the reservation policy.

References

Ambedkar (1979). *Evidence Before the Southborough Committee*, in (ed.) Vasant Moon, Babasaheb Dr. Bhimrao Ambedkar Writings and Speeches, Vol. 1, Bombay: Government of Maharashtra.

Ambedkar (1997). *Constitution (First) Amendment Bill*, in (ed.) Vasant Moon, Babasaheb Dr. Bhimrao Ambedkar Writings and Speeches, Vol. 15, Bombay: Government of Maharashtra.

Guhan, S (1991). Reservations: The Tamilnadu Experience, *Manushi*, March-June, No. 63-64.

Kuppuswamy (1978). *Backward Class Movement in Karnataka*, Banglore: Banglore University.

Thimmaiah, J (1997).*Karnataka Governments Reservation Policy* in (ed.) Panindikar Pai, Politics of Backwardness, New Delhi: Konark.

Notes

1. https://www.forwardpress.in/2018/05/shahu-ji-maharaj-the-saviour-king-of-the-backwards-and-dalits/ accessed on 18 July 2019.
2. https://www.britannica.com/topic/public-opinion accessed on 22 July 2019.

Chapter - 4

The Republic of Reservations and the Roster Struggle

— *N. Sukumar*

Abstract

The RSS supremo, Mohan Bhagwat again tinkered with the Pandora's Box that is reservations. He wishes that both the opponents and supporters of reservations have a harmonious dialogue. For him and his ilk, reservations reflect the ugly underbelly of caste oppression in Hindu society. For the supporters of reservations, it is the only way for them to access the constitutional provisions envisaged by Babasaheb Ambedkar. The principal of merit is largely undefined. However, the social and economic worth of individuals and institutions are valued on this amorphous principle. Any standard definition of merit will again feed the myth of the "family farm" comprising of parental background, educational alma mater, economic occupations, physicality and geographical location. Needless to say, these privileges are available only to a chosen few who are then considered as 'meritorious', 'worthy' and the 'best'. For ages, the idea of merit was instrumental in barring dalit-bahujans, adivasis and women surviving on the margins into the domain of Sarasvati. We need to recall that the edifice of merit is constructed on Eklavya's thumb.

Introduction

The autarchic Indian society was rudely jolted by colonialism and in order to create a servile bureaucracy, the British invested in education. Gradually, knowledge became secularized and scriptural traditions were being critiqued by Jyotiba and Savitribai Phule, Iyothe Thass Panditar, Pandita Ramabai, Begum Rokeya, Ambedkar and Periyar to name a few. Intense intellectual battles were fought to safeguard 'pristine tradition' but women and dalit-bahujans got a foothold in accessing education. After independence, the Constitution provided for reservations in education and employment for the scheduled castes and tribes for socio-economic mobility.

Constitutional Provisions

On January 26, 1950, India ended its 'Dominion' status, became a republic, and put in effect its new constitution. The strategy of affirmative action is usually deployed to win over the support of the marginalized or under-represented sections of society. The public policies in support of affirmative action are generally justified in the name of equity, justice and democracy. The underlying goals said to be served by affirmative action policies in higher education generally comprise compensation to the victims of past discrimination and maltreatment, redistribution of resources and opportunities from the privileged sections of society to those worse off, motivating students from lower socio-economic and disadvantaged classes to aspire for better positions in society, better appraisal of students in terms of potentiality and productivity, higher quality education and learning due to prevailing diversity on campuses, better access to social capital in terms of useful contacts and networks for improving career opportunities, improved chances of integrating the societal elite in terms of race and ethnicity, fostering a more legitimate and vital democratic order, etc.

With an entire section dedicated to 'Fundamental Rights,' the Indian Constitution prohibits any discrimination based on religion, race, caste, sex, and place of birth through Article 15(1). This law extends to all public institutions, such as government-run educational facilities, to access hotels and restaurants, public employment and public wells, tanks and roads. The practice of untouchability is declared illegal by Article 17. Significantly, Article 15, which prohibits discrimination, also contains a clause allowing the union and state governments to make "any special provision for the advancement of any socially and educationally backward classes of citizens or for the Scheduled Castes and Scheduled Tribes." This provision was added in 1951 within weeks of a Supreme Court decision outlawing quotas in school admissions. The speed of the amendment is indicative of the strong political support for reservations. Similarly, Article 16, calling for "equality of opportunity in matters of public employment," contains clauses permitting the "reservation of appointments or posts in favour of any backward class of citizens which, in the opinion of the State, is not adequately represented in the services under the State" and another allowing "reservation in matters of promotion" for Scheduled Castes and Scheduled Tribes.[1]

A separate section of the Constitution, "Special Provisions Relating to Certain Classes," requires the reservation of seats in the "House of the People," or Lok Sabha, and the Legislative Assemblies of the states for the

Scheduled Castes and Scheduled Tribes.[2] The numbers of reserved seats are determined by the proportion of the Scheduled Caste and Scheduled Tribe members to the general population, based on population estimates from the most recent decennial census. The President of India and the Parliament, in consultation with the state governments, determine the list of groups qualifying as Scheduled Castes, Scheduled Tribes, and "backward classes." Regarding the reservation of jobs, Article 335 of the Constitution mandates that the "claims of the members of the Scheduled Castes and Scheduled Tribes shall be taken into consideration, consistently with the maintenance of efficiency of administration." Finally, a National Commission for Scheduled Castes and Scheduled Tribes[3] was created to investigate, monitor, advice, and evaluate the progress of the Scheduled Castes and Scheduled Tribes under the schemes aimed at the socio-economic development of these groups. Another Commission was also created to investigate the conditions of the socially and educationally backward classes. It is interesting to note that reservations explicitly single out certain castes for special preferential treatment. It also contradicts the Constitution's prohibition on discrimination based on caste, race, and other such criteria. Furthermore, India's caste system itself, with its strict hierarchy dictated by birth, is at odds with the ideals of equality and social justice.

Reservations or quotas can be methods for promoting affirmative action but are not affirmative action per se. Affirmative action is different from a reservation or quota in that it is open-ended and without any fixed number. Yet all such devices aim at serving as a "corrective" for past governmental, social or individual bias against women, certain individuals, groups or minorities based upon caste, class, creed, gender or ethnicity. The disadvantaged groups have often been subjected to unfair, derogatory or discriminatory treatment for no fault of their own. The scope for affirmative action may or may not be provided for in the constitution itself but it is common to speak of "affirmative action" or "positive discrimination" in the sense of providing justice to those who are ill-treated, discriminated against or under-represented due to inherent socio-economic and cultural traits or of preventing those in power from doing any further wrong to caste/class/creed-based minorities.

It was precisely the denial of social opportunities, sanctioned by law and custom, which pushed vast numbers of dalit-bahujans and adivasis into a life of penury, lacking both cultural and social capital. In order to bridge the gap, affirmative action was made constitution-ally mandatory so as to enable the deprived populace to regain their dignity. Education, long regarded as a liberating and modernising force, formed an important part of the social justice campaign. But although the Indian welfare state recognises its moral obligation to guarantee every child an education, this is a dream that is still far from being realised. The first generation of learners from the marginalised communi-ties must not only come to terms with an alien curriculum, they must also battle entrenched pedagogical prejudices. The debate on reservations in the public domain intensified when V. P. Singh announced the implementation of the Mandal Commission Report in 1989. It lead to widespread protests and renewed the debate on caste based reservations and its efficacy.

Merit and the Language of Hate

As observed by Uma Chakravarti, at the height of the anti-Mandal agitation in Delhi, newspapers carried photographs showing women college students in Delhi demonstrating in the streets. They were carrying placards that read 'We don't want unemployed husbands'![4] Women students protested not for themselves but on behalf of their potential husbands. In Lucknow, medicos and other students were polishing shoes and cleaning cars and taking out processions in which they ply rickshaws - to make the point that this is what they are likely to end up doing if the Government reserves more jobs[5]. Such prejudiced expressions in the public domain reflect the sense of entitlement embedded amongst the upper caste 'meritocracy' who are unwilling to relinquish their hold on intellectual resources. This has prevented the implementation of reservations and there is negligible representation of dalit-bahujans in academia. Till date, the 200 point roster model was utilized by the UGC/MHRD to ensure fair representation such as 27% for OBCs at entry level (Assistant Professors), 15% for SCs and 7.5% for STs at all levels. In an RTI response, the UGC furnished the following data as on 30th June 2016 for faculty positions in all Central Universities, across all categories as per the 200 point roster

Grant Total (NON-NER CUs + NEW CUs + NER CUs)	*Statement of Teaching staff strength (Category wise) as on 30.06.2016 in Central Universities*					
	No. of Vacant Posts					
Prof.	895	238	117	0	34	1284
Associate Prof.	1396	448	254	0	87	2185
Assistant Prof.	950	377	219	861	107	2514
Total No.	**3241**	**1063**	**590**	**861**	**228**	**5983**

If fairly implemented, this would ensure that out of 200 posts, 99 will go to SC, ST and OBC and 101 will be left for general category. However, this seldom happened and the Allahabad High Court[6] found this system faulty and ordered for reservations to be applied department wise. Hence, the 13 point roster was reintroduced. This would prevent any SC/ST/OBC candidates from nursing academic and employment ambitions. If the department is considered as a unit, in smaller departments with less than seven seats, departments with specialized categories like Indian History, European History, Medieval, Modern, Ancient History etc, specialized area studies programs, chairs etc the doors are shut for dalit-bahujans. However, in all its wisdom, the court failed to mention anything about the existing backlog in faculty recruitment and how this issue will be addressed.

The fine print of the Allahabad Court judgment[7] requests the UGC to deliberate over the subject with the MHRD and then decide the course of action. On the contrary, the UGC sought to implement the decision and many universities like BHU and Central Universities of Punjab (CUP) and

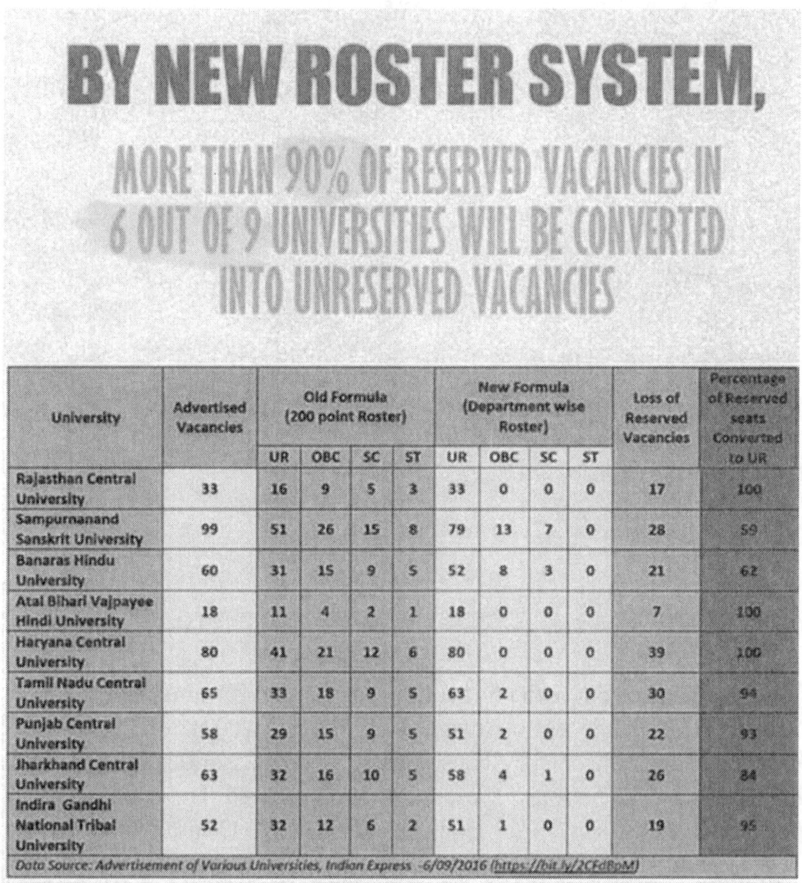

BY NEW ROSTER SYSTEM,

MORE THAN 90% OF RESERVED VACANCIES IN 6 OUT OF 9 UNIVERSITIES WILL BE CONVERTED INTO UNRESERVED VACANCIES

University	Advertised Vacancies	Old Formula (200 point Roster)				New Formula (Department wise Roster)				Loss of Reserved Vacancies	Percentage of Reserved seats Converted to UR
		UR	OBC	SC	ST	UR	OBC	SC	ST		
Rajasthan Central University	33	16	9	5	3	33	0	0	0	17	100
Sampurnanand Sanskrit University	99	51	26	15	8	79	13	7	0	28	59
Banaras Hindu University	60	31	15	9	5	52	8	3	0	21	62
Atal Bihari Vajpayee Hindi University	18	11	4	2	1	18	0	0	0	7	100
Haryana Central University	80	41	21	12	6	80	0	0	0	39	100
Tamil Nadu Central University	65	33	18	9	5	63	2	0	0	30	94
Punjab Central University	58	29	15	9	5	51	2	0	0	22	93
Jharkhand Central University	63	32	16	10	5	58	4	1	0	26	84
Indira Gandhi National Tribal University	52	32	12	6	2	51	1	0	0	19	95

Data Source: Advertisement of Various Universities, Indian Express -6/09/2016 (https://bit.ly/2CEdRpM)

ANNEXURE-I

REFERRED TO IN REPLY TO PARTS (a) TO (e) OF LOK SABHA STARRED QUESTION NO. 267 TO BE ANSWERED ON 31.12.2018 REGARDING "INDIAN INSTUTES OF TECHNOLOGY" RAISED BY DR. UDIT RAJ:

Details of Faculty in respect of IITs

S.No	Institute Name	Sanctioned posts	Posts earmarked for		Posts filled	
			SC	ST	SC	ST
1.	IIT-Kharagpur	1203	*	*	8	0
2.	IIT Bombay	1034			5	0
3.	IIT Madras	800			13	2
4.	IIT Delhi	776			10	2
5.	IIT Kanpur	694			3	0
6.	IIT Roorkee	745			10	2
7.	IIT Guwahati	596			16	3
8.	IIT BHU	556			19	3
9.	IIT Jodhpur	90			2	0
10.	IIT Ropar	150			4	0
11.	IIT Indore	150			2	0
12.	IIT Patna	155			6	0
13.	IIT Gandhinagar	160			1	0
14.	IIT Hyderabad	254			6	1
15.	IIT Bhubaneswar	170			4	0
16.	IIT Mandi	125			0	0
17.	IIT(ISM) Dhanbad	711			29	6
18.	IIT Jammu	93			1	0
19.	IIT Tirupati	93			2	1
20.	IIT Palakkad	93			4	0
21.	IIT Dharwad	93			1	1
22.	IIT Goa	45			1	0
23.	IIT Bhilai	70			2	0
Total		**8856**			**149**	**21**

Tamil Nadu came out with notifications for faculty recruitments. The CUP advertised on 1st July 2018 (Advt. No. CUPB/18-19/003), for 57 positions in different departments for all positions. All 15 Professors and 25 Associate Professors and 12 Assistant Professors are unreserved. There are only two positions for OBCs and 3 for PWD at entry level. In Central University of Tamil Nadu, (Advt No 04/2018, dated 14/06/2018) out of 39 positions advertised at various levels, all are for unreserved category. There are two PWD positions under the same category. The Central University of Rajasthan, (Advt No, CURAJ/R/F.99/2018/761, dated 25th May 2018), advertised for 33 positions at various levels and all are unreserved in different departments. In the same category, two positions are reserved for PWDs.

Unraveling Modinomics

Ideologically, the RSS-BJP government is against any notion of reservations as it invalidates their metanarrative of 'Hindu brotherhood'. If they acquiesce to reservations, they need to admit the existence of caste, which is akin to committing political hara-kiri. Akhand Bharat and Mandal are antithesis to each other. The past few years have witnessed repeated agitations by Patidars, Jats, Marathas and Kappus. In order to satisfy them, the government announced 10% for the economically weaker sections among the upper castes. This policy is riddled with contradictions. In the absence of a caste census, how is the weaker section enumerated? Any person with a land holding of one acre is worth lakhs if not crores in urban areas. As per the income tax ceiling in India, if your income is two and a half lakhs per annum, you need to pay your taxes. How does one justify then that an income of eight lakhs per annum makes one economically poor? Even an assistant professor in any state or central university does not earn eight lakhs per annum. The same income is the creamy layer slab for OBCs. How does one rationalize Modinomics?

Such desperate measures violate the constitutional provisions for reservations as representation under Articles 15 and 16. When the Women's Reservation Bill and Reservation in the Private Sector Bills are pending for ages in Parliament, within 48 hours, the 10% quota was rushed through both Houses of Parliament. Is it to appease the upper castes post the defeat in the recent state elections? With unseemly haste, UGC and MHRD rushed to implement the fresh orders from the current academic year. This begs the question, what about the backlog vacancies in the SC/ST and OBC positions which are yet to be calculated and filled. The brahmanical institutions were never interested in filling up these posts. Clearly the powers that be have goofed up their math.

On 29th January 2019, the Honourable Prime Minister pontificated on exam stress via 'Pareeksha Pe Charcha'. Who will alleviate the stress experienced by this nation through the midnight robbery of demonetization, RBI and CBI crisis, mob lynching, citizenship woes, widespread misogyny and hatred? When will 'naukri pe charcha' happen? To illustrate, there are around 5000 adhoc, temporary, guest teachers in Delhi University and constituent colleges. Some of them have been teaching for decades. Their positions were filled as per the 200 point roster. If the 13 point roster is implemented in Delhi University, 90 % of them will be jobless. Maybe they should turn self employed by selling 'pakodas' after working hard to achieve PhDs, NET/JRF and years of teaching and research experience. This motivated the youth to organize protest vociferously. Their well orchestrated movement convinced the Modi government to issue an ordinance before the general elections of 2019.

The Roster Movement

The Allahabad High Court Judgment on the roster for employment delivered a severe blow to the placid life in many a university campus. In the meantime, various universities advertised faculty positions based on the 13 point/ department wise roster. The message was loud and clear. If the Constitutional provisions have to be protected, one has to organize and agitate in order to save reservations in public institutions. A Joint Forum for Academic and Social Justice was formed which spearheaded the roster struggle. For more than a month after the Court Judgment, in Delhi University the SC/ST/ OBC teachers sat on a relay hunger strike which transformed the academic space into a vibrant arena of debate and discussion on the judgment and its consequences on the community. There was also a sense of despondency that after years of relentless struggle, young scholars would be deprived of a seat in academia. This was more highlighted in Delhi University as scores of adhoc/guest/temporary teachers realized that the notion of job security was reduced to a chimera.

Coincidentally, an academic body constituted by Delhi University authorities recommended the removal of Kancha Illaiah's books from the reading list of political Science courses. This uncalled for interference in academic issues stirred a major controversy as Dalit bahujan students and teachers felt that any alternative reading of the prevalent hegemonic discourse is being thwarted. Teachers and students groups cutting across ideologies, except the right wing took a united stand that such blatant withdrawal of books was totally unwarranted. Kancha Illaiah also addressed a mammoth gathering near the Arts Faculty in Delhi University.

In January 2019, the state also announced a 10% reservation for Economically Weaker Sections and the Supreme Court also endorsed the judgment of the Allahabad High Court making the department as a unit for preparing the roster to implement reservations. The EWS Bill was passed without much debate and discussion. This measure diluted the idea of social justice which Ambedkar envisaged when he proposed for reservations. Realizing the implications of such measures which will adversely affect the future generations, a group of Dalit bahujan teachers and students met to discuss about a plan of action. On 24th January 2019, an 'Aakrosh March' (a rally to express their anger) was organized in Delhi. A team was formed to coordinate with different universities to conduct a candle march and mass protests on 25th January to restore 200 point roster. Around 2500 teachers and students from ideological groups barring the BJP-ABVP participated in the march. A few sympathizers (who belong to the SC/ST/OBC) from the right wing groups also joined the protests. This was a tremendous show of strength seldom witnessed in the university. Similar candle marches were also organized in Banaras Hindu University Hyderabad Central University, Gujarat Central University and other institutions. Gradually, the idea picked up and the protests spread to other cities. Despite the huge marches on the streets of Delhi, apart from social media, there was practically no print or television media coverage of the anger simmering in the campuses.

From 26th January 2019, letters were written by members of Parliament from various parties-RJD, BSP, SP, AAP and Congress representing the roster problem. The members of the legislative assemblies from Rajasthan and Madhya Pradesh also actively campaigned against the new roster regulations. In the Delhi Assembly, the Minister of Social Welfare took the initiative to demand the roll back of the 13 Point roster. The Joint Action Committee called for a week long protest which brought the campuses of Allahabad, Punjab, CCSU Meerut, BHU, HCU, GCU, Pondicherry, Wardha to a standstill with the support of progressive groups. IN order to sustain the pressure, a group of teachers and students from the JAC met MPs and MLAs to represent their issues. To mobilize support for the agitation, JNUSU organized a public meeting on 30th January at the Sabarmati Dhaba. The JAC and DUTA (Delhi University Teachers Association) jointly decided to organize an 'Aakrosh Rally' on 31st January 2019 from Mandi House to Sansad Marg in coordination with political parties and civil society groups. The teachers associations from Jamia, JNU, Ambedkar University officially supported the agitation. A few individual teachers from IGNOU and Indraprastha University also participated. Student organizations like BAPSA, YFSJ, AISA, SFI, NSUI, KYS, DSU, JNUSU, Pinjra Tod, civil society organizations like UAH (United Against Hate), Bahujan Sahitya Sangh, Bhim Army, Delhi Teachers Initiative, NACDOR, All India SC/ST/

OBC Employees Organizations in various sectors and political parties like CPI, CPIM, AAP, Congress, SP and RJD addressed the rally and supported the cause. The same day, parallel agitations took place in other institutions. There existed a tacit support from different levels of the bureaucracy in Delhi which provided valuable inputs for the struggle.

The JAC continued to sustain the pressure and called for a Bharat Bandh on 5th March 2019. The struggle had percolated to the rural areas also, thanks to the social media network. The bandh was a complete success in Bihar, Uttar Pradesh, Madhya Pradesh, Delhi and Rajasthan. The other regions, the bandh witnessed a sporadic success. The protestors were lathi charged; scores of them were detained in various states. This made the state to realize the simmering anger of the Dalit bahujan public and an ordinance was issued to retain the 200 point roster on March 7th 2019.

The Roster Movement: Some Reflections

One of the chief gains of this movement was that the slogans of 'Jai Bheem', 'Brahmanvaad ke chaati pe Birsa, Phule, Ambedkar'[8] etc gained currency. The protesters marched with the portraits of Birsa, Jyotiba and Savitribai Phule, Ambedkar, Rohith Vemula, B P Mandal etc. After the Mandal agitations, this was the first time that the national capital was witnessing the emergence of the Dalit Bahujan counterpublic. The fact that the brahmanical powers which controlled the state would swindle them of their constitutional rights united the dalit bahujans to collectively oppose such attempts.

The roster movement also demonstrated the socio-economic faultlines in the Indian society. The southern states took advantage of the opening up of the Indian economy in the 1990s. The investments in software and computing technology enabled the youth in these states to access alternative sources of education and employment. They are less dependent on only government/public sector or university jobs. Their English language skills also are an asset for upward mobility. On the contrary, the states of North India have witnessed les investments in education, industry and social welfare. The focus on Hindi language hampers their upward socio-economic mobility. The people are still enchained to caste and religious conservative values. The sole source for leading a good dignified life is to get into a government job. For the majority of the youth from North India, Delhi is a Mecca to realize their dreams of UPSC or academics. Hence, for the youth the fact that with the change in roster, their dreams will also vanish as many teaching positions will be declared unreserved and the seats in the university will be decreased came as a rude shock. One also needs to question as to why the identity politics and the political parties which thrive on it fail to provide any possible alternatives to the Dalit bahujans. The success of pushing back the 13 point roster and reinstating the 200 point roster which demonstrated the strength of the movement miserably failed in reining back the fascist forces. One needs to retrospect the massive gains made by Hindutva in the Hindi heartland despite the antagonism of the dalit bahujans.

References

Birsa, Phule and Ambedkar are sitting on the chest of Brahminism.

In 1990, a five-member commission replaced the Officer for Scheduled Castes and Scheduled Tribes.

Saba Naqvi Bhaumik, Decision to implement Mandal Commission report stirs up protests across India, September 30, 1990, https://www.indiatoday.in/magazine/special-report/story/19900930-decision-to-implement-mandal-commission-report-stirs-up-protests-across-india-813545-1990-09-30, Accessed 17th Jan 2019.

SLP (C) Diary No 14318/2018, Supreme Court of India, Record of Proceedings, Section XI.

Court No . 37, Writ-A No. 43260 of 2016, Allahabad High Court Judgment Copy, 7/4/2017.

The Constitution defines the "State" as the "Government and Parliament of India and the Government and the Legislature of each of the States.

The draft constitution, produced by the Constituent Assembly's Drafting Committee headed by B.R. Ambedkar, included Muslims and Indian Christians among the beneficiaries of reservations in legislatures.

Uma Chakravarti, Gendering Caste Through Feminist Lens, Stree, 2006, p. 3.

Notes

1. The Constitution defines the "State" as the "Government and Parliament of India and the Government and the Legislature of each of the States.
2. The draft constitution, produced by the Constituent Assembly's Drafting Committee headed by B.R. Ambedkar, included Muslims and Indian Christians among the beneficiaries of reservations in legislatures.
3. In 1990, a five-member commission replaced the Officer for Scheduled Castes and Scheduled Tribes.
4. Uma Chakravarti, Gendering Caste Through Feminist Lens, Stree, 2006, p. 3.
5. Saba Naqvi Bhaumik, Decision to implement Mandal Commission report stirs up protests across India, September 30, 1990, https://www.indiatoday.in/magazine/special-report/story/19900930-decision-to-implement-mandal-commission-report-stirs-up-protests-across-india-813545-1990-09-30, Accessed 17th Jan 2019, 10.40 pm.

6. SLP (C) Diary No 14318/2018, Supreme Court of India, Record of Proceedings, Section XI.
7. Court No 37, Writ-A No-43260 of 2016, Allahabad High Court Judgment Copy, 7/4/2017.
8. Birsa, Phule and Ambedkar are sitting on the chest of Brahminism.

Chapter - 5

Reservation and Social Justice: Historical Perspective

— *Prof. Adapa Satyanarayana*

Abstract

Historically, social justice is not of recent origins but its seed was planted during the early times and was also analyzed by the concerned social thinkers. Beginning with Gautama Buddha in Ancient times through the medieval Bhakti saints and modern day anti-caste social reformers like Jotiba Phule, Ayyankali, Ayoti Das, Periyar, Baba SahebAmbedkaretc. have articulated the concept of social justice and emancipation of sudras and ati-sudras.[1] *The visualization of the concept of inequality brings to the fore the necessity for the achievement of social justice. The Constitution makers felt that India being a country of unequal there should be an answer to the wretchedness of the ostracized, stigmatized and segmented sections of the downtrodden people. The answer to this has been provided for in our Constitution by the right to equality (Articles 14 to 18) to make equality meaningful, and thereby placing the weak and the strong on the same platform. This paper is going to trace the idea of the reservations and its evolution.*

Introduction

In modern India, unlike the elitist nationalist, it was JotibaPhule who articulated the notion of equality and social justice for the emancipation of the oppressed communities. In his battle against discriminatory Brahmanism; JotibaPhule was inspired by the egalitarian philosophy of the Buddha and Kabir. He was an admirer of the emergent liberal democracies of the West, but he consciously built his protest movement on the ideological and cultural bedrock of the indigenous shamanic tradition. In fact, he saw his own movement as continuation of those of Buddha, Kabir and Tukram. Phule's exposure to modern intellectual currents after coming into contact with Christian missionaries during his school days, and his reading of Paine's

The Rights Man and The Age of Reason in 1847 had left a deep imprint on him. Phule's critique of Brahmanic Hinduism drew sustenance from different sources including the Christian and European rationalism but the most critical input, was provided by the indigenous shamanic tradition of equality and reason coupled with Phule's own experiences and observation of socio-economic realities.[2] Like Jotiba Phule, Ayyankali in Travancore also asserted and fought for social equality and social justice in the 19th century. A scholar wrote:[3]

> During the late 19th century Aiyyankali of Travancore (1863-1941) led the struggle of the Pulayas that kindled a new awareness of freedom and self-respect. He was born in 1866 in a poor Pulaya family at Venganoor near Trivandrum. He determined to emancipate Pulayas from their social and economic servitude and to become members of modern secular society. Ayyankalihim self experienced all kinds of inequalities meted out to the Pulayas. They are engaged in agriculture as the servants of the Sudra land owners. Ayyankali could not tolerate all the inequalities and deprivation imposed upon the Avarnas and he reacted against this and this earned him the title '*Urupilla*'. A notable event of his early social activism was his forceful entry into the caste Hindu 'public Sphere'- the historic Viluvandi journey in the year 1893. The first attempt of Ayyankali was mobility in public spaces and he was very well aware about the fact that some sort of physical force should be applied for social change. For this purpose, he organized a group of physically trained youth called 'AyyankaliPada' with the help of his followers he walked along the public roads in his village at Venganoor near Thiruvananthapuram. The caste Hindus who tried to use physical force against them were 'met with physical force. As a result of defiance and confrontation, the Pulayas under Ayyankali's leadership won the right to walk on the public roads in most of the areas of Travancore by 1900, though there were many private and special roads prohibited them for many more years. He travelled in a bullock cart (*villuvandi*) from Venganoor to Trivandrum along the public road in l898. It shook the very foundation of the upper caste structure. The caste Hindus threw stones and sticks on him. But he rode the cart as a majestic knight. This incident proved him as the undisputed leader of the Pulayas. Then he and his band the famous 'AyyankaliPada' charted out a series of programmes to stifle the upper caste predominance and to secure their basic rights".

In south India Ramaswami Naickar, popularly known as Periyar launched a vigorous struggle against Brahmanical domination, caste discrimination and propounded social justice. About the significance of his self-respect movement BrijRanjan Mani wrote thus:[4]

> "His extraordinary life and carrier puts in bold relief the problematic history of congress politics and nationalism. He left the 'Brahman-dominated Congress ' to organize a 'Self – Respect movement' for Dravidian people which represented not only the radical phase of the non- Brahman movement. A trenchant critic of caste hierarchy, ritualism and idolatry, Periyar – like Phule and Ambedkar – conflated Hinduism with casteism and brahmanism and lambasted Hindu laws and institutions and inhuman instruments of 'bramanic' 'male and 'Aryan' exploitation. The Self – Respect movement was 'fundamentally opposed to the holy alliance of region, caste and nationalism, an alliance which it understood as embodying a social and political order that was inherently in-egalitarian. In 1920, he had presided over a separate session of non- Brahmans at the 26thProvincial session of the Congress at Tirunelvelli. In this conference, resolutions were adopted demanding the reservation of constituencies and government posts for non-Brahmans. Periyar unmasked Congress hypocrisy again in 1928, when the Justice Party- supported S. MuthiahMuddaliar cabinet issued a government order giving adequate representation to all the communities. Its non- Brahmanism was a radical blueprint for societal and cultural transformation. It visualized the tern 'non- Brahmanism was radical blueprint for societal and cultural transformation. It visualized the term 'non Brahman' as a grand fraternity comprising all those whom the Brahman and Brahmanism held to be low, desired, and less than human. The basic thrust of the Self- Respect movement was to free non-Brahmans from their shudra hood and to prepare them to come together with the ati-shudras and others to realize an ideal society in which castes would have no place. In other worlds, whereas the Justice party had been mainly concentrated about ending the Brahman raj in public spheres through its politics of proportional representation, the Self-respect movement aimed at bringing about a cultural revolution on the bedrock of egalitarianism and rationalism".

Having influenced by egalitarian thought of earlier social thinkers and reformers in general and Phule's thought in particular, Baba Saheb Ambedkar inscribed the principle of social justice as the foundational principle of constitutional measures of reservation and representation. Ambedkar marked in the Constituent Assembly thus: "I am using the term social justice in a comprehensive sense so as to include economic and social justice." So, reservation in legal terminology might imply preferential treatment. The Preamble of Constitution envisions the achievement of a socialist State with social, political and economic justice. Tis constitutional principle had a long history in the making. Therefore, I focus on some aspects reservation, representation and social justice in a historical perspective, based on my own research findings. In the conventional social science discourse it is wrongly presumed that the demand for reservation is not made from the egalitarian world view. Infact, it is the egalitarian and social justice principles that inspired the historically disadvantaged sections of people to demand reservation and representation as their legitimate right. It is not essentially asking for compensation for past sins. It is to get rid of social injustice and social inequality that reservation is demanded. Structurally, the socio-economic injustice is imposed by *varna-jati*(caste) system. This system and the disabilities imposed by it originated in India several centuries ago. The socio-religious system and the disabilities arising out of it still continue. Under the system of *varna-jati*, the Brahminical upper castes have undue, unearned and unjust privileges, whereas the Sudra and atisudra castes suffer from suppression, neglect and discrimination. Because of the graded inequality based on the mere incident of birth of a person in a caste group, the lower castes were denied educational opportunities and a share in the administration by the priestly and the ruling classes. The system and its effects still continue to make them socially and educationally backward.

The socio-cultural and educational disabilities perpetuate inequalities and injustices. Then, how could there be free, fair and equal competition among unequals? Reservation is demanded as a right to set rights the wrongs and disabilities arising out of the unequal caste structure. The wrongs and the consequent disabilities are historical because they originated in the past, but they are not things of the past, but are realities even today! The Brahminical upper castes are even now a privileged lot socially, economically religiously and culturally. So they are placed in an advantageous position in economic, political, administrative and other spheres as well. The Scheduled Castes, Scheduled Tribes and Other Backward Classes (castes) are a traditionally deprived lot denied of equal rights and opportunities. Therefore, having become aware of the prevalence of injustice, they want to undo it and move towards an egalitarian social order. So they demand the implementation of policies based on the principle of social justice to eradicate the continuing social injustice. Historically, Dalits have been suffering from indignities and Sudras from disabilities for about two thousand years. As a matter of fact, the Brahminical upper castes who have reserved for themselves (on the basis of scriptures and religious practices) the benefits of education, wielding authority and owning vast resources, experience high social status and deny equal respect and human dignity to other castes. The under-privileged sections are able to assert gradually their self-respect only after getting education and jobs by reservation in modern India. As the struggle for Independence was going on, the question of reservation was also raised to usher in social justice for the suppressed sections of the society. So the policy of reservation was quite firmly and secularly established during the closing years of the British Rule and this policy was more or less designed to redress the communal inequalities in public services. However, representation through preferential treatment was thought of as device to redress the structurally rooted socio-economic inequalities of the disadvantaged sections of the society because of past societal discrimination. The concept of equality together with social justice which implies there should be prohibition of discrimination on grounds of religion, race, caste, sex etc. against any citizen was not enough to make social justice and human rights a reality for the weaker sections.

In this chapter perceptions of social justice, freedom, and socio-political emancipation in modern India will be highlighted. It also seeks to interpret the alternate visions and voices pertaining to representation articulated by the lower caste organic intellectuals in theory and praxis. The concept of Nation and its constituents as perceived by them was fundamentally different from the idea of Nation and its totality as articulated by the upper caste elite nationalists. In the existing historical writings the emergence and articulation of a distinct dalitbahujan self-perception, sensibility and ideology did not receive adequate attention. What the dalitbahujan communities, as members of civil society, themselves thought about the meaning of Nation and its essence in their own terms and how did they related themselves is also not adequately analyzed by scholars. The dalitbahujan critique of the upper caste representations of Nation and its ideology (nationalism) needs to be interrogated. The fact that there emerged in the first three decade of the twentieth century, a well-informed dalitbahujan thinkers and activists provides an ample opportunity to examine the ways in which they perceived and interpreted certain concepts like nation, self-rule and freedom.[5]

The traditional nationalist historiography maintained that the rise of political consciousness during the colonial period was due to the activities of elite-led associations and political parties, like the Indian National Congress. This perspective is based on the assumption that the dominant nationalist ideology articulated by the upper caste-class truly mirrored the will of the people of India. The identification and equation of the rise of socio-political consciousness with the emergence of the pan-Indian organizations seeks to legitimize and justify the movements launched by the Congress party in national-political terms and tends to exclude and undermine other forms and processes. Nineteenth century India in general, and South India in particular witnessed diverse forms of socio-political awakening and mobilizations characterized by unevenness among different segments of the population, more so among the lower castes/communities. Recent debates generated by the subaltern historiography, in particular, drew the attention of scholars to undertake and explore the diversity, multiplicity and complexity of ideas, intellectual traditions, cultures etc. at the micro-regional level.[6] Macro level discourses on Indian nationalism lacked sensitivity to the diversities of ideas or thought processes. The grand, mega-narrative of the nationalist movement and its agenda tended to highlight the vision of "the leaders" who were supposed to have shaped the destiny of Nation and accorded sanctity to their thought. Any contrary or divergent ideas and ideologies, visions, perceptions, aspirations by sections below the upper caste-based middle class intelligentsia has been termed as parochial, narrow, sectarian, communal, castiest and hence non/anti-national. There is also inadequate discussion in the existing historical literature on the visions and perspectives of the non-elite, local, vernacular-based intellectuals and spokesmen. How different segments of Indian society, both across time and space, have understood, interpreted and articulated the ideology of nationalism and the visions of nation is not adequately explored so far. There is also an urgent need to focus on the context, local traditions and articulations by the organic intellectuals of the disprivilezed sections of Indian society.

The subaltern historians have pointed out that in the course of the anti-colonial movement, long before the political nationalist ideas were articulated by the elites, common, illiterate masses have projected their own vision of a future society, however hazy and vague it might have been. But the mainstream historians paid very little attention to the initiates taken by the non-dominant groups, which often had a profound effect on the growth of nationalist consciousness, socio-political movements as well as in shaping the nationalist agenda. They tended to discount "Brahmin/ Bhadralok nationalism" and had expressed doubts about the validity of their movements and at times disagreed with their program, since it was unconcerned with their life experiences. The articulate groups among the lower castes began to ask questions like whose Nation it was going to be. And what kind of a Nation that was sought to be built? In a sense, the ideal upper caste nationalism was at variance with the popular nationalism, as articulated by the disprivileged groups. The popular nationalism articulated by the dalitbahujan intellectuals was influenced by Ambedkar's thought. What is a nation?" asked Ambedkar rhetorically; and explained that 'nationality' (or nation ness) is a social feeling. It is a feeling of corporate sentiment of oneness which makes the people feel that they are kith and kin. And it is also a feeling of "consciousness of kind", "like-mindedness", "and possessing things in common" in a life of communication, participation and of sharing with all those who constitute one nation. In Ambedkar's writings the terms nation, society and democracy are used interchangeably to express a social reality. In this sense nation is a society where there is an unlimited scope of 'social endosmosis. Nation is a democracy and a mode of associated living.

Dalitbahujan communities in India aspired for secularization, humanization and liberalization of civil society as much as the elite nationalists. Their conception of nationalism is inclusive of socio-economic and political justice. A Sudra intellectual opined: "The exclusion of most of the castes from sharing in the political life of the country has left little room for the growth of feeling of common interest and public spirit. The caste system, which is born of the most abject spiritual slavery, has resulted in the political slavery... The spirit of caste is inimical not only to the growth of national unity but also to the emancipation of the individual.... Priest-ridden, karma-obsessed, maya-enslaved mentality is the source of all the miseries under which the Hindus are groaning.... Spiritual slavery, fatalism and superstition have smothered all power of self-reliance and all sense of freedom."[7]

The non-brahmin organic intellectuals vehemently denounced the caste system and desired to dismantle it. Their urge for ritual equality was very much rooted in their secular conception of a modern society and nation. They visualized a nation and society free of inequality and social oppression. They intended to emerge as free and equal citizens of the civic and political community of the emerging nation. A spokesman of the Justice Party wrote: "...The idea of a nation involves the oneness of culture and implies the binding together of a similar portion of mankind by other than mere political ties. Nationality does not depend upon but transcends political allegiance, religious belief and economic interest. Nationality is a form of consciousness of kind, which binds men together irrespective of their political allegiance, religious beliefs and economic interests....When caste and status delimit life, men are driven to be either fools or hypocrites. No democracy can be built on restrictions, which hinder individual liberty and free association.

No democracy can grow in a social environment in which the distinction of inferiors and superiors forms an essential and permanent idea."[8]

The intellectual ferment thus generated unleashed forces that led to the emergence of a powerful political non- Brahmanism in the then Madras Presidency consisting of Tamil Nadu, Karnataka, Andhra and Malabar Kerala. The south Indian Liberal Federation, commonly known as the Justice Party, was formed in 1916, on an anti- Congress, anti- brahmincal plank with objective or radical redistribution of socio- political power. Thyagaraya Chetty and T.M. Nair Played a pivotal role in the 'shudramovement' by issuing in December 1916 the Non- Brahman Manifesto against the overwhelming preponderance of Brahmans in the fields of education, public shrive, and politics.[9] Brahman domination in the public sphere was clearly reflected in statistic. While 80% of the Brahman populace was literatim barely four percent of non- Brahman people had learnt the alphabet, let alone derived the benefits of higher education. Leading Justicites hammered home the point that the Brahmans had usurped all real power, while the toiling masses, cultivators and others who constitute 9% of the population had not eve a semblance of power on their hands. Demanding democratic representation for non-Brahman castes in the girls of education, administration and legislation, Justice leader lashed out at the brahma – dominate congress nationalism. Presenting the Justice road- map, leaders like Thygaraya Chetty and Nair exuded confidence that the non-Brahman could attain a unity and wholeness, both in their resistance to the Brahman power and though assertion and practice of an alternative culture and community with their own values and conventions. Chetty extolled the 'genius of Dravidian civilization' and held that it does not recognize difference between and man by birth. In 1920, the Justice party won a remarkable victory in the elections to run ad diarchic government in the Madras Presidency. On assuming Office, It passed a Government order on 16 September1921 directing an increase in the proportion of posts in government offices held by non- Brahmans. In Justice' fresh initiative to ensure the representation of various castes and communities at all grades a levels in government appointments was again derided by the Brahman lobby as divisive and dangerous. It is interesting to note that this statement of a Justice Party leader clearly echoes the opinions of the spokes persons of various caste associations. A social activist remarked in 1936: "Owing to a combination of modern influences such as education, social and political reform, and irreligious propaganda, the Harijans are becoming more and more restless and discontented with their social status and economic position and are here and there already in revolt, discarding the religion of their birth for others and none at all. Should that revolt become general and the Harijans fall away en-masse, the prestige of Hinduism will be damaged."[10]

In colonial Andhra, various social reform movements and ideologies also facilitated the assertion of dalit identity and self-respect during the first quarter of the twentieth century. In addition to the Christian missionaries, a number of social reformers, liberal and progressive forces also denounced untouchability and caste discrimination. Indeed, generations of dalitbahujan educated youth and intellectuals were nurtured by many reform organizations such as Brahma Samaj, AryaSamaj, Adi-Andhra Mahasabha etc., and they fostered in them a sense of self-respect, dignity and individualism. Consequently, a host of dalitbahujan intellectuals through their writings, speeches, associations etc., launched an attack on the Brahmanical ideology. They were quite instrumental, in intellectual and ideological terms, in critiquing, delegitimizing and undermining the ascriptive social order and social inequality based on birth. The distinct and autonomous dalitbahujan identity and assertion of 1920's and 30's was rooted in the socio-political turmoil of colonial Andhra; and the Adi-Dravida, Adi-Andhra Mahasabha, Justice Party, Self Respect Movement, Harijan Sevak Sangh, Poona Pact etc. played a significant role in it. A political commentator remarked in the early 1930's thus: "The mere possibility of political change has awakened the depressed classes from their age-long torpor, and their insistent demand that the institution of untouchability should disappear, has become one of the most live questions of modern India...*That the choice lies between the caste system with its attendant social tyranny and political power on the one hand, and democratic institutions with the possibility of social progress and political power on the other, has been clearly grasped*...This is the reason why the fight for the equality of untouchables has become a tremendous struggle between the political forces of the country in alliance with all the impulses of social reform and educated thought on the one side, and religious orthodoxy, political reaction and social obscurantism ranged on the other."[11] The first quarter of the 20th century also witnessed the emergence of a distinct dalit literary tradition and creation of "texts of resistance" and 'protest literature" reflecting the changing consciousness and ideology of dalits' quest for social justice, visions of modern nation and freedom. An examination of the proceedings of the Adi-Andhra Mahasabha, journalistic writing of dalit intellectuals in the vernacular press, (in *Navajeevana,* for instance) and other sources indicate that dalits resented monopoly of socio-economic resources by upper castes and demanded access to education, employment in public places as well as a reasonable share in the institutions of administrative and political power.

At the turn of the twentieth century Andhra society witnessed a sort of internal churning/turmoil, because of new awakening among many non-Brahmin communities and castes pertaining to their status. In the awakening of the non-Brahman communities both the socio-cultural and political dimensions were evident. Indeed the Justice Party initiated and led socio-political protest against Brahminical domination and it had played an important role in moulding their consciousness in the 1920's and 30's. Political and intellectual assertion of the lower castes became more sharp and pronounced in a situation, in which the Brahmin community disproportionately held privileged positions in the spheres of education and employment. Hence, educated sections from among the lower Sudra castes felt that the Brahmins blocked their opportunities. Invariably, the non-Brahmin ideologues (including dalits) articulated notions of "equitable distribution of resources", "equality of opportunity", "equal rights and privileges" "proportional representation" and emphasized democratization of civil and political society. They were also unequivocal in rejecting the ascriptive ideology of caste and Brahmanical supremacy.

According to LaxmiNarasu, a leading intellectual of the Non-brahmin movement. "A polity of caste and privilege can never be consistent with social equality….only out of equal rights and privileges for all will emerge justice, human dignity, human solidarity and unity".[12] Furthermore," equality of opportunity meant that success should be determined by talent and energy and not by the accident of birth. The abolition of special privilege, the wider and more equal distribution of wealth, the extension of facilities for education …is some of the means of affording equality of opportunity". The anti-Brahmins consciousness and a broad non-Brahmin identity was conditioned and shaped by emotional and political expediencies. The non-Brahmin movement was perceived as "self-expression" of the majority. At the socio-cultural level, it was claimed that

> "The justice movement is organized for the vindication of self-respect. The desire to reconstruct society on a more rational basis expressed itself in its varied activities. Social Justice is the basic principle of its foundation. Social Justice is the main plank on which it first concentrated its efforts. The Principle of self-respect has caught the imagination of the people of rural areas. The leaders of the movement realized that political power could not be permanent without the practical application of the principle and equal opportunities for all,

> including those who are termed non-political or depressed. The keynote of its work has been the service of the people hitherto despised as 'unpolitical masses'.[13]

Prominent non-Brahmin intellectuals also visualized "a national society based on unity and fraternity, a new nation, of a new form of congruence between culture and power and a new way of relating the self with the other". To quote a Justice Party ideologue:

> "The dream of Indian nationalism will be realised fully with the passing away of caste from our land. Power cannot be safely vested in the people unless the mental habit, which sanctions and enforces the customary treatment of lower castes, is changed. The emancipation of the people from suspicious communalism is the first milestone in the progress of responsible self-government of the country. National evolution will move on sound lines when all the component parts of the body politic are sound and strong enough to contribute their energy, experience, and intelligence, and when the organic connection and vitality of each link is healthy. With every unit of society growing strong and contended the whole society will be safe; otherwise national progress will be one-sided and irregular."[14]

There was a broad convergence of ideas among the lower caste articulation regarding the nature and content of democracy, freedom, nationalism, nation state etc. Likewise, the preponderance of Brahmin caste and the ideological foundations of their supremacy became the most common areas of conflict and contestation between the upper and lower castes. The protest of dalit-bahujan communities against social and ritual dominance of the Brahmin community was also governed by their material conditions. They denounced the existing caste system and social arrangements not to uphold but to change and modify them. The so-called sanskrisation efforts of some of the non-Brahmin castes were surely aimed at it. By negating the Brahmanical monopoly of interpretation of the texts they were demanding the democratization of priesthood and the right for priesthood for others. It could also be interpreted as a protest against "Brahmanical exclusivity and sacerdotal monopoly". The dalit-bahujan movement might not have professed a "radical/revolutionary" ideology to over through the existing system by violent means, yet their conscious efforts were directed at delegitimizing and destabilizing it; to what extent they succeeded is altogether a different question. But it was a fact that there was consistent demand to reduce the monopoly of certain social groups and equitable distribution of available opportunities/ and resources. It is in this unity of ideas/perceptions that one can visualise commonness in the social consciousness of dalitbahujan castes in terms of articulation of emancipatory ideology. Notwithstanding social, ritual and material differences, majority of their spokesmen envisaged a future set-up based on the principles of egalitarianism and social justice.

A dalit spokesman wrote: "Independence (*swarajyam*) will be obtained by the collective efforts of all the people. It requires unity. In India it is lacking.... If untouchability were eradicated, there would be equality. It would facilitate unity among the people. With unity and united action freedom could be achieved".Dalitbahujan intellectuals felt that social equality, self-respect and dignity are an inalienable and integral part of independence i.e., *Swarajyam/swantantram*. They doubted the sincerity of the caste Hindu Nationalists in establishing an egalitarian Nation-State and asserted that unless social equality is achieved, freedom would be worthless and visualized freedom with social dignity, honour and social justice. Therefore, for them, *SamanatwameSwantantram* (Equality is Freedom).

To conclude, The emerging consciousness of dalit-bahujan communities has been grounded on such ideological and intellectual articulations. The opposition of higher castes to the growing assertion of lower castes also helped cement broader non-Brahmin identity. The mainstream nationalist press and upper caste ideologues tended to denigrate non-Brahmin assertion. For instance the Brahmin-dominated *Andhra Patrika*commented: "the non-Brahmin movement is an artificial creation, that it has the support of only a small number of followers, and the bulk of the non-Brahmin community.... stood aloof from it". (25 August 1919); "The attitude which the non-Brahmins of Madras are displaying against Brahmans is a self-destructive one and a national evil" (27 August 1919); "This community (non-Brahmans) being more influential in the matter of wealth, numerical strength etc than the Brahman community needs no separate representation" (19 February 1920). Similarly, *Krishna Patrika* another Brahmin controlled newspaper noted: "This (caste representation) being once accepted, there will be no end to the consequent complications... The suggestion of the Andhra Congress Committee that the non-Brahman representation should be discussed by various bodies leads to the undesirable increase of mutual feuds". (31 January 1920) Some papers also dismissed the idea of abolition of caste as 'specious arguments which are not in our interests", because "the caste system conduces to national advancement. The various castes in a nation are something like the numerous departments, which constitute the huge machinery of administration. The caste system is thus not a great evil after all." ("*Swadeshabhimani*, 23 November 1917). But on the contrary, the spokesmen of lower castes resisted discrimination and pleaded recognition of their just claims. They asserted that caste is "social Imperialism"[15] a "crippling disease" and described the Brahmins as a "privileged oligarchy". "Throughout the whole system permeates the dogma of Brahmanic superiority. This is the foundation on which the whole edifice is created…the maintenance of institutions based on such obviously unjust principles, involved a conscious and deliberate policy, political, religious and educational, on the part of the Brahmins. In order to safeguard their interests, it was necessary for them to dominate councils of the State, to mould the religious development and control the educational machinery and literature of the community. This the Brahmins tried to do, and we know that they have been eminently successful from the fact that their predominance in Hindu social life continues unbroken even to the present time. For more than 3000 years the Brahmins have maintained…a complete sway over the masses of the Hindu population". It has been argued that the attainment of liberty and justice has always been a negative process. Without rebelling against unjust social institutions and destroying age-old customs, "there can never be the free exercise of liberty and justice".

Available source materials such as press reports, resolutions of caste associations, autobiographical and biographical accounts amply make it clear that not all the castes and communities responded uniformly, but to the extent that certain caste groups became assertive, a broad pattern could be discerned in their thought process and ideological formation. Of course, the context, factors and actors which facilitated such an articulation and mobilisation also differed, for instance between the dalits and other lower Sudra castes (bahujans). But what were common to all of them were certain notions of social justice, egalitarianism and socio-economic mobility. There was a broad convergence of ideas among the lower caste articulation regarding the nature and content of democracy, freedom, nationalism, nation state etc. Likewise, the preponderance of Brahmin caste and the ideological foundations of their supremacy became the most common areas of conflict and contestation between the upper and lower castes. The protest of dalit-bahujan communities against social and ritual dominance of the Brahmin community was also governed by their material conditions. They denounced the existing caste system and social arrangements not to uphold but to change and modify them. The so-called sanskrisation efforts of some of the non-Brahmin castes were surely aimed at it. By negating the Brahmanical monopoly of interpretation of the texts they were demanding the democratisation of priesthood and the right for priesthood for others. It could also be interpreted as a protest against "Brahmanical exclusivity and sacerdotal monopoly". The dalit-bahujan movement might not have professed a "radical/revolutionary" over through of the existing system by violent means, yet their conscious efforts were directed at delegitamising and destabilising it; to what extent they succeeded is altogether a different question. But it was a fact that there was consistent demand to reduce the monopoly of certain social groups and equitable distribution of available opportunities/resources. It is in this unity of ideas/perceptions that one can visualise commonness in the social consciousness of dalit-bahujan castes in terms of articulation of emancipatory ideology. Notwithstanding social, ritual and material differences, majority of their spokesmen envisaged a future set-up based on the principles of egalitarianism and social justice. The uniqueness of the social-political assertion and consciousness of the dalit-bahujans in modern south India lies in the fact that they attempted to undermine the ideological underpinnings of the Brahmanical social order and the tyranny of caste. They also attempted to pave the way for a relatively more equal spread of secular power in modern society, by attacking the socio-cultural foundations of the old order. The movements led by them such as the Self-Respect Association, Justice Party, Adi-Andhra Mahasabha etc., were based on the notion of egalitarianism and a vision of "homogenization of power within culture and society".

References

A.P. Patro, "The Justice Movement in India", in *The Asiatic Review,*vol.xxviii, no. 93, 1932, p. 28.

BrijRanjan Mani, *Debrahmanising History: Dominance and Resistance in Indian Society,* New Delhi, 2015. And G. Aloysius, *Nationalism without Nation in India*, New Delhi, 1998.

BrijRanjan Mani, *DebrahmanisingHistor*.... p. 259.

C.J. Baker, The Politics of South India, 1920-37, New Delhi, 1976, and E. Irschick, Politics and Social Conflict in South India; The Non-Brahmin Movement and Tamil Separatism, 1916-29, Berkeley, 1969.

E. Sudha Rani, "The 125th Bullock Cart (Viluvandi) Sojourn of Mahatma Ayyankali in Travancore in 1893", in: TRC Journal of Telangana Studies, April-June, 2019, Vol. 1, No. 1 p. 63.

G. Aloysius, *Nationalism..op.cit.*

K.M. Panikkar, *Caste and Democracy*, London, 1933, p. 38.

Lakshmi Narasu, *A Study, op.cit.,*

M. Arokiaswami, "The Birth of the Harijan Movement" in *The New Review*, vol.iv, July-Dec. 1936, p. 183.

P. Lakshmi Narasu, *A Study of Caste*, Madras, 1922, p. 112.

R Guha (ed.), *Subaltern Studies*, vol.1, New Delhi, 1987.

Notes

1. For details see, Brij Ranjan Mani, *Debrahmanising History: Dominance and Resistance in Indian Society,* New Delhi, 2015. And G. Aloysius, *Nationalism without Nation in India*, New Delhi, 1998.
2. Brij Ranjan Mani, *Debrahmanising Histor....* p. 259.
3. E. Sudha Rani, "The 125th Bullock Cart (Viluvandi) Sojourn of Mahatma Ayyankali in Travancore in 1893", in: TRC Journal of Telangana Studies, April-June, 2019, Vol. 1, No. 1 p. 63.
4. Brij Ranjan Mani, *DebrahmanisingHistor....* p. 322-24.
5. Ibid and G. Aloysius, *Nationalism..op.cit*
6. For detail see, R Guha (ed.), *Subaltern Studies*, Vol. 1, New Delhi, 1987.
7. P. Lakshmi Narasu, *A Study of Caste*, Madras, 1922, p. 112.
8. *Ibid.,* p. 110.
9. See, C.J. Baker, The Politics of South India, 1920-37, New Delhi, 1976, and E. Irschick, Politics and Social Conflict in South India; The Non-Brahmin Movement and Tamil Separatism, 1916-29, Berkeley, 1969.
10. M. Arokiaswami, "The Birth of the Harijan Movement" in *The New Review*, Vol. iv, July-Dec. 1936, p. 183.
11. K.M. Panikkar, *Caste and Democracy*, London, 1933, p. 38.
12. Lakshmi Narasu, *A Study, op.cit.,*
13. A.P. Patro, "The Justice Movement in India", in *The Asiatic Review,* vol.xxviii, no. 93, 1932, p. 28.
14. *Ibid.*
15. K.M. Panikkar, *Caste; op.cit.* p. 18.

Chapter - 6

Trends in Reservation Policy of India: An Analysis from Social Justice to Economic Justice[1]

— Dr. E. Venkatesu

Introduction

There are various nomenclatures for the special treatment of certain social categories such as indigenous ethnic groups, socially, educationally and economically disadvantaged communities in different parts of the world. The nomenclatures are including affirmative action policy in the United States, positive discrimination in Britain, reservation policy in India, standardization in Sri lanka, reflecting the federal character of the country in Nigeria and sons of the soil preferences in Malaysia and Indonesia. The group preferences and quotas have existed in Israel, China, Australia, Brazil, Fiji, Canada, and Pakistan, New Zealand and the Soviet Union and its successor states (Sowell, 2004).

India is one of the countries, in the world, which has been following reservation policy for more than a century beginning in the late 19th century in the Colonial Presidencies, Princely states and post-independent period.

Review of the Literature

In the scholarly works (Galanter, 1984) the term backward classes, as refereed in the Constitution has been denoting of several social categories, which come under the reservation category in Indian context. These are

1. As a synonym for Depressed Classes, untouchables, Scheduled Castes.

---

1. Revised version of the paper presented in the 3rd Conference of International Public Policy Association at National University of Singapore.

2. As comprising the untouchable, aboriginal and hill tribes, criminal tribes,etc.
3. As comprising all the communities deserving special treatment, namely those included in (2) above and in addition the lower strata of non-touchable communities.
4. As comprising all non-tribal communities deserving special treatment.
5. As comprising all communities deserving special treatment except the untouchables.
6. As comprising the lower strata of non-untouchable communities.
7. As comprising all communities above the untouchables but below the most "advanced" communities.
8. As comprising the non-touchable communities who were "backward" in comparison to the highest castes.
9. As comprising all communities other than the highest or most advanced.
10. As comprising all persons who meet given non-communal tests of backwardness (e.g., low income).

In India, reservation policy is being used as an instrument for the upliftment of the historically marginalized such as Scheduled Castes (SCs), Scheduled Tribes (STs), Other Backward Classes (OBCs) also known as Socially and Educationally Backward Classes (SEBCs), who were subjected to the social deprivation (Venkatesu, E, 2014). In the wake of dominant castes agitation, certain articles are published. One of the article on Marathas reveals that Marathas, from sociological origin point of view, are Kshtriyas, they have grabbed disproportionate political positions on Congress party including Chief Minister position and controlling the economy of Maharashtra (Deshpande, 2014). On *Patels*' Quota for *Patels*? The Neo-middle-class Syndrome and the (partial) Return of Caste Politics in Gujarat'[1] The *Patels*in Gujarat politically highly mobilized and even occupied Chief Minister, they are the beneficiaries of Cooperative societies, businessmen of Diamonds, Detergent barrens, Motels in USA etc (Jeffrelot, 2016). *Jats*are not only prosperous and socially powerful in Haryana, western Uttar Pradesh and Rajasthan but also call the shots in politics and governance in these States (Dogra, 2014). The survey of literature reveals that there is hardly any write up on the demand of kapus for the OBC quota. The review of the literature reveals that the policy has got long historical legacy, which can be classified into three phases.

The historical account of reservation policy in India reveals that, broadly, there are three phases, which includes (1) the origin and genesis of special treatment or reservation policy for socially deprived communities from late 19th century to commencement of the Constitution in 1950. (2) Efforts to extend the reservation policy for Other Backward Classes/ Socially and Educationally Backward Classes 1950s -1990s and (3) Dominant castes demand for Reservations from 1990s and state response. To achieve the objectives of the paper, the secondary sources includes books, articles, Commission reports and primary sources such as surveys are used for the historical analysis.

The origin and genesis of policy for socially deprived communities from late 19th century to commencement of the Constitution in 1950

The traditional India was a highly stratified and hierarchically structured social system, which was formed based on caste. Caste is an informal social institution of kin relationship and those who have practiced similar occupation assigned on the basis of birth in a caste (Srinivas, 1996). In the process of colonial modernisation with the penetration of western education and ideas, there was a social upsurge from the lowest social order of the society for human dignity and self-respect during the 19thcentury (O' Hanlon, 1985).

The genesis of Backward Classes can be traced back to 1872 when British Government in Madras Presidency identified the lack of representation to the Muslims in education and employment. To make the Muslims as part of colonial education, the government had started schools in the Muslim localities and in Urdu, Persian and Arabic medium (Radhakrishnan, 1990). The Education Commission of 1882 focused on aboriginals and lower castes to provide special facilities in terms of education and employment. Backward classes proper also appeared in 1884 as a reference to 'aborigines' and 'low castes' in the remarks of the Madras government sent to the government of India in chapter nine of the Education Commission's report on the education of classes requiring special treatment (Ibid). During this period, the Education Committee identified that there is no proper accommodation of all the social groups, emerging pressure from the Caste Associations and social resistance, the British and Native rulers had introduced reservations in the education and employment opportunities for the lower castes. As a result, in 1883 the British rulers of Madras Presidency recognized 39 castes as Backward Classes and introduced reservation system in educational institutions and government jobs. The number of castes in this list grew to 238 by 1943 (Ibid).

In 1880s, the *Sahu Chatrapathi Maharaj* of *Kolhapur Sansthan* (indigenous princely state) took special steps for the representation of *Shudras* in government jobs. The *Mysore Maharaja* implemented reservation for the Backward Classes since 1895. *Travancore* and *Cochin Maharaja* took special steps for the representation of the oppressed in proportion to their population in the administration.

Efforts to extend the reservation policy for Other Backward Classes/Socially and Educationally Backward Classes 1950s-1990s

The legacy of 19th century social resistance had become rich social capital for the incorporation of 'Right to Equality', 'Social Justice', 'fraternity' in the Constitution of India, which came into existence on 26th January 1950. The makers of Indian Constitution such as BR Ambedkar raised the issue of caste centric annihilation and need for Constitutional status to the policy that was supposed to be introduced in the form of reservations/affirmative action/positive discrimination for the amelioration of the historically marginalized, indigenous and socially and educationally backward classes (Galanter).

The post-independent Indian Constitution ensured reservation policy through the following Articles. Article 15(4) Nothing in this article or in clause (2) of article 29 shall prevent the State from making any special provision for the advancement of any socially and educationally backward classes of citizens or for the Scheduled Castes and the Scheduled Tribes. (5) Nothing in this article or in sub-clause (g) of clause (1) of article 19 shall prevent the State from making any special provision, by law, for the advancement of any socially and educationally backward classes of citizens or for the Scheduled Castes or the Scheduled Tribes in so far as such special provisions relate to their admission to educational institutions including private educational institutions, whether aided or unaided by the State, other than the minority educational institutions referred to in clause (1) of article 30.

Article 16(4) Nothing in this article shall prevent the State from making any provision for the reservation of appointments or posts in favour of any backward class of citizens which, in the opinion of the State, is not adequately represented in the services under the State.

(4A) Nothing in this article shall prevent the State from making any provision for reservation in matters of promotion, with consequential seniority, to any class or classes of posts in the services under the State in favour of the Scheduled Castes and the Scheduled Tribes which, in the opinion of the State, are not adequately represented in the services under the State.

(4B) Nothing in this article shall prevent the State from considering any unfilled vacancies of a year which are reserved for being filled up in that year in accordance with any provision for reservation made under clause (4) or clause (4A) as a separate class of vacancies to be filled up in any succeeding year or years and such class of vacancies shall not be considered together with the vacancies of the year in which they are being filled up for determining the ceiling of fifty per cent. reservation on total number of vacancies of that year.

Article 46 Promotion of educational and economic interests of Scheduled Castes, Scheduled Tribes and other weaker sections.—The State shall promote with special care the educational and economic interests of the weaker sections of the people, and, in particular, of the Scheduled Castes and the Scheduled Tribes, and shall protect them from social injustice and all forms of Exploitation.

Article 335 The claims of the members of the Scheduled Castes and the Scheduled Tribes shall be taken into consideration, consistently with the maintenance of efficiency of administration, in the making of appointments to services and posts in connection with the affairs of the Union or of a State: [Provided that nothing in this article shall prevent in making of any provision in favour of the members of the Scheduled Castes and the Scheduled Tribes for relaxation in qualifying marks in any examination or lowering the standards of evaluation, for reservation in matters of promotion to any class or classes of services or posts in connection with the affairs of the Union or of a State.]

Article 340(1) The President may by order appoint a Commission consisting of such persons as he thinks fit to investigate the conditions of socially and educationally backward classes within the territory of India and the difficulties under which they labour and to make recommendations as to the steps that should be taken by the Union or any State to remove such difficulties and to improve their condition and as to the grants that should be made for the purpose by the Union or any State and the conditions subject to which such grants should be made, and the order appointing such Commission shall define the procedure to be followed by the Commission.

(2) A Commission so appointed shall investigate the matters referred to them and present to the President a report setting out the facts as found by them and making such recommendations as they think proper.

(3) The President shall cause a copy of the report so presented together with a memorandum explaining the action taken thereon to be laid before each House of Parliament.

While following the Constitutional provisions, the post-independent Indian state introduced 22.5% reservations in public sector employment, education and political representation for the SCs and STs in proportion to their population right from the commencement of Indian Constitution.

Other Backward Classes can only get justice as per Article 340 of the Constitution. The Article 340 proclaims that the President of India can appoint a Backward Classes Commission to look into the concerns of the Backward Classes, investigate them and make recommendations to the State and Central Government.

(1) The Government of India, on January 29, 1953 appointed a committee under the Chairmanship of *Kaka Kalelkar*and with 11 other members. The terms of references of the committee were to find out the reasons for Backwardness and make recommendations to bring them out of social and educational backwardness. The commission evolved certain indicators such as place in the social structure, educational level, and representation in government jobs, trade and business. On the basis of these indicators, the commission identified 2,399 castes as Other Backward Classes. The Committee concluded that 32% ofthe Indian population belonged to social, educational and economic backwardness and recommended the government to take necessary steps for their welfare.

However, the Chairman of the Commission *Kaka Kalelkar*, while submitting the report, recorded his dissatisfaction over the report in black and white for taking caste as the indicator to measure the level of backwardness. The report was submitted in March 1955 but there was hardly any discussion in the Parliament. The then Home Minister declared that the development of Backward Classes come under the purview of State governments, therefore, the Central government would not take any action. Because of chairperson's dissatisfaction, lack of initiation from Prime Minister to discuss in the Parliament and putting it on the state governments by the Ministry of Home Affairs, there was hardly any attempt for the advancement of OBCs so long as the Congress party was in power at the national level.

By 1970s, because of the land reforms, green revolution and the political movements led by *LoknayakJayaprakash Narayan* and *Ram ManoharLohiya*, the upper castes were losing their importance in village politics, which led to the changes in power dynamics at the local level. With the rise of new social groups in the local politics, the Congress party was defeated and Janata party came to the power. The Janata government in 1979, constituted the Second National level Backward Classes Commission under the Chairmanship of *Bindeshwar PrasadMandal*.

(2) The Second Backward Classes Commission evolved three broad indicators and eleven sub- indicators to identify the social and educational backwardness. The indicator sincludes

A. Social

(i) Castes/Classes considered as socially backward by others.

(ii) Castes/Classes, which mainly depend on manual labour for their livelihood.

(iii) where at least 25% female and 10% male above the State average get married at an age below 17 years in rural areas and at least 10% female and 5% male do so in urban areas.

(iv) Castes/Classes where participation of female in work is at least 25% above the state average.

B. Educational

(i) Castes/Classes where the number of children in the age group of 5-15 years who never attend school is at least 25% above the state average.

(ii) Castes/Classes where the rate of student drop-out in the age group of 5-15 years is at least 25% above the State average.

(iii) Castes/Classes amongst whom the proportion of matriculates is at least 25% below the State average.

C. Economic

(i) Castes/Classes where the average value of family assets is at least 25% below the state average.

(ii) Castes/Classes where the number of families living in kuccha houses is at least 25% above the state average.

(iii) Castes/Classes where the source of drinking water is beyond half a kilometre for more than 50% of the households.

(iv) Castes/Classes where the number of households having taken consumption loan is at least 25% above the state average.

The Commission, as per 1931 census, estimated the population of OBCs at 52%. and also recommended for initiating measures to bring about social, educational, economic and political transformation among OBCs. The commission strongly opined that the OBCs constitute about 52%, therefore, they must have 52% reservations in the central government institutions. Due to existence of Supreme Court ceiling of not exceeding the percentage of reservations more than 50%, the Commission recommended 27% reservations for OBCs along with several other measures for their development.

The Commission submitted its report in 1980, by that time, again, Congress was in power at the center. Therefore, the *Mandal* Commission Report gathered dust for about a decade. During 1989 Parliament election, the National Front in its election manifesto promised that they would implement the *Mandal* Commission Report. After the formation of a non-Congress government headed by National Front at the center, the Prime Minister *V.P. Singh* on 7th August, 1990 announced that 27% reservation Due to several initiatives such as land reforms, importance of adult franchise, green revolution and political mobilisation from 1960s, the OBC emerged as a powerful challenge to then ruling political parties. Therefore, it was an inevitable to recognise their hold in the electoral politics in the form of Mandal Commission. The Bharatiya Janata Party opposed the Mandal Commission from implementation, but accommodated the OBCs in the political positions (Jeffrelot, 2003). One of the recommendations of the Mandal Commission was to provide the 27% reservations in education and employment of the central government institutions. After a sever battle, the 27% reservations was started to implement from 1993 onwards. But in the process of implementation, there are several issues have been coming up. will be implemented for Other Backward Classes in all the Central Government Institutions.

However, there was an outcry from upper caste political leaders, government officials, trade and commerce, dominant civil society, media and others against the union government decision. In opposing the 27% quota of OBCs, the castes, which are demanding for OBC quota also joined. The political parties under the leadership of Backward Classes, non-Parliamentary leftist parties, Dalit, civil liberty associations, progressive intellectuals stood up for the cause of reservations to OBCs. As the pro and anti-reservation agitation was going on, *Indira Sawhney* challenged 27% reservations in the Supreme Court. The Supreme Court of India upheld the 27% reservations through its verdict in 1992. The verdict was entered into Gazette of India in 1993, from then onwards 27% reservations have been in implementation in central government institutions, especially in employment and from 2007-08 onwards in educational institutions. In the implementation of 27% reservation policy, there are certain hurdles such as Creamy-layer, lack of awareness to the beneficiaries and difficulties in obtaining caste certificate from the government, therefore, hardly 14% of reservations have been filled in the public sector. These issues are elaborated as follows[2].

1. **The problem of identifying OBC population:** The two National level Backward Classes Commissions have prepared their reports according to 1931 Census. The two reports identified and estimated the OBC population but they were set aside. The BC list prepared by the state governments' is being taken into consideration for the implementation of 27% reservations. Until today, the initiatives for the development of OBCs are being taken up without accurate data of the OBC population.
2. **Constitutional limit to reservations:** As per the Supreme Court directions - the reservations including *Dalit*, *Adivasis*, Other Backward Classes, put together, should not exceed 50%. This limit is against the Constitutional principles of 'Equality and Social Justice' and proportional representation. According to minimum democratic principle 'All citizens are equal', everybody should get their due share in polity and development. The basic purpose of reservations is to make a vertical social order into a horizontal one that means equality in an unequal society. Therefore, there is need to make a Constitutional amendment about the judicial restriction of ceiling on the percentage of reservations.
3. **Creamy layer:** While the Supreme Court of India gave its verdict upholding the 27% reservations, it exempted the creamy layer from reservations. The Court identified two types of 'Creamy layer'. One - those who have income more than the permissible income limit. Two: Children of the parents who are working in the state, central government high rank positions. Though there is a point in Creamy Layer, in implementation process it has become very difficult in terms of identification.
4. **Difficulties in getting caste certificate:** to get the privilege of reservations either in education or employment, one must need to

2. These issues are extracted from the article on 25 Years of OBC Reservations and Emerging Challenges' written for the Souvenir of Backward Classes Centre for Empowerment, 2015, Hyderabad.

produce an evidence in the form of caste certificate. It is true that caste certificate is a basic requirement to get the Constitutional entitlements, but the people of OBCs have been facing a great deal of difficulty in getting the certificate. It is because the revenue department is not having proper records regarding castes, lack of duplicate caste certificate as an evidence for fresh one, lack of computerization and lack of awareness among the social categories which come under reservations about the importance of caste certificate. Another importance issue is that the OBCs are supposed to renewal their caste certificate once in every six months to proof that they are not coming under the 'creamy layer' category.

5. **Inclusion and exclusion in the Other Backward Classes list:** The Government of India, while implementing the 27% reservations, takes into consideration the BC list prepared by the state governments. In this regard, the central government has made provisions to add or delete some castes from that list. However, while including or excluding any caste from that list, the National Backward Class Commission has to deeply delve into the social, educational and economic factors and then take a decision. However, right from the *Vajpayee* government to *Manmohan Singh* government, few hundreds of castes were included in the Backward Classes list due to political pressure rather than any scientific criteria and it was done without increasing the reservation ratio. Due to political pressure, the *Jats* from North India and *Marathas* from *Maharashtra* were also included in the Backward Classes list. But the thing is that both these castes are economically and politically strong and dominant ruling castes in their respective states. Therefore, the judiciary has rejected them from inclusion in the OBC list. Interestingly, those dominant groups such as *Kapus* in *Andhra Pradesh, Patels* in *Gujarat* etc., which opposed the *Mandal* report. The hidden agenda of the dominant castes to include them in the OBC list is to perpetuate and continue their dominance in the society under the umbrella of OBC identity.

Dominant castes demand for Reservations from 1990s and state response

From late 19th century to 1990s, it was the downtrodden sections of the society especially SCs, STs and OBCs fought for the reservations. However, from 1990s, the dominant castes, such as *Kapus* in *Andhra Pradesh, Marathas* in *Maharashtra, Jats* in *Hary ana* and *Patels* in *Gujarat* started demanding for the reservations in the OBC quota. Dominant caste means numerically the strongest in the village or local area and economically and politically exercises a preponderating influence (Srinivas MN 1959). These communities have not only benefited from the post-independent political system through occupying key positions but also industrial development and Green Revolution in the country but also vehemently opposed the reservation policy at the state and National level to the Backward Classes up to 1990s. Because of State initiative, judicial intervention and support of the civil society organizations, the Backward Classes/OBCs have got reservations but the dominant communities have been trying to grab the cake of backwards through violent agitations for putting a pressure upon the State.

The demand of dominant castes for OBC status was rejected by the National and State level Backward Classes Commissions, struck down by High Courts and Supreme Court and opposed by the Backward Classes Associations on the demand of dominant castes. Even civil society is also opposing the reservations for dominant groups, which is being well established in a survey on Youth (Lokniti, 2017).

Table 6.1 on Measuring youth Support for demand of non-OBC farming Communities to be included in the OBC category (%)

	Fully Support	*Support but only after increasing existing OBC quota*	*Oppose*	*No Response*
Youth (overall)	26	10	34	30
Hindu Upper Caste	18	6	53	23
Hindu Dominant Farming Castes	23	11	41	24
Hindu Peasant OBC	32	11	30	28
Hindu Artisanal and Service OBC	26	10	33	31
Hindu SC	33	11	30	27
Hindu ST	13	5	17	64
Muslim	26	11	30	33
Others	23	14	39	24

Source: CSDS- KAS: Attitude, anxieties and aspirations of India's Youth: changing Patterns- A report.

The survey found youth to be more opposed to this demand than in support. While every fourth youth (26%) was found to be in favour of inclusion of such communities within the OBC category, about one in every three or 34 percent were averse to the idea. One in every ten gave conditional support to the idea; that is, they were in favour of inclusion but only after increasing the existing OBC quota beyond 27 percent.

While responding to the emerging demand of the dominant caste, The NDA government headed by Narendra Modi, passed the 103rd Constitutional Amendment Act in 2019 to provide 10% reservations for Economically Weaker Sections of society. The basic purpose of amendment is to insert certain clauses to Article 15 and 16 of the Constitution to avoid the legal hurdles for the reservations based on economic criteria.

The 10% economic quota is not a new one in India. In the past economic criteria based reservations were introduced but the court has struct down on the ground that the basic purpose of reservations is to make unequals as equals in terms of social discrimination in India, while citing article 15 and 16 of the Constitution. In order to over the legal issues, the amendments are made to insert clause 6 to article 15. Clause 6 is that nothing in this article or sub-clause (g) of clause (1) of article 19 or clause (2) of article 29 shall prevent the State from making-

(a) any special provision for the advancement of any economically weaker sections of citizens other than the classes mentioned in clauses (4) and (5); and

(b) any special provision for the advancement of any economically weaker sections of citizens other than the classes mentioned in clauses (4) and (5) in so far as such special provisions relate to their admission to educational institutions including private educational institutions, whether aided or unaided by the State, other than the minority educational institutions referred to in clause (1) of article 30, which in the case of reservations would be in addition to the existing reservations and subject to a maximum of ten percent of the total seats in each category.

For article 16, clause 6 is added and reads as nothing in this article shall prevent the State from making any provision for the reservation of appointments or posts in favour of any economically weaker sections of citizens other than the classes mentioned in clause (4), in addition to the existing reservation and subject to a maximum of ten percent of the posts in each category.

Conclusion

From the historical analysis of the origin and genesis of reservation policy in India has been revealing that there has been a shift from social basis of reservations to economic criteria. The demand for the special treatment for historically disadvantaged social categories was started in the late 19th century and through ought the 20th century, in a cumulative manner, it has gained momentum due to increase in number of lower castes to get benefit as well as percentage of reservations.

In the context of globalization from 1990s, the ruling dominant sections of the society, who were opposing reservations at a particular point of time, has started demanding for the reservations when the public sector economy is getting rapidly privatised. However, the same category of people never opposed the privatisation of the economy but intensified the demand for reservations in the public sector, where the cake is shrinking.

Moreover, the ruling party at the national level passed the constitutional amendment Act in 2019 just before the 17th Loksabha election for providing 10% reservations to Economically Weaker Sections (EWS). However, the 10% quota of EWS is being challenged in the Supreme Court of India. One will have to wait and see for the final verdict that whether it is in tune with the basic principles of the Constitution or contentious?

References

Galanter, Marc, (1984), Competing Equalities Law and the Backward Classes in India, Oxford University Press, Delhi, 1984, p. 155)

Backward Classes in India Exclusion, Empowerment and Modernisation 22-24 March, 2014 at Osmania University, Hyderabad.

Deshpande, Rajeshwari, (2014), Seeking OBC status: Political Strategies of Two Dominant Castes, SAGE Publication, Vol. 2 (2), pp. 169-183.

Dogra, Chander Suth, (4th April 2014), The Hindu (English Daily), Chennai.

Jaffrelot, Christophe, (2016), Quota for Patels? The Neo-middle-class Syndrome and the (partial) Return of Caste Politics in Gujarat, SAGE Publication, Vol. 4(2) 218-232.

——Jeffrelot, Christoph, (2003), India's Silent Revolution-the Rise of Lower Castes in North India, Columbia University Press, New York.

——Lokinit (CSDS)-Konrad Adenaauer Stiftung (2017), Attitudes, anxieties and aspirations of India's youth: Changing patterns- A Report -Ibid, p. 29.

O' Hanlon Rosalind, (1985), Caste, Conflict and Ideology Mahatma Jotirao Phuleansd Low Caste Protest in Nineteenth-Century Western India, Cambridge University Press, London.

Radhakrishnan. P, (1990) Backward Classes in Tamilnadu: 1872-1988, Economic and Political Weekly, March 10, Mumbai.

Srinivas, MN, (1996) Castes Its Twenty First Century Avatar, and Penguin Books, India. -Srinivas, MN (1959).

Sowell. Thomas, (2004), Affirmative Action Around the World An Empirical Study, Yale University Press New Haven and London.

Venkatesu, E, (2015), Other Backward Classes, Twenty Five Years of Reservations and Emerging Challenges, Souvenir released by Backward Classes Centre for Empowerment on 6thSeptember at Hyderabad.

— Venkatesu, E, (2014), Social Deprivation, Mobilization and State in the Identity Formation and Affirmative Action Policy-An Analysis of Other backward Classes, paper presented in the national seminar on The Other 103rd Constitutional Amendment Act, 2019.

Chapter - 7

History of Reservations Policy in India: An Overview

— Dr. Panthukala Srinivas,
Dr. Sareen Chatla

Abstract

Caste Based Reservations in India Started in the second (2nd) Century BCE. In the Manusmriti *- the law book of Brahmins according to which all the laws were based on Caste and no Merit was ever considered. It divided people into High and Low Castes on the basis of their birth and not on the basis of Merit. Wealth, Political power, Spiritual leadership, Education, Ownership of Land, Trade and all lucrative positions were reserved for the higher castes. The correct term used for "Reservation" in the Indian Constitution is "Representation". Anyone engaging with Reservations, first of all must understand the true meaning and the essence of the very concept of "reservations". It is not given to anyone in his or her individual capacity. Reservations is given to any individual as a representative of the under-privileged community. The beneficiaries of reservations are in turn expected to help their communities to develop economically, leading to social equality. Reservation is a democratic principle to provide representation to the castes that hitherto remained unrepresented, hence pushed to margins, in multiple arena of governance of the country. This paper will discuss the history of Reservations policy in India and will critically engage with the concept, its operation and multiple implications at various levels of the social operation.*

Introduction

The British Government commissioned the Hunter Commission to investigate the status and condition of Education in India. A written memorandum relating to representation in administration was submitted by Jotirao Phule to the Hunter Commission. Detailed information about the troubles faced by the Shudras and Ati-Shudras because of the operating multi-layered caste system in the Indian society and the crusaders of the same system Brahmins occupying the key Administration was put forth by Jotirao Phule in this memorandum. He uses the word *Kalam-Kasai* (Marathi) i.e., "Pen yielding Butchers" to characterize the Brahmins in the Administration. It is important to know that the reservations for the backward classes were introduced for the first time on 26th July 1902 by Chatrapati Sahuji Maharaj of Kohlapur Presidency. Later, in 1919 it was implemented by the King of Mysore on the recommendations of the Miller Committee. It was suggested by the Committee that there has to be a fair representation of non-Brahmins in matters of employment and education. This practice was replicated in the Madras Presidency in 1921, where for every 12 posts, five had to go to non-Brahmins, two to Brahmins, two to Muslims, two to Anglo-Indians or Indian Christians and one to the depressed classes (read Untouchable castes). Reservation in services was extended to the Scheduled Castes in the year 1942 as a policy of the British government.

The Role of Dr. B.R. Ambedkar in the History of Reservations

In order to get insights in to whole range of issues, it is necessary to go back to the formative stage of reservation policy in India for which systematic intellectual efforts were made by Dr. B. R. Ambedkar, who articulated the Reservation policy from 1919 through 1947. Ambedkar's efforts began in 1919 and carried through the 1930's and 1940's till the reservation policy was finally accepted in the present form in 1947.

Systematic articulation of arguments in favour of remedies against caste discrimination were spelt out in Ambedkar's first statement submitted in January 1919 to the South borough Committee, at the time of the reform of Government of India Act 1919. About ten year latter in May 1928, when the second attempt was made to revise the Government of India Act, during 1930/31 through series of Round table conferences, Ambedkar submitted two Statements, one to the Simon Commission in May, 1928 and another two years later in 1930 at the First Round Table Conference. The final statement came in 1947 in the "States and Minorities –What are their Rights and how to Secure them in the Constitution of Free India" at the time of framing of India's Constitution. An analysis of these documents provides insights into the origin of reservation policy in India and also lessons for the present discussion on private sector reservation. In their intellectual exercise these documents are basic to the understanding of the malady of the Hindu society and the remedies proposed by Ambedkar against denial of equal opportunity to untouchables. (See Dr. B. R. Ambedkar 1919, 1930 and 1947)(6).

From these writings in the 1920 through 1940's it become clear that Ambedkar grounded the case for remedies against discrimination of untouchables in the framework of the rights of citizens. In the first systematic written statement, "Evidence before the South borough's Committee" for Constitutional Reform in January 1919" he argued,

> The enforced servility and bar to human intercourse, due to untouchability involves, not merely discrimination in public life, but actually works out as a positive denial of all equal opportunity and the denial of those most elementary of civil rights on which all human existence depends"
>
> He further observed:
>
> Not only the untouchability arrested the growth of personality of untouchables but also comes in the way of their "material well being. It deprived them of certain civil rights ——The untouchable is not even a citizen. Citizenship is bundle of rights such as personal liberty, personal security, right to hold private property, equality before law, liberty of conscience, freedom of opinion, and speech, right of assembly, right of representation in country's Government, and right to hold office under the state".—The untouchability of untouchable puts these rights far beyond their reach." (Evidence before the Southborough's Committee, 1919, 256, 261).

Substantiating the claim before the Simon Commission Ambedkar argued, about thirty years later in 1928 at the time of reform of the Government of India Act "— Depressed classes cannot be employed in the army, navy, and police because such employment is opposed to the religious notion of majority. They cannot be admitted in schools, because their entry is opposed to the religious notion of majority. They cannot avail themselves of Government dispensaries, because doctors will not let them cause pollution to their persons or to their dispensaries. They cannot live cleaner and higher life, because to live above their prescribed station is opposed to the religious notions of the majority." Ambedkar added: "So rigorous is the enforcement of the social code against the Depressed classes that any attempt on the part of Depressed classes to the exercise their elementary rights of citizenship only ends in provoking the majority, to practice the worst forms of social tyranny known to history' (Statement to Simon Commission, 1928, 445). "Repeating the same argument in First Round Table Conference in Plenary Session on November 1930 Ambedkar argued "What is worse that this servility and bar to human intercourse, due to their untouchability, involves, not merely the possibility of discrimination in public life, but actually work out as a positive denial of all equality of opportunity and the denial of those most elementary of civic rights on which all human existence depend" (Plenary Session, 20 November 1930, First Round Table Conference, 504).

Finally in 1947 while justifying the need of safeguards against discrimination for the Scheduled Castes in the Constitution of independent India, Ambedkar argued "Unequal treatment has been the inescapable fate of the untouchables in India" — and added that "in a country like India where it is possible for discrimination to be practiced on a vast scale and in a relentless manner fundamental rights have no real meaning for untouchables." (States and Minorities 1947, 406, 407). Dr. B. R. Ambedkar incorporated Articles 330 and 332 in the Constitution to provide political reservation for the Scheduled Castes and Scheduled Tribes (SCs and STs). He also incorporated Article 15(4) and 16(4) to provide reservations in the executive and administrative services for the SCs and STs.

Reservations as Participation in Governance

Reservations are to be viewed as the right to active participation in the governance of the State and not merely be at the receiving end where the people are objects of law but not subjects of a state. According to Cicero (106-43 BCE), the Roman political thinker, the State is not a hierarchical structure of people but belongs to all people and exists for their welfare. All are concerned with State; and the State is the wealth of the people and not any community or group or caste. Cicero says: "A State is nothing else than partnership in Law". (Cited from H.R. Mukhi, A *Simple History of Western Political Thought: Plato and Burke*, Surjeet Deport, Delhi, 1986, p.222.). Cicero comments that every man possesses reason equally. He believes that error, bad habits and false opinions create inequality among the people. For him, all races are equal and he denounces racial inequality, propagating equality of men. The ideal state is that which possesses the virtue of justice. The 5th century Christian philosopher Saint Augustine says in the *City of God*: "Justice being taken away, then, what are kingdoms but great robberies? For what are robberies themselves, but little kingdoms?" Without justice – social, political and economic – our understanding of democracy has no meaning at all. To enhance the cause of justice we need to have some kind of reservations that will balance an unequal system.

Social Justice and the Policy of Reservations

The modern Indian society is divided into thousands of castes. In a textbook for the X class students M. Radhakrishna Sharma says: "The caste system represents a culture of repression. It is opposed to the democratic principles of liberty, equality and fraternity." (M. Radhakrishna Sarma, (eds.), *Social Studies,* Text book of class X, Government of Andhra Pradesh, Hyderabad, 1998, p.257.) There is a philosophical basis for the reservation system in the concept of justice. In other words, one should understand that justice is the root cause of reservations, because as John Mackenzie says, "The constitution of society is ...unjust when large classes in it are so enslaved by others as to be unable to develop their own lives. It is unjust for instance, when there is any class in it so poor. Or so hard worked or so dependent on others as to unable to cultivate their faculties and make progress towards the perfection of their nature. It is unjust when the idlers are protected and set in power, and the hard workers are crushed down and degraded."(John S. Mackenzie, *A Manual of Ethics*, Oxford University Press, Delhi, 1929, p.287.) Thus, according to Mackenzie, a society may be defined as just society, when the lives of all its members are developed skilfully at the optimum level. In view of these conditions, as elaborated in earlier sections, the reservations were introduced before India's independence in some provinces and were made Constitutional after independence.

Dr. B. R. Ambedkar incorporated Articles 330 and 332 in the Constitution to provide Political Reservation for the Scheduled Castes and the Scheduled Tribes. He also incorporated Articles 15(4) and 16(4) to provide Reservation in the Executive/Administrative Services for the Scheduled Castes and the Scheduled Tribes. Having made such a provision for the Scheduled Castes and the Scheduled Tribes, Ambedkar prepared a Draft to provide Reservation for the Other Backward Classes. Why did Ambedkar fight for the Other Backward Classes in the Constituent Assembly?

Dr. B. R. Ambedkar Resigned For the Rights of the OBCs

The Constitution of India came into effect from 26th January 1950. During this time Dr. B. R. Ambedkar was the Law Minister in Nehru's Cabinet and he raised the issue of constituting a commission as per Art 340 of the Constitution of India to identify the Other Backward Classes (OBCs), but his demand was not accepted. When his demands (Hindu Code Bill and Constitution of Backward Classes Commission) were not accepted, he resigned as Law Minister. We can understand that the OBCs do not know this fact. Due to the pressure of these OBC members Kakasaheb Kalelkar could identify 2218 Castes as OBCs. A resolution was passed bearing the signature of Kakasaheb Kalelkar and was sent to the then President Dr. Rajendra Prasad. The Resolution said that the OBCs should get the

Right of Reservation like the Scheduled Castes and the Scheduled Tribes. This Backward Classes Commission was constituted as per the directive of Art. 340 of the Constitution.

Constitution of Mandal Commission

In 1977, Indira Gandhi imprisoned the opposition leaders. Later she announced elections. As the elections were announced, Indira Gandhi had to release the opposition leaders from jail. The released opposition leaders were in a state of fear. They came together and formed a new Party called the "Janata Party". They released the election manifesto of their Party. They announced that if they get a majority they would implement the Kalelkar Commission. The Elections were over and the "Janata Party" got a clear majority. Morarji Desai became the Prime Minister of India. A delegate of the Backward Classes went to meet Morarji Desai to remind him of the Election Manifesto that he signed. The Election Manifesto declared that after formation of the new Government the Kalelkar Commission would be implemented. As the Election Manifesto carried his signature, the Backward Class Delegation asked Morarji Desai to implement the Kalelkar Commission. Morarji Desai felt confronted with danger. To save himself from this danger, Morarji Desai found a way out. He stated to the Backward Class Delegates that the Kalelkar Commission was old, as it was constituted in 1953. He further opined that conditions had changed quite a lot. Instead Desai suggested that a new Commission must be constituted. Desai thought in his mind that the Report of the newly constituted Commission will only come 2-4 years later. He thought that even the government would not last that long. So it happened that the Desai Government did not last for more than 18 months. Bindeshwar Prasad Mandal was appointed the Chairman of the newly Constituted Commission constituted by Morarji Desai and hence the Commission was called the "Mandal Commission".

Refusal to Table the Mandal Commission Report in Parliament

The Desai Government ended. Indira Gandhi formed her Government again. In 1981, just a few months after Indira Gandhi formed her Government, the Mandal Commission submitted its Report to Indira Gandhi. The Mandal Commission identified 3743 Castes belonging to the Other Backward Classes. The Report recommended that like the Scheduled Castes and the Scheduled Tribes the Other Backward Classes must get Reservation several sectors. Further it recommended that the more meritorious students belonging to the Other Backward Classes must not be included in the reserved category. Many such recommendations were made by the Mandal

Commission. Indira Gandhi did not table the Mandal Commission Report in the Parliament for discussion. Earlier the Kakasaheb Kalelkar Commission Report was also not tabled in the Parliament by her father Jawaharlal Nehru. Seeking inspiration from him, Indira Gandhi took the same steps her father had taken.

Mandal Commission Report was implemented less but sabotaged more by V. P. Singh

The National Front Government, under the leadership of the Janata Dal supremo V. P. Singh as the Prime Minister, stood on two legs. One leg belonged to the BJP and the other leg belonged to the Communist Party. When the decision to implement the Mandal Commission was taken, the BJP people were annoyed and Advani embarked on his Rath Yatra. When this Rath Yatra reached Bihar, Laloo Prasad Yadav who was the Chief Minister of Bihar at that time arrested Advani. Because of Advani's arrest, Atal Bihari Vajpayee withdrew his support given to the V. P. Singh's government. V. P. Singh fell on his face. Thirty-one constitutional experts approached the Supreme Court to end the Mandal Commission. V. P. Singh too did a cunning thing. He denied Reservation in Education while giving Reservation in the Services. If there is no reservation in Education then reservation in services is also meaningless. Also, only 27% Reservation was given to the 52% OBC. This means the Mandal Commission was implemented less and sabotaged more by V. P. Singh.

The upper castes were greatly annoyed with the 22.5% reservation given to the Scheduled Castes and the Scheduled Tribes. Due to the implementation of the Mandal Commission the overall Reservation increased by an additional 27%. The upper castes thought that the Structural System of the elite domination in the Legislature, Executive and the Judiciary would be endangered by the increase in Reservation.

The provision of Reservation is in Art.15 (4) and Art.16 (4). Before 1950, this was not the case. When was the amendment of 15 (4) and 16(4) done? The Constitution came into effect from 26th January 1950. No sooner the Constitution came into effect than a person belonging to the General Category approached the High Court against Reservation.

In 1951, the case "The State of Madras V/s Smt. Champakam Dorairajan" came for hearing before the Madras High Court. This person said that his fundamental rights were violated as students belonging to the Scheduled Castes and the Scheduled Tribes got admissions on lesser marks. Equality before law is a fundamental right. This person's argument was accepted by the Madras High Court. Dr. B. R. Ambedkar opined that the High Court's interpretation was incorrect. Further he said that the person belonging to the General Category did not suffer any discrimination in India. They could exercise all fundamental rights. The provision of "Equality before Law" was not for the Savarnas but the law was for those people who were denied the right to equality. The person who approached the High Court did not belong to the exploited class but he belonged to the General Category. The upper castes of India are not victims of Inequality. Ambedkar had incorporated "Equality before Law" in the Constitution to guarantee equal rights to those who were victims of Inequality. Dr. B. R. Ambedkar replied to the court that as the Madras High Court has given a decision about violation of fundamental rights, a provision must be included in the fundamental rights itself. To save Reservation it must be included as a fundamental right. Reservation can be saved only by making it a fundamental right. Thus, in India the first Constitutional Amendment was done by Dr. B. R. Ambekar for Reservations. This important event must always be remembered in the History of Reservation.

Decision of the Supreme Court — 'Reservation is not a Fundamental Right'

On 16th September 1999 the Supreme Court gave a decision that Reservation is not a Fundamental Right. Whereas history proclaims the fact that to save Reservation, it was included amongst the Fundamental Rights. The Decision of the Madras High Court was refuted and Reservation was included in the Constitution as a Fundamental Right. If this is judicial history and if people outside the Judicial System know this fact then such judges who violate the principles of the Constitution should be penalised under the law.

Reservations in Private Sector and New Economic Policy (LPG)

The New Economic Reforms and Policies came into effect during the then Prime Minister P. V. Narsimha Rao's regime with Dr. Manmohan Singh as the Finance Minister. The new economic policy started to be implemented in 1990's to terminate the reservation policy. The ruling classes do not want to give reservations to the SCs, STs. However, they are forced to implement reservation system in our democratic platform. In the context of the Liberalisation, Privatisation and Globalisation (LPG) owing to class polarisation, the Dalit movement is being guided by the elites among the Dalits within the larger framework of upper caste vested interests that are being perpetuated through class dichotomies. The poorest of the poor continue to be poor as ever while the rich and the bourgeoisie are benefiting from the fruits of the LPG. The entire movement revolves around atrocities while we in fact observe that there is no proper consolidated effort towards real liberation of the Dalit masses who are also the labor-producing classes in India. Reservations are the only weapon for the emancipation of the oppressed castes; hence, the fruits of reservations must be accessible, in terms of education, employment, social welfare schemes in turn contributing to political representation, to all the needy among Dalits and Adivasis. Until now though only around 10 percent have benefitted from reservations while the rest 90 percent of the masses have not yet reached a situation where they could garner the fruits of the Reservation policy. In this global context reservations should apply in the private sectors as well. Needless to state therefore the chunk of Indian populace, particularly those marginalised and oppressed due to historical reasons remain neglected. This has perpetuated caste and various other forms of discrimination and gross inequalities. Therefore there is not only the need of affirmative action but also of participation of marginalised sections of society in the areas where state is withdrawing from its responsibilities. The very participation of the marginalized group proportionate to their population in the organized services, sectors of the state i.e. Judiciary, Media, Education and Defence is still a distant dream. After Dr. B. R. Ambedkar's long and painful struggle for social justice and equality people have begun to be aware of their right to education, employment and political representation. Although these things have been achieved to some extent at present affirmative action in private sector is a necessity for the development of marginalized groups and individuals.

Demands for Liberty, Equality and Fraternity

"After the historic declaration of his intention to give up Hinduism in 1935 at Yeole, a conference was organized in Mumbai in 1936, at the instance of Dr. Ambedkar himself, to explain his decision of not being a Hindu to the leaders of the movement. Ambedkar, in his historic speech, which is famous in Marathi-speaking circles with the title "*mukti kon pathe*?" (Which way is the liberation?), started by highlighting the actual plight of masses" (Anand Teltumbde 2010). This can be interpreted, in the present context as the plight of the Dalits among the Dalits, who launched their struggles to liberate themselves from all kinds of exploitations including the internal ones. Nevertheless, these struggles have been misinterpreted and (re)presented by the established 'Scheduled Castes intellectuals' as mere struggles for classification, or say division. However, these struggles should be understood as struggles for distribution of resources among all members of the community and uniting Dalits by practically applying Ambedkar's dream principle of "Liberty, Equality and Fraternity" to all. Somewhere we have to stop the class polarisation among the Scheduled Castes and Schedule Tribes as well.

There are multiple Dalit voices from all parts of India, which are asserting their immediate need for "self-respect, identity, equality and unity" such as the Mala, Madiga, Adi-Andhra and Relli in AP; Parayar, Pallar and Arundhatiyars in Tamil Nadu; Chamars, Balmikis and Ravi Dasis in Punjab and Haryana; Pashwans and Mahadalits in Bihar; Jatavs, Chamars, Khori and Valmikis in Uttar Pradesh; Mahar, Mang and Bhangi in Maharashtra; Holeya and Madiga in Karnataka. However, the above mentioned concepts have varied meanings and interpretations to each community, mentioned above, based on their social, political and cultural situation along with their representation in the 'mainstream' movement within their state of domicile. Moreover, none of the above concepts can be pursued in an isolated fashion as they are very much interlinked and intertwined with each other contributing to each other's necessity. Reservations are the only alternative platform for community development.

Reservations and Politics: New Economic Policy to terminate Reservations

Why did the Supreme Court give such a Decision? What are the Reasons? The Supreme Court gave such a decision in 1999. The New Economic Policy came into effect from 1990. In 1999, nine years had already passed since the New Economic Policy came into effect. The New Economic Policy was started to end Reservations. The Ruling Castes do not want to give Reservations to the Other Backward Classes. But they were forced to give. So they thought of a way of not giving anything in reality—by implementing the New Economic Policy the Ruling Castes downsized the Government Bureaucracy by 10%. There would be no new Recruitment. If new (Government) jobs are not available, then the issue of giving 27% Reservation to the OBCs ends there and then.

Those who support such views are indirectly supporting Privatisation. They expect that they will get justice by supporting Capitalism. In this context Ambedkar's speech given at Manmad (Maharashtra) assumes much more significance and relevance. In that speech he said, "Shudras and Ati-Shudras have two enemies. One is Brahmanism and the other is Capitalism." In short, our enemy wishes to terminate our Constitutional Reservations through our help and support. Therefore, we need to create awakening amongst our people to oppose this policy of the Ruling Castes.

Unfortunately owing to the liberalization policy of the government Ambedkar's objective and spirit has been killed by elite intellectuals and politicians from various castes and class groups. The inequalities are increasing along with the injustices as well. Even the BSP Supremo Mayawati has promised to give reservations to Upper castes on the base of economical backwardness by putting the word "Sarvajana" in place of "Bahujana". Ambedkar's vision is compromised by vested interests. This needs to change. In order to create a caste-free society we've to create a society where everyone is equal. That is what Reservations hopes to achieve. There are many castes raising the voice for the Reservations of their community for example the recent Rajasthan Gujjar's movement for reservations. There are many communities fighting for reservations and political parties trying to use them for vote bank politics. Other side of the story is Upper castes demanding reservations for economically poor among upper castes through economic criteria. Kapu's in Andhra Pradesh, Reddy's in Telangana, Jat's, Gujjar's in Rajasthan, Patel's in Gujarath, Meena's in North India demanding reservations for their community. Who are not demanding reservations is a million question? They are demanding either to give them reservations or to remove reservations completely. It's a compulsion for political parties for assurance of communities to get vote bank of these communities or polarization of votes of the communities.

Here, we should understand Dr. Ambedkar's spirit on Reservations. It is not just about one or two or few castes but the development of all disadvantaged sections. Unless there is this development of various downtrodden and exploited castes and sub-castes there is no meaning to reservations. Nonetheless, Ambedkar's vision is very important in the present context because it takes each and every exploited section into consideration. We need to have reservations in all developmental sectors in order to bring about equality and social justice. The root of this idea can be seen in all of the works and the life of Dr. B. R. Ambedkar as well.

Lost Generations Trapped in the Struggle for Survival

Despite the fact that reservations are enormously important for the development of the disadvantaged it must be borne in mind that there are communities and tribes that have not reached the stage of acquiring the benefits of reservations because they are caught in survival struggles. They are unable to get the fruits of reservation for lack of information, education and terrible economic backwardness. They live in remote integrated areas, in tribal hamlets and backward region. By and large across India the Scheduled Castes and Scheduled Tribes do not have proper food, home, clothes and basic rights which are absolutely essential in order to even think about the usage of reservations. There are generations and generations still far from the Constitutional safeguards that are given by the law. They're the lost generations and we need to keep them in mind when we think of Dr. Ambedkar's vision of an egalitarian society. The fruits of reservation have been distributed among those who come from well-to-do backgrounds with education, economic success, and a strong cultural and urban background. However it is more significant to include those who come from rural and tribal backgrounds because as Fanon says they are the "wretched of the earth." We're forgetting the poor and the downtrodden and more is being given to those who already have. This has generated some criticism of reservation policy in recent times. Because of the LPG there is a social partition which divides Scheduled Castes and Scheduled Tribes into rural Vs urban and literate Vs illiterate and male versus female. In conclusion we can say that while reservations ought to be provided in the private sector as well in order to reduce the gap between the haves and the have-nots we also have to remember the marginalized sections that are in the majority, who are deprived of information and basic education and continue to live in a state of poverty and degradation. This gap that is increasing day by day needs to be addressed from a larger perspective in order to implement Dr. B. R. Ambedkar's vision for the upliftment of the disadvantaged in a global context.

Reservations for Economically Weaker Sections among the Upper Castes

Recently the Government of India passed the Bill Reservations for the Economically Weaker Sections among the upper castes. It has framed the economic conditions and status for eligibility criteria. One way reservations are automatically eliminated by globalisation and other way upper castes are demanding for reservations. In this context state has to think the permanent solution for social justice, equality in the society. Recent studies emphasised that 70% wealth is in the hands of 01% rich in the society. So 30% wealth is distributed to the rest of the 99% of the society. It is clearly visible that huge economic imbalance and regional disparities are prevalent in the Indian society. Now we have to think beyond reservations in the global context for the betterment of the society. In the present context of the Liberalisation, Privatisation and Globalisation we have to work towards the equal distribution of every opportunity and resources for real social transformation and economic emancipation in turn promising absolute equality and social justice.

Bibliography

1. Dr. B. R. Ambedkar. Castes in India: their mechaniam, genesis and development. Bpatrika Publications, India.
2. Dr. B.R. Ambedkar –Writings and Speeches, Vol. 1 (1979)," Education Development, Government of Maharashtra.
3. Dr. B.R. Ambedkar –Writings and Speeches -In the Bombay Legislative, with the Simon Commission and at the Round Table Conference-1927 to 1939, Vol. 2," Education Development, Government of Maharashtra. (pages 546 to 556) and (2) "State and Minorities –What are their rights and how to secure them in the Constitution of free India (Ambedkar 1947) in Vasant Moon (Edited) (1982)
4. Srinivas. M. N. Caste: Its twentieth century avatar. Penguin Books. India. 1996.
5. Bhagawan Das, Moments in a History of Reservations, Economic and Political Weekly, Vol. 35, No. 43/44 (Oct 21-Nov 3, 2000) pp. 3831-3834.
6. Illaiiah, Kancha, Reservations: Experience as Framework of Debate, Economic and Political Weekly, Vol. 25, No. 41 (Oct 13, 1990) pp. 2307-2310.
7. DN, Reservations and Class Structure of Castes, Economic and Political Weekly, Vol. 25, No. 2 (Jan 13, 1990) p. 83.
8. D.L. Sheth, Reservations Policy Revisited, Economic and Political Weekly, Vol. 22, No. 46 (Nov 14, 1987) pp. 1957-1962.
9. Chalam, K.S., Caste Reservations and Equality of Opportunity in Education, Economic and Political Weekly, Vol. 25, No. 41 (Oct 13, 1990) pp. 2333-2339.
10. Pradeep Kumar, Reservations within Reservations: Reak Dalit-Bahujans, Economic and Political Weekly, Vol. 36, No. 37, (Sept 5-21, 2001) pp. 3505-3507.
11. Balagopal.K, A Tangled Web: Subdivision of SC Reservations in AP, Economic and Political Weekly, Vol. 35, No. 13 (Mar 25-31, 2000) pp. 1075-1081.
12. Jangam Chinnaih, BJP and Reservations: Quota Politics or Electoral Convenience? Economic and Political Weekly, Vol. 38, No. 30 (July 26- Aug 1, 2003) pp. 3143-3145.
13. John Stuart Mill. Representative Government. Internet.
14. Saint Augustine. City of God. Internet.
15. John S. Mackenzie, *A Manual of Ethics*, Oxford University Press, Delhi, 1929, p. 287.
16. H.R. Mukhi, A *Simple History of Western Political Thought: Plato and Burke*, Surjeet Deport, Delhi, 1986, p. 222.

Chapter - 8

Religion, Representation and the Politics of Reservation: Critical Reflections

— *Prashant Kumar Kain*

Abstract

When people are divided into discrete social categories, it also leads to division in their experiences, worldviews, histories and politics. This division is clearly visible on the question of reservation. The arguments both in favour and opposition of reservation have certain historical and social locations. The reservation debate is not new and has not been created just now today. It has been carried forward from the history with its own cultural specificity. What is the meaning of reservation?. Why it was given at first place?. Where and when it was implemented?. How state was brought into this whole debate?. Who are demanding it and why some are opposed to this? Why there is so much of controversy and debate on backward "class" reservation?. Why some are demanding economic criteria now?. The groups that are opposing reservation and those who are seeking or defending this have certain dialectic and historical continuity in their arguments. These (in)consistencies and contradictory arguments, views and positions cannot be understood without bringing into inquiry the epistemology and knowledge production processes. The reservation discourse cannot be understood without bringing philosophy, religion, culture, economy and history into consideration. The question requires that we take a comprehensive and critical view of this concept and do an analysis backed with facts.

Keywords: *Caste, Reservation, Representation, Social Justice, Discrimination, Social Inequalities.*

Introduction

The controversies regarding reservation are not new to this country. There has been consistent resistance and opposition against it ever since the policy had been drafted and implemented. Whenever the question of reservations is raised, it leads to arguments and counter arguments both in favour and opposition from different corners of the society. Some project it as discrimination while others perceive it as a question of representation and a remedy to bridge up the gap between different groups. There are clear, deterministic and contradictory positions, perspectives and approaches on this question by different groups. There has not been any other government policy which has been subject of such great controversy, resistance and opposition. This clearly reflects how important the question of caste is, and a proof how divided society is within, on the question of caste.

When we think of reservation, it is usually associated with a state policy which is devised to give representation to the historically marginalized groups in education, employment and political sphere. The policy has been implemented by the state to ensure just and fair representation according to their population. Contradictorily, it is often perceived as discriminatory by those groups that have historically monopolized these spaces and privileges. The historical bias is continued in the present as well in the very ways the question of reservation is projected and represented. The opponents have repeatedly raised concerns and doubts about the "efficiency", "merit", "quality" "aptitude" of these groups. They have used humiliating language, demeaning symbols and icons even in their protest against reservation. This clearly shows continuity of their historical privileges, prejudices and biases to demean them over and again. The same terms and concerns are not raised on the question of women reservation.

The groups that are opposed to caste based reservation are also in opposition to follow caste on the question of gender. Those who favour applying economic criteria on the question of caste based reservation are hesitant or silent to apply same on the question of gender. There is an inbuilt contradiction and inconsistency in their argument. This duality is important as on the one hand they wish to treat women as a homogenous question while contradicting in on the question of caste. This clearly brings out the clear caste prejudices of the opponents of caste based reservation. Interesting and noteworthy is the fact that woman reservation bill has stuck in the parliament due to the lack of consensus. Some political parties have been demanding equal and just representation of women of different groups within this heterogeneous category of women. This highlights a clear and deep relationship between caste and gender on one hand and the politics of representation on the other.

The concept of "reservation" is deep, pervasive and multi-dimensional phenomenon. It can be associated and related with various things depending upon its uses in different contexts. In its pervasive sense and meaning, it signifies certain conditions like fixation, insulation, isolation, securing, preservation, control, compartments, protection, difference, segregation, segmentation, monopoly, exclusivity, etc. These are natural, normal and even conditions as they come with certain specific meanings, relations and associations. These specific meanings and associations have their own socio-historical ideological origin. The concept of reservation, thus become pervasive and involve, transcend, penetrate many other identities and categories like religion, region, race, gender, work, time, polity, labour, nation, and sexuality etc. There are complex interactions and inter-linkages within and between these. These complex inter-linkages and interactions cannot be understood without a reference point. These reference points or representations are built well within the history and culture. Hence culture and history are two important sites of subjugation and resistance. One has to be well aware of the historical and cultural specificities to avoid the judgmental errors.

Religion, Representation and Segregation

Caste is one of the most important determinants of social reality in India. It is one phenomenon which runs deep into the social and cultural fabrics of the society. The origin of the institution lies in the social structure of the society. India holds the distinction of being the most stratified, hierarchal and divided societies in the world. The sources of these inequalities are to be found in the religious doctrines, texts and mythology. People are assigned fixed identities, ritual position and social status. In this social arrangement, groups are so hierarchically placed to each other in such a manner that there are differential and hierarchal rights, duties and privileges. Those who are placed at the top have traditional, historical and cumulative advantages while those at the bottom have pain, sufferings and disadvantages. The interactions among people are guided and controlled by their ritualistic and social positions within society.

In Hindu cosmology and worldview, People are divided into different *Varnas* (categories) on the basis of their *Gunas*. "These three Gunas (qualities or nature) are *Satva* (goodness), *Rajas* (activity) and *Tamas* (darkness). When one of these three qualities predominates, the body becomes distinguished by that quality" (Ketkar, 1909: 114). In this graded classical division, certain human beings (as Varna) represent Satva, some Rajas and some Tamas. The Satva is a quality of supreme Varna, Rajas is the quality of higher yet lower Varna while the Tamas is the quality of inferior Varna. These qualities are intrinsic and permanent to the nature of human beings therefore are universal and non-contestable. These are ontological in nature therefore cannot be transferred, altered and changed by human consciousness and acts.

The Hindu texts also mention a category of people usually called *Avarnas* (without Varna) as contrasted with *Savarna* (with Varna). The Avarnas were not part of Varna system they are known with different names like *Chandals, Pischaha, Acchut, panchama*. They are often called "untouchable" in contemporary world and are identified as Dalits or SCs in government records and documents (Wagmore, 2007: 9, Thapar, 2002: 63). According to Deliege, "Untouchables were known as *Chandala*, *Nishad*, a term that designates those who were not allowed to dwell in a town or a village but had to live in special quarters outside the village or town limits, in theory, their main task was the carrying and cremation of corpses…the law books stipulate that chandalas must eat their food from broken vessels and avoid any contact with higher castes, high castes individuals could be reduced to the stats of chandalas by merely touching the latter" (Deliege, 2001: 11).

The Brahmins are located at the top of this social pyramid. "They stand apart from, and above, the others in the social hierarchy for four principle reasons according to the Brahmin authors of Vedic texts: (1) they were created prior to others therefore take precedence; (2) they are the most complete and perfect instance of the human being; (3) they are learned in the Veda; and (4) they had a monopoly on the priesthood and control of the powerful sacrifice" (Smith, 1994: 32). This hierarchal and differentiated power arrangement was based on the basis of origin, order of origin and the Gunas (nature) they possess. Therefore, "the studies of Vedas, austerity, and knowledge, and purity, etc. are of the quality of goodness. Delighting in adventure, want of firmness, indulgence in sexual pleasure are marks of the quality of activity. Cruelty, covetousness, evil life, etc. are marks of dark qualities" (Ketkar, 1909: 114).

According to Manu; the "scared" law giver, Different categories of people have different kinds of role, duties, and function in this world. Therefore, Brahman has the exclusive right to 'knowledge' (Vedas). The *Kshtriyas*, as the warriors, have to rule the world as per the *Dharmashastra*, he has to preserve the (given) order, the *Vaishyas* to do the business and trade, and the fourth one the Shudra to serve the above three categories (Thorat & Despande, 2001:71). The classical division of people into these categories also categorized and reserved their role, function, material assets, duties, privileges, prestige, and power in the economy, polity and culture. The religion derived worldviews divided the whole society in such a way that it led to de-factor monopolies and concentration of the resources in different groups. Land, temple and ritual hierarchy became the source of power and status. The Brahmins acquired authority and power in the matter of religion and temple, the Kshtriyas acquired power and control in the matter of polity, preservation of order and rule and Vaishyas acquired the monopoly in the trade and commerce on so on. In all spheres, these above Varnas complimented and legitimized each other exclusive rights and order making it a pervasive structure and system.

The Varna based scheme brought temple as a centre of economic and political activity. The kings became de-facto owners of the whole property in their kingdom. It was their responsibility to maintain the "order". They were the patrons in the villages due to their social ranking. They were also the patrons of the village temples. Menon writes, "The development of land relations under the feudal Cholas is of importance, when in a certain period grant of villages were made to groups of Brahmins, in order to maintain them. The further development of this practice, for various reasons, seems to have led to a deliberate attempt by certain rulers to restrict land ownership to only the Brahmins caste in such *Brahmadeya* villages. This meant that exclusive land ownership rested with a particular caste in certain villages" (Menon, 1979: 57). Temples became a source of power and gradually acquired huge influence in the civil and political life.

The Pallavas, the Pandyas and the Chola kings were great patrons of temples. They made huge grants to the temples and spent lavishly for its upkeep. The king used to make grants on the day of his birth day, coronation, at the time of leading expeditions, on the occasion of victory in a battle, on the birth of a son, for the prosperity of his son, at the time of renovating, or setting up of divinities, at the time of visiting the temple, while he was camping, for long life, health and victory, while performing *Hemagarbha* and *Tulabhara* and at the request of others (Geetha, 2008: 1-18). Kalugumalai is in Tirunelveli district of Tamilnadu state for centuries. Its temple enjoyed the patronage of the Rajas of Ettaiyapuram, the local Zamindars, within whose ancestral estate it lay. "The records show that in December 1849 the Raja donated the whole village to the temple, agriculture revenue, as well as land and building rents, thenceforth went towards the temple's upkeep. At the same time he instituted the main festivals, built car streets for procession by temple deity and granted house sites around them to temple servants" (Good, 1999: 70). Temples were exempted from tax so were its servants. Not only they were exempted they were also attached with additional villages so that there is proper maintenance of the temple.

The Brahmins acquired an absolute control over the land especially in some villages which were exclusively reserved for them. Menon writes, "Apart from land monopoly, the incidence of landownership by Brahmins has traditionally been high in Thanjavur. In 1807, the Tanjore committee in its report recorded that "there is hardly a family of this colony which does not hold land on ordinary *Mirasi* tenure in Tanjore". To substantiate this statement, they quoted the fact that the Brahmins constituted over 27 percent of the total number of Mirsadars (62,048). An 1876-77 Jamabandi is even more revealing. Out of 136,532 Pattas the Brahmins held 37,736, although the entire Brahmin population formed only 6.42 percent of the district's total population" (Menon, 1979: 58). The Brahmins used their superior ritualistic power to gain control over the economic resources and polity. It led to concentration of economic resources in the control of few groups and emergence of huge disparities between different sections and segments in terms of ownership of assets and means of production. Temples did not remain merely a site of worship rather gradually became a source of power and means of production itself as they started controlling the labour and determining the status of different occupations, wages and conditions of work.

Colonial Power, Intervention and Structural Changes

The situation in India has been more or less stagnant and there was no dynamism except the frequent wars between kingdoms, conflicts, competition to match each others in luxuries and brutal display of power. Social life and economy did not change significantly even during the Muslims' rule. Although there was growth in the trade and the commerce but the larger village life remained unaffected. The village economy was stagnant and controlled by traditions. There were all kinds of superstitions, social evils of human sacrifice, inhuman and cruel practices like female feticide, sati, illiteracy, lack of industrialization, non availability lack of means of transportation, under utilization of the resources, no improvement in the science and technology, wide spread poverty, exploitation and absolute power of the Brahmins and the aristocracy.

Like any primitive society, India too, was heavily dependent on agriculture. The agricultural has been the backbone of the economy and all the other subsidiary activities were dependent on it. Majority of the masses were directly dependent on it for their survival and livelihood. The other economic activities too were dependent on the products of agriculture. Aloysius writes, "complex and advanced agricultural societies were broadly marked by an unequal, hierarchal distribution of power among diverse groups, following somewhat rigid, hereditary occupations this ascriptive inequality permeated all spheres of social relations and tended to divide the entire society into relatively isolated segments such as orders, status-groups, caste etc" (Aloysius, 2010: 24). The same is true for India as it had been an agriculture based society, like any other society it also had huge inequalities in land and resources.

The land has historically been under the control of dominant sections and groups. The land was virtually owned and controlled by Brahmins, kings, Rajas and later on by Nawabs, Zamindars and others. The farmers and peasants were cultivators of the land without the ownership rights. Therefore the economy, occupations and labour were socially controlled and regulated which marked differential power arrangements between groups. When British came, they gradually brought whole of India under their jurisdiction. This structural unification came along with economic transformation, expansion of civil society and introduction of liberal, secular ideas and reforms affected the social, cultural, economic and political spheres. They introduced the legal system which was applied to the whole of British governed India. prashad says, "Without the aid of a new legal system it would have been impossible for the English to rule distant and heterogeneous million with a handful of military personnel" (Prashad, 1964: 76).

The British introduced various system of revenue collection on the type, nature, productivity of the land. These systems are called *Mahalwari*, *Ryotwari* and *Zamindari* (Dutt, 1904: 273-323). "The British gradually transformed land ownership into private property and established the legal basis for capitalist production relations among landlords, tenants, village servants, and agricultural laborers. After various experiments, the government made household of the managerial castes separately responsible for specific amounts of revenue in 1822-23. In 1865, it issue individual tile deeds to share of varying sizes in the village lands, although actual field were not permanently parceled out until 1891-92" (Gough, 1978: 29). British actions led to the commoditization and commercialization of the land and the crops. They forcefully or though coercion made the princely class accept their dominance in various spheres. "After the mutiny (1857), British rule and military preparedness became stronger than ever and the rural upper classes of landlord and prices were either crushed totally or co-opted by the British through concessions" (Gough, 1974: 1392).

The British rule broke the monopoly of some groups in the land by making it a attaching an economic value to it. They transformed land into a commodity which had a value and that value can be transferred to anyone who could provide them their revenues. They auctioned land rights to those who provide maximum land revenues to them. This broke the traditional monopoly of the kings and Brahmins and other dominant groups but it also created a special class of oppressors in the form of money-lenders, taxation staff, zamindars, administrative and bureaucratic officials. "Under the new British administration, each Ryot had to pay his land tax to the government in cash and this enabled money lender to gain an effective control over village landlords for the first time" (Beck, 1970: 791).

The successive British policies commercialized and commoditized the land and crops. There occurred significant changes in the land relations both the land owners and the British authority and the laborers who worked on those land. The land became a transferable commodity subject to the payment of the revenue. Many were displaced due to nonpayment of the revenue or through coercive measures like succession. This also changed the relationship of people with the land. The *Jajmani* system started collapsing which were the backbone of the traditional village economy and also the source of sufferings for the poor masses. The old system started collapsing and there were significant changes in the village structure and economy. New opportunities and employment were emerging due industrialization, emergence of railways, opportunities in public works and increase in the trade and commerce.

There was no systematic attempt to study India, its fragmented diversity, human population, animal livestock and natural resources before the arrival of British. To exploit the resources more effectively and to gain knowledge about the native society and their customs, they undertook exhaustive studies. On religion and culture, they studied the people, their customs, manners and attitudes, their social relationships, beliefs and practices, rituals and village structure. They introduced various social legislations to ban certain practices which they considered to be inhuman. One of them was related to the slaves and slave trade. Under the Diwanship of Col. Munroe the slavery was abolished in Travancore in 1812 by the royal decree. It became illegal to sell or buy the lower caste slaves in the territory of the state (Jebakany, 2011 :144). This brought not only dignity but also respite from the ruthless exploitation.

A similar measure had been undertaken by the rulers of the State of Cochin under the leadership of its able Diwan Nanjappa in the year 1821 of CE (Philip, 2005: 36-7). Later in 1843 the viceroy and his council decided to enact an act for the emancipation of slaves throughout India in 1843.

(Beena, 2011: 188). In 1829 Widow burning was prohibited and in 1856 government passed an act legalizing the marriage of Hindu widows. Similarly, in 1891 age of consent act was passed raising the age of marriage from ten to twelve. Under the pressure from the Christian missionaries and the British authority, the king of Travancore issued a Proclamation in 1863 that the women of *Ezhavas* and all other caste had the right to cover the upper part of their body (Mila, 2009: 113). The missionaries played an important role not only in awakening the downtrodden, raising their consciousness, spreading western education but also bringing employment opportunities to them.

The labour acquired a new meaning and value during the rule of British; it became a scarce resource and a commodity. Those groups who were traditionally slave and attached to land though *Jajmani* system benefitted as new opportunities arose outside the village. Roy says "Large streams of migration began from the mid-nineteenth century, aided by the railways and the telegraphy after 1850, to facilitate this huge reallocation of labour. Men increasingly had to leave home for careers elsewhere. And as competition for land intensified, those with inferior rights to land had to do so more often than before" (Roy, 2005: 9). The labour which was till now controlled and regulated by the traditions and customs got freed from the village based traditional economy. The mass migration was not merely to get better livelihood but also caused by the famines, failure of crops, shrinking of agriculture activities, caste oppression in the villages etc.

The industrialization brought significant mobility, flexibility among the lives of people "While this process of disintegration was going on the British rule (backed by a more powerful techno-economic power in the wake of the industrial revolution) delivered the final blow. The introduction of centralized administration and the revenue system, the institution of police and law-courts, the extension of modern means of communication (railway, motor bus) broke the isolation of the villages. Local produce began to be exported and the imports found their way in the country side" (Singh, 1960: 95). These changes had huge implications to the wide mass of people which controlled and sufferings from the bondage of traditions and customs. There were more new openings in the public works in constructions, railways network, ports, mines, factories, small scale works in the cities.

One of the important aspects of colonial rule was the secularization of work and universalisation of education. The British maintained huge bureaucracy, military, police, revenue collectors and civil servants. This required some standard procedures in recruitment of their servants. "The

British began to recruit civil servants for coveted government jobs on the basis of education and not (in principle, at least) on the basis of caste affiliation, as had previous rulers. All this, plus the development of new markets, and a rapid increase in transportation and communication facilities, served to multiply the possible routes to prestige and power" (Beck, 1970: 791). They opened up new opportunities in education, employment, trade and commerce. This led to mass migration from the "Shudra" and "Ati-shudra" castes in search of better life, dignity, economic stability and political awakening of their rights.

State, Reservation and History

Reservation as an official state policy came during the colonial rule. The religion driven social structures created huge socio-economic inequality and disparities between different groups and sections of the society. The colonial authorities were forced to address the question of caste determined inequalities due to its political significance. "The Madras Revenue Board passed the standing order no. 128 as far back as in 1851, instructing all district collectors to ensure that appointment are not dominated by few influential families" (Cynthia, 2006: 18). This was an effort to check the monopoly of certain sections in the government jobs. Hence then, the state acquired an important significance and role in democratic distribution of the public resources. The state attempt to democratize itself was projected and branded as "divide and rule" policy by the Brahmins and other vested interests. They branded state as being divisive to hide the Brahmins hegemonic dominance in the government jobs and education. According to 1901 census, they constituted about 3% of the population but accounted 94 % of the civil service. While 80 percent of them were literate and the rate was 4 percent among the others.

Another major and important intervention came from the princely state of Kolhapur. The then princely state of Kolhapur under the leadership of Chhatrapati Shahu Ji Maraharaj issued an order (during a visit to Britain) in 1902 reserving 50 percent public employment for socially backwards. He played an important role in promoting education, public employment, and removing social disabilities. Another important intervention came from the princely state of Mysore which is now known as Karnataka. The Maharaja of Mysore, Krishnaraja Wadiyar IV appointed Sir Leslie Miller as committee head to study the representation of deprived communities in the public services. The report was based on caste-wise demographic and English literacy data from the census 1911. The recommendations included emphasis on primary and secondary education, education to women, political representation, scholarships for backward classes (read castes), relaxation of age limit for public service appointment, changes in the merit-based examinations, and fair proportion of backward classes in recruitment as school teachers, among many other things. The committee recommendation met with tough resistance from the Brahmins and other privileged groups. Mass protests were organized and a staunch opponent C.P. Ramaswamy Iyer passed resolution stating that such "reservations were detrimental to the best interests of the country and (that) such divisive move(s) would prove highly injurious to the Hindu society" (ibid: 19).

The movement for representation acquired huge significance and a political turn in the wake of emerging political and social consciousness among the masses. An important and major event happened what is popularly known as Poona Pact in 1932. This is also known for the bitter dialogue and open confrontation between Ambedkar and Gandhi on the question of representation. Gandhi declared himself to be representative of the whole nation and common masses while Ambedkar insisted for a separate identity of the depressed classes. Gandhi rejected the 'communal award' for depressed class as being divisive for the Hindu society. He compelled Ambedkar to forgo his demand for separate electorate and instead agree to reservation in assemblies, employment and education. The Gandhi used his 'fast unto death' as an arm twisting and a moral blackmailing keeping aside the interests of the marginalized. Reservation was only a compromise against the very issue of political freedom and separate identity of the depressed classes.

After independence there were debates and discussion on the nature of state. Significant time and labour was invested to prepare the draft. Finally, the constitution was adopted on 26 January 1950. There was no specific mention of any particular caste as backward. The ruling elites of that time used it as an excuse to abrogate the government order on reservation. The reservation issue was challenged in the madras high court which held it unconstitutional. This was also upheld by the Supreme Court later on. E.V.R. Periyar became highly vocal and critical about it. He gave a call and people responded in mass and brought state to halt on august 14 august 1950. "This forced the union government to introduce the very first constitutional amendment incorporating article 15 (4) which enables the state to make special provision, notwithstanding articles 15 (1) and 29 (2) for the advancement of the social and educational backward classes as well as the SCs and STs" (Cynthia, 2006: 23). Reservation became an important and potent tool for social and political mobilization. This political consciousness also brought in more aggressive demand for the democratic distribution of public resources. The governments both at center and state have responded to those demands and have expanded and included more castes over period of time.

The issue of the reservation for the SC and ST was settled to some extent although there have been periodic controversies. The growing awareness of the rights and political representation also led to movement and demands from various categories and sections of the society. On January 29th 1953, first backward classes commission was established under the chairmanship of Kaka Saheb Kalekar under the provision of article 340 of the constitution. The report was submitted on 30th march 1955 which was later discusses in the parliament. There were adequacies and contradictions in its report. The commission noted that "our society was built essentially on the medieval ideas of birth, caste and social hierarchy, but not on an economic structure" but, the commission desired to "disassociate the caste from the social backwardness at the present juncture" (Anuradha, 2011: 172). The commission could not provide clear criteria for backwardness therefore it stuck in the controversies. One of them was the caste data as the practice of caste enumeration for census was abandoned in 1951. However, some recommendations of commission were significant. One of which was the recognition of all women as class as "backward".

The demand of fair share in education, public employment and development did not die with the failure of first commission. It started acquiring a shape of a movement and political assertion with the passage of time. It led to the establishment of Mandal commission in February 1978 to study the social and educational backwardness of the large chunk of masses known as Shudras erstwhile and later on OBC or BC. The commission used caste census data of 1891 and 1931 and used 11 indicators to define backwardness. It recommended radical land reforms, 27 percent reservation in public employment, reservation in promotions, relaxations in upper age limit, financial help, subsidized loans, category wise roaster system, etc. The stated reservation has to be applicable in toto in all central and state government recruitments and public sector undertaking including banks. These recommendations had far reaching implications to the society.

The fight for social equality and backward class movement led the emergence of new leadership among the Shudra castes especially in the regions which had huge socio-economic disparities in land ownership and social relations like Bihar and Uttar Pradesh. Jai Prakash Narayan, Karpoori Thakur, Ram Manohar Lohia were prominent one who wanted a non-violent social transformation. Karpoori Thakur played an important role in changing the socio-economic conditions in Bihar. He introduced reservation to backward class in 1978 in Bihar leading to great social awakening of the masses. All these leaders were attracted by a socialist dream of creation of an equal and just society. These leaders are considered to be a mentor for present day's leaders like Lalu Prasad Yadav, Mulayam Singh, Ram Vilas Paswan, Nitish Kumar etc. The quest for social equality and justice started revolving around just share in public employment and education. Reservation became an important and potent tool for political mobilization. Many governments had to budge to the growing public demands of social justice and just representations. V.P.Singh used social justice plank in the late 80s and early 90s to consolidate the OBCs.

The growing political consciousness among the Shudra castes led to be aggressive assertion which started affecting the political landscape of the country. In order to survive, many governments used reservation as a sure and certain guarantee for political success and dividends. This led to politicization of the reservation and naturalization of the caste. Reservation started being branded as politics and a tool of appeasement by the opponents. In a balancing act, many governments tried to give reservation to the upper castes in the cover of economic criteria. In September 1991, an office memo issued by the then P.V. Narasimha Rao government reserved 10 percent of posts for "other economically backward sections" however it was not successful. In 2006, the then HRD minister, Arjun Singh promised 27 percent reservation for OBCs in educational institutions. Over the few years, many regional and national parties in different states have promised reservation to different groups at state level. The BJP has resisted and branded reservation to Muslims and Christians as vote bank politics and appeasement. However it has given in to political pressures in many states and advocated and implemented the same for OBCs. The recent 10 percent reservation initiative of BJP is on the same line without much demand and mobilization by the upper castes themselves. It is designed to consolidate the upper caste votes in its favour after bitter and humiliating defeat in the three states.

Predudices, Resistance and Hidden Language of Caste

The arguments and debates surrounding reservations have been cultivated and shaped up by the intellectual and academic world. The social scientists have played an important role shaping and representing this issue. The social science knowledge in India was dominated by traditionally elite groups hence it was careless and far away of the views and concerns of the masses. The earliest social anthropologists were occupied with the positivist concerns of objectivity and neutrality. They avoided those writings which they found political and critical. In a thought provoking essay titled 'how egalitarian are the social sciences in India?' Noted political scientist Gopal guru writes, "it is frustrating, if not tragic, for dalits to languish in raw empiricism"... Indian social science represents a pernicious divide between theoretical Brahmins and empirical shudras" elaborating it further he says, "social science discourse in India is being closely disciplined by self appointed juries who sit in the apex court and decide what is the correct practice according to the canons. These juries decide what is theory is and what is trash. It is different matter that these canons lack authenticity as they are borrowed from the west unreservedly. The apex court in social science with its full bench in Delhi keeps ruling out subaltern objections as absurd and idiosyncratic at worst and emotional, descriptive-empirical and polemical at best" (Pandian, 2008: 34).

The early sociologist and social anthropologists like G.S. Ghurye, M.N. Srinivas, T.N. Madan, R.K. Mukerjee, etc. were from privileged Brahmin background. It is reflected in their priorities, theorization and treatment. They could not separate themselves for their own social background and biases. The ignorance, biases and prejudices were manifested in their treatment when they projected reality. Among them the G.S. Ghurye is usually credited for contributing towards "Anthropologisation of Indian sociology" (Oommen, 2008: 60). These writings had nostalgic and romantic account of the past with anti-colonial (or say nationalist) contents and tone. Partha chatterjee, while discussing Tarinicharan Chattopadhayay's *The History of India*, notes, "if the 19th century Englishman could claim ancient Greece as his classical heritage, why should not the English educated Bengali feel proud of the achievement of the so-called Vedic civilization?" (Pandian, 2002: 1736).

The social background had its effect in their theorization, conceptualization and writings. One of the most important historical works on caste especially on colonial period is '*Castes of Mind: Colonialism and the Making of Modern India*' by Nicholas dirks. This work has been heavily criticized because it out rightly blamed British for the invention of caste. Couple of years back Nicholas Dirks writes an article in 2013 titled '*G.S. Ghurye and the politics of sociological knowledge*' in which he writes, "Ghurye has influenced my own work on caste and Indian society. He was the first anthropologist to turn his attention to the dangerous effects of colonial discourse and colonial institutions on the fundamental institutions of Indian society" (Dirks, 2013: 240). This clearly shows how the earliest sociologists and sociological knowledge had nationalist visions and priorities in their writings. These writings lacked reflexivity therefore were far away from the actual reality. These writers had their own pre-conceived notions, biases and prejudices which are reflected in their treatment, theorization and selection of field sites. For instance, M.N. Srinivas did not stay in Dalit Basties (Residential clusters) for his field works. At one place he acknowledges that "I would have obtained a new angle on the village (read caste) if I had spent more time in their (untouchable) areas" (Deliege, 2001: 28). This absence or prejudice is also reflected in his selection of the references. It is very rare to find reference of the B.R. Ambedkar in Srinivas' writings.

M.N. Srinivas holds a prestige and reputation of a serious scholar in Indian sociology and is known all over the world for his concept of *Sanskritisation*. When his concept of Sanskritisation was criticized by Edmund Leach for its' being Brahman centric and did not reflect the Sudra or untouchable views. Srinivas Responds, "…my stressing of the importance of the backward classes movement, and of the role of caste in politics and administration, are very probably the result of my being a south India, and a Brahmins at that. The principle of caste quotas for appointments to posts in the administrations, and for admissions to scientific and technological courses, produced much bitterness among Mysore Brahmins. Some of these were my friends and relatives, and I could not help being sensitive to their distress" (Pandian, 2002: 1738). M.N. Srinivas has produced huge writings on the Indian society and he consistently wrote on many contemporary issues like politics, reservation, caste mobilizations, backward caste movement etc. He was the one who devised and popularized many terms like "vote bank" "dominant caste" "divide and rule" etc. There is a consistent and hidden perspective and position in his writings. Not surprisingly, his concepts and writings have been used by the opponents of reservation to strengthen their arguments.

There has been so much of bitterness against reservation among the so called "upper castes". This bitterness has all the ingredients like concerns for nation, efficiency, merit, quality, justice, equality etc. Reservation has always been labeled as being discriminatory, divisive and as a sign of backwardness. These can well be understood by the articulations of first Prime Minister Jawaharlal Nehru. Jawaharlal Nehru wrote a letter to all chief ministers on 27th June 1961 expressing his oppositions to reservations. He writes, "I dislike any kind of reservation, more particularly in services. I react strongly against anything leads to inefficiency and second rate standards…the only way to help a backward groups is to give opportunities of good education…everything else is provision of some kind of crutches which do not add to the strength or health of the body…if we go in for reservations on communal and caste basis, we swamp the bright and able people and remain second rate and third rate...let us help the backward groups by all means, but never at the cost of efficiency" (Anuradha, 2011: 151).

There has been a history of resistance against reservation since colonial times. Jawaharlal Nehru views are merely the reflection of the popular sentiments against reservation prevalent among specific sections. There is a concern for the "body" (read nation) and a worry for the "able and bright" (read meritorious). This is not surprising given the fact that traditional elites have always resisted the democratization of the public resources be it universal education or public employments. Peary Mohan Mukerjee, a member of Governor-General's Executive Council (the most powerful body in British India) argued against the introduction of compulsory education. He argued that the government should aim to make the masses into useful members of the society like 'servants, shepherds, apprentices and not scholars' as 'the educated mock at all distinctions of caste, wealth and lineage which had enthralled them for centuries' (Rao, 2016 :155). The fear of the educated competing for jobs as well as challenging the feudal order was evident in the opposition to the introduction of the mass education.

The reservation has been one kind of affirmative action which was devised to ensure just and equal distribution of public resources. However, it has been a contested issue since beginning. It was never given voluntarily rather came as a compromise against the demand for separate electorate. Therefore there has been a consistent opposition to it from different quarters of the society. These kinds of arguments have been given everywhere in the world wherever the affirmative policy has been implemented. The opponents have articulated their negative views about it. These are not mere opinions rather inbuilt fears of losing their monopolies. They have used all kinds of arguments to prevent diversity and democratic distribution of resources. In an interesting paper titled 'we'd love to hire them, but...' by kirshenman and Neckerman (1991) discovered that employees believed black men were unreliable, unruly, poorly educated, and low skilled" (Jodhka, 2012: 52). The same arguments are repeated with a different language even today. Reservation is till date is equated with inefficiency and labeled as promoting substandard (or less efficient) students at the cost of bright, compromising merit, promoting brain drain, ruining and pulling the nation backward etc. These ambiguous and shallow arguments are merely the cover to hide and divert attention from the traditional and historical privileges, monopolies and caste determined inequalities.

Denial, Discrimination and Destitution

There is a clear duality, selectivity and ambiguity in the arguments of the opponents of reservations. They are silent on the question of caste determined inequalities and inter-group disparities in land distribution, access and quality of education, health, incidences of untouchability, discrimination and quality of life that mass of people live. The opponents have always directed their anger against those who have managed to break the chains of caste and become independent. Their "creamy layer" concerns and arguments are constructed to target, sabotage and control their mobility attempts as they are the ones who are giving competition to them and challenging their hegemony in various fields. This fear and hate is well evidently visible when 50 IIT alumni quit their job to form a political party called "Bahujan Azad Party". When the news was published, it received huge comments (1853). People were abusing mayawati, reservation, raising question on their merit, making filthy jokes, used filthy and abusive language against them. These comments clearly show their prejudices, fear, hate and hidden concern to lose their privileges on the one hand and their dominance on virtual spaces.

Universal education is often cited as a means to overcome exclusion and disadvantages. It is argued that education will play a leveling effect and empower them. However the fact is that there are already inbuilt inequalities and graded hierarchies in the education system itself. Moreover, those who have managed to overcome educational barrier find it difficult to get appropriate placements due to biases, prejudices and discrimination in the labour markets as found by many studies. If one goes back to the history one finds there was severe opposition to universal education by traditional elites. The argument against universal education at that time was to oppose the entry of lower castes and women in public space and employment. Today contrastingly, there is argument in favour of universal education to oppose reservation. There is typical continuity in their argument with a different language and articulations. They want to retain their historical privileges and monopolies. Hence they restrict their argument only to state and public employment and shy of engaging with culture, religion and history as site of marginalization and exploitation.

The discrimination, opposition and resistance against the Shudra and Ati-shudra castes are not new to Indian society. They have remained invisible, exploited and at periphery for thousands of years. The situation has remained unchanged to a large extent despite periodic assertion, revolts and contestations. The monopolies of certain groups in the state services have not checked or changed even after OBC reservation implementation. There are powerful sections within the state and outside that are opposed to the idea of equality and democratic distributions of the resources. Even after more than 70 years of independence certain groups have not been able to reach to their proportionate representation in the state services. This clearly reveals how the ideology is controlling and preventing the access of public resources. The table below clearly reveals the status and representation of various social groups in central government employment (where reservation is applicable) as on 1st January 2010.

Status and Representation of Different Social Groups in Central Government Employment

Group	*Number of persons*									
	Total number of employees	*SCs*		*STs*		*OBCs*		*Upper castes* (Derived)*	
		numbers	*%*	*numbers*	*%*	*numbers*	*%*	*numbers*	*%*
A	*88896*	*10315*	*11.6*	*3998*	*4.5*	*7505*	*8.4*	*67078*	*75.5*
B	*173493*	*26495*	*15.3*	*9923*	*5.7*	*10648*	*6.1*	*126427*	*72.9*
C	*2070666*	*330167*	*15.9*	*153844*	*7.4*	*306176*	*14.8*	*1280479*	*61.9*
D (excluding Safai karamcharis	665739	123780	18.6	47702	7.2	101114	15.2	393143	59
Safai karamcharis	71324	35729	50.1	4314	6.0	7822	11.0	23459	38.9
Total (excluding Safai karamcharis	2998788	490727	16.36	215467	7.19	425443	14.19	1867151	62.26
Total (including safai karamcharis	3070112	526456	17.15	219781	7.16	433265	14.11	1890610	61.58

Source: Annual Report 2011-12, Ministry of Personnel, Public Grievances & Pensions, GoI, Pp. 38.

*Note: this category consists of Hindu upper castes and non OBC Christians, Muslims and other minor groups for whom reservation is not extended.

** Refer Sacchar committee report to see the position of Muslims in public employment.

The situation is not very different rather pathetic in the state institutions of higher learning. These are absolutely controlled by the traditional power elites of the society. Recently, many newspaper reports have been published highlighting the severe under representation of SC, ST and OBC faculty in the institutions of high learning like IITs and IIMs. There are merely 2 ST, 8 SC and 27 OBC faculty members out of the total sanctioned posts of 784 in 18 IIMs. 590 posts have occupied by the general category people while rest are lying vacant. SC, ST and OBC together make up just 6 percent of the total faculty members. Similarly, there are 8,856 sanctioned strength of faculty in 23 IITs (both old and new). 4876 are from general category, 329 from OBC, 149 from SC and merely 21 from ST. the total strength of SC,ST, OBC is merely 9 percent of the total strength in 23 IITs. This is alarming and indicates the caste bias of the management and administrators who are openly defying reservation policy of government. The situation is gruesome and more alarming if one look at the representation of SC/ST/OBC at the level of Vice-Chancellors in higher educational institutions. An RTI reply by the UGC reveals that there were 496 vice-chancellors across India in 2015-16 as per the AISHE (All India survey of higher education). There were 6 SC, 6 ST and 36 OBC and rest 448 came from general. This means SC, ST and OBC together had mere 9.67 percentages whereas the general category people occupied more than 90 percent posts.

There are clear constitutional guidelines to implement the reservation and ensure just representation. However, there appears to be forces which defy the constitutional provisions. The table and data above clearly shows how brahmanical ideology of graded inequality functions. The Varna hierarchy clearly reproduced in the distribution of jobs. There is a clearly link between the social status of a group and status of their jobs. The share and percentage of lower castes increases as one go down. Contrastingly, the share and percentage of upper castes increases as one goes up. Certain categories of jobs are disproportionally represented by certain specific groups. The table above clearly shows there is monopoly, segregation, segmentation, discrimination and under representation of various groups under different category of employments. The under-representation of some groups proves the hypothesis that, either there is institutional discrimination against them or they are still far away reaching to the levels of upper castes in education and availing other opportunities.

Reservation is often projected as a panacea or a problem of all the problems by defenders and opponents. The above table only shows the representation of groups where reservation policy is implemented. One has to be careful of the coverage of reservation while discussing the issue. Firstly, the reservation is applicable to only to public sector. Even with optimum estimates, public sector employment, including centre, states, quasi-government and local bodies may not go beyond 2 percent of total population. This means 98 percent of the population is still outside of the purview of reservation. Secondly, there are certain areas like defense and judiciary where reservation policy is not applicable. Defence alone constitutes roughly 30 percent of all central government jobs. Thirdly, there has been huge reduction in public employment over the years due to privatisation. The share of organized sector jobs has reduced considerably in the economy. According to Director General of Employment and Training (DGE&T), Under Ministry of Labour & Employment (MLE), there has been a loss of 19.18 Lakhs formal jobs between the years 1995 to 2011 in the public sector alone as per the information received by March 31, 2011.

This means those groups that were already under represented in state services have further lost significant opportunities.

The Indian society is going through a transitional phase after the opening of its economy. The competition in the economy has increased, intensified and sharpened due to privatization and globalization. There has been uneven growth of different sectors post reform period. Agriculture has been the backbone of the Indian economy for a long time. It has been one of the major sources of employments traditionally. The agriculture has suffered very badly over the last two decades. According to government sources, the percentage of people dependent on agriculture is 53.2 while its share in GDP has reduced to mere 12.35 percent. Contrarily the percentage of people dependent on service sector is 25.3 whereas its share in the GDP is 57.09. The percentage of people dependent on manufacturing sector 11.0 where its share in GDP is 16.17 for the period 2009-10 at 2004-05 base prices (GOI). Inequalities in the society and economy have increased by huge volume. Agriculture has emerged as the worst affected sector after liberalization. Agriculture today contributes mere 12.35 to the GDP whereas people who are dependent on it are more than four times.

This clearly shows the pathetic condition of agricultural sector. Agriculture today is becoming a liability and loss making venture. It is not without reasons that farmers suicides are increasing and it has become a political issue today. Various governments are using this as an opportunity to encash their vulnerabilities in the form of votes by promising debt relief. The unemployment and vulnerabilities in the agriculture sector have grown both by magnitude and degree. There have been violent and non violent movements by the farmers and peasants to address their problems. It is manifested by the demand for reservation by the traditionally agriculture castes like Jats and Gujars in Rajasthan and Haryana, Patels/Patidars in Gujarat, Marathas in Maharastra and Kapus in Andhra Pradesh. Similarly, the trade liberalization has led to entry of foreign goods and capital in the market creating excessive pressure on the small sector. According to planning commission report, there has been stark decline in the employment in the manufacturing sector from 2004-05 to 2009-10. The manufacturing sector has lost 31 Lakh jobs in between 2004-05 to 2009-10. The declining trend has continued even after that period. There is intense crisis in the labour market these days and there is stiff and cut throat completion for the available jobs. The crisis can be understood by the fact, in many states, science graduates, engineers, M.Phil and Ph.D holders are applying for the class IV jobs in government sector.

Conclusion

Indian society is probably the most stratified and highly unequal society in the world. Caste has been one of the most significant and pervasive features of social reality in India. People are divided into thousands of groups with each group differing from other on the basis of their history, origin, beliefs, cultural practices, ideological and political orientations. The question of caste ceases to die and keeps emerging in different forms and level both publically and politically. One of the most important pretexts this question violently comes is on the question of reservation. There has not been any government policy which has been subject to such huge debate and controversies in India. There has been constant opposition and resistance to it by historically privileged groups. The policy is projected as discrimination and promoting inequality in the society.

The reservation policy has been drafted to provide representation to those groups that have faced historical violence, inequality and discrimination. Ironically enough, the policy has been duped as discriminatory by the opponents. Reservation is an often associated with certain kind of negativity in India. The terms which often come in context of reservation are "reserved nation", "merit", "quality", "inefficiency", "creamy layer", "quota people" "identity politics", "divide and rule" "backwardness" etc. The beneficiaries are made to feel apologetic and humiliated when these labels are thrown at them. It also creates violence of its kind and they have to tolerate or suffer humiliation and harassment on a daily basis. The erstwhile humiliating caste nomenclature and terms have been replaced with the new and modern ones creating secular violence.

The power to give nomenclature and names is still lying with the historically privileged groups. They are the ones who decide the discourse and its contents. The significance of caste never eroded from the public life nor it has changed. The only that has come is that we have stopped listening it and pretending it not to be there. It is often perceived caste as a rural phenomenon but the most violent opposition to equality (reservation) has come from the urban areas. It is perceived that education mellows down ignorance and makes a person sensitive. However the fact is that almost all anti-reservation protests have taken places in the urban cities by well educated people. The institutions of higher learning have been their hot spots for protest against reservation. It is not surprising that many bright, promising and aspiring youths chose to commit suicide rather than living with day to day humiliations. There are hundreds of Rohit Vemulas in this country who died untimely due to caste oppression.

There are still people in this caste obsessed society who have not been able to accept equality as a natural principle. There are still many who take pride in their caste identity and purity of their blood. They openly defy the constitution and make sure that it is not implemented. The brahmanical ideology of graded inequality produces itself as a structure. There is however stiff counter resistance to it from different corners of the society. The reservation issue is not going to die soon given the historical and empirical complexities. It is going to be bitter with time as the society progresses to be democratic and egalitarian both in outlook and content. The fight for reservation is going to be intensified with the passage of time and more and more groups likely to put pressure for their fair inclusion and democratic distribution of public resources.

References

Annual Report 2011-12, *Ministry of Personnel, Public Grievances & Pensions*, GoI.

Agha, E. (2017, Sept. 4). Hardly any Backward Caste Teachers at IIMs, Reveals Study. *News 18*, accessed on 20/04/2019, Retrieved from https://www.news18.com/news/india/hardly-any-backward-caste-teachers-at-the-iims-reveals-study-1508973.html

Agha, E. (2019, Jan 14). IIM-Ahmedabad Alumni Write to Director, Compare Lack of Diversity in Faculty Bodies to Apartheid. *News 18*, Accessed on 20/04/2019, Retrieved from https://www.news18.com/news/india/iim-alumni-raise-concern-over-deficit-in-faculty-social-diversity-petition-for-affirmative-action-in-programs-2001641.html

Aloysius, G. (2010). *The Brahmanical Inscribed In Body-Politics*. New Delhi: Critical Quest.

Anuradha, (2011). *Reservation Policy and Law: An Analytical Study of Its Criteria*. (Unpublished Ph.D Thesis). Department Of Law, Regional Campus, Ladhewali, Guru Nanak Dev University. Jalandhar. Punjab.

Basham, A.L. (2004). *The Wonder That Was India: A Survey of the History and Culture of the Indian Subcontinent before the Coming of Muslims*. London: Picador.

Beck, B.E.F. (1970). The Right-Left Division of South Indian Society, *the Journal of Asian Studies*, Vol. 29, No. 4 (Aug.), Pp. 779-798.

Beena, E. (2011). *Advent Of Christian Missionaries In Travancore: A Socio- Religious Identity Of The Oppressed*. (Unpublished Ph.D Thesis). Department of History and Research Centre, Scott Christian College, Manonmaniam Sundaranar University, Tirunelveli,

Commons. (2019, feb 13). Diversity deficit in IIMs, IITs - just 23 STs and 157 SCs in 9,640 faculty posts. *ThePrint*, accessed on 20/04/2019, Retrieved from https://m.dailyhunt.in/news/india/english/the+print-epaper-theprint/diversity+deficit+in+iims+iits+just+23+sts+and+157+scs+in+9+640+faculty+posts-newsid-108664531

Cynthia, S. (2006). The history of reservations in India from the 1800s to the 1950s. *Integral liberation*, Vol. 10, No. 2, pp. 17-25.

Deliege, R. (2001). *The Untouchables of India*. UK: Berg.

DGE & T (2014). *Census of Central Government Employees.* Ministry Of Labour & Employment, Goi. New Delhi: Available At: Http://Dget.Nic.In/Upload/Uploadfiles/Files/Publication/Census_Report_2011_.Pdf

DIPP. (2003). *Report Of Working Group On Leather & Leather Products, Twelfth Five Year Plan Period (2012-17),* Ministry Of Commerce & Industry, GOI. Available At:Http://Planningcommission.Nic.In/Aboutus/Committee/Wrkgrp12/Wg_Leath0203.Pdf.

Dirks, N.B. (2013). G.S. Ghurya and the Politics of Sociological Knowledge. *Sociological Bulletin*, Vol. 62, No. 2, Special Issue on the Bombay School of Sociology: The Stalwarts and Their Legacies (May-Aug.), Pp. 239-253.

Dubois, A.J.A. (1906). *Hindu Manners, Customs and Ceremonies*. Oxford: The Clarendon Press.

Dutt. R. (1902). *The Economic History of India under Early British Rule Vol. I* Trubner: Kegan Paul.

Dutt. R. (1904). *The Economic History of India under Early British Rule Vol. II* Trubner: Kegan Paul.

Geetha, V. (2008). *Land Grants to Temples in Tamilnadu, 550-1200 A.D.* (Unpublished Ph.D Thesis). School Of Historical Studies, Madurai Kamaraj Uiversity, Madurai, Tamilnadu, (India).

Good, A. (1999). The Burning Question. Sacred and Profane Space in a South Indian Temple Town. *Anthropos*, Bd. 94, H. 1/3, Pp. 69-84.

Gough, K. (1974). Indian Peasant Uprisings. *Economic and Political Weekly*, Vol. 9, No. 32/34, Special Number (Aug.), Pp. 1391-1412.

Gough, K. (1978). Agrarian Relations In Southeast India, 1750-1976. *Review* (Fernand Braudel Center), Vol. 2, No. 1 (Summer), Pp. 25-53.

(GoI). GDP of India and major Sectors of Economy, Share of each sector to GDP and Growth rate of GDP and other sectors of economy 1951-52 onward. Retrieved from https://data.gov.in/catalog/gdp-india-and-major-sectors-economy-share-each-sector-gdp-and-growth-rate-gdp-and-other

Jebakany, C. J. (2011). *Socio-Religious Movements in South Travancore (1806-1956)*. (Unpublished Ph.D Thesis). Department Of History & Research Centre, Nesamony Memorial Christian College, Marthandam, Manonmaniam Sundaranar University, Tirunelveli, (India)

Jodhka, S.S. (2015). Cast(e) On The Hill: 'Divine' Power, Social Cohesion and Hierarchy in Humachal Pradesh. *Economic and Political Weekly*, Vol. L, No. 21, Pp. 59-69.

Joshi. S & Malghan, D. (2018, Jan. 18). Diversity Deficit: Why Are There Still Such Few SCs, STs And OBCs at IIMS? . *Business Standard*, Accessed On 20/04/2019, Retrieved From https://www.business-standard.com/article/current-affairs/diversity-deficit-why-are-there-still-such-few-scs-sts-and-obcs-at-iims-118011900156_1.html

Ketkar, S. V. (1909). *The History of Caste in India*. Ithaca, N.Y: Mkssrs. Taylor & Carpenter.

Kirshenman, J. & Neckerman, K.M. (1991). We'd Love To Hire Them, But…:Meaning Of Race For Employers, In jenks, C. & Peterson, p. (Eds), *The Urban Underclass*, Washington, DC: The Brookings Institution, Pp. 203-34.

Menon, S. (1979). Response To Class And Caste Oppression In Thanjavur District, 1940-1952: Part Two. *Social Scientist*, Vol. 7, No. 7 (Feb.), Pp. 57-68.

Mila, D.R. (2009). *Social Upheaval In South Travancore*. (Unpublished Ph.D Thesis). Department Of History, S.T. Hindu College, Nagercoil, Manonmaniam Sundaranar University, Tirunelveli, (India).

Oommen, T.K. (2008). Disjunctions between Field, Method and Concept: An Appraisal of M.N. Srinivas. *Sociological Bulletin*, Vol. 57, No. 1 (January-April), Pp. 60-81.

Pandian, M.S.S. (2002). One Step outside Modernity: Caste, Identity Politics and Public Sphere. *Economic and Political Weekly*, Vol. 37, No. 18 (May 4-10), Pp. 1735-41.

Pandian, M.S.S. (2008). Writing Ordinary Lives. *Economic and Political Weekly*, Vol. 43, No. 38 (Sept. 20-26), Pp. 34-40.

Philip, G. (2005). *A Historical Anatomy of the Evolution of Social Revolution in Travancore*. (Unpublished Ph.D. Thesis). School Of Gandhian Thought and Development Studies, Mahatma Gandhi University, Kottayam, Kerala, (India).

Prashad, G. & Prashad, G. (1964). Law and Colonialism. *The Indian Journal of Political Science*, Vol. 25, No. 3/4, Pp. 76-84.

PRS legislation Research. (2015, Dec. 8). Vital Stats: Overview of Central Government Employees. Accessed on 18/04/2019, Retrieved from https://www.prsindia.org/sites/default/files/parliament_or_policy_pdfs/1449721528~~Vital%20Stats-%20Overview%20of%20Central%20Government%20Employees.pdf

Rao, P.V. (2016). *New Perspectives in the History of Indian Education*. Hyderabad: Orient Blackswan.

Report of Working Group on Leather & Leather Products, 12th Five Year Plan Period (2012-17), *Department Of Industrial Policy & Promotion*, Ministry Of Commerce & Industry, GOI.

Roy, T. (2005). *Rethinking Economic Change in India*. London: Routledge

Sharma, K. (2019, feb. 13). Diversity deficit in IIMs, IITs — just 23 STs and 157 SCs in 9,640 faculty posts. *ThePrint*, accessed on 20/04/2019, retrieved from https://theprint.in/india/education/diversity-deficit-in-iims-iits-just-23-sts-and-157-scs-in-9640-faculty-posts/191246/

Singh, V.B. (1960). *Economic History of India: 1857-1956*. New Delhi: Allied Publishers Private Limited.

Singh, V.B. (1960). *Economic History of India: 1857-1956*. New Delhi: Allied Publishers Private Limited.

Smith, B.K. (1994). *Classifying the Universe: The Ancient Indian Varna System and the Origins of Caste*. New York: Oxford University Press.

Thapar, R. (2002). *The Penguin History of Early India from the Origins to Ad 1300*. New Delhi: Penguin Books.

Thorat & Despande, (2001). Caste System and Economic Inequality: Economic Theory and Evidence. In G. Shah (Eds), *Dalit Identity and Politics*. New Delhi: Sage Publications.

Wagmore, S. (2007). Exploring the Unexplored: Dalit Worldview in Development Discourse. *The Indian Journal of Social Work*, Vol. 68, Issue 1: Pp. 7-23.

Woodburne, A.S. (1922). Can India's Caste System Survive In Modern Life?. *The Journal of Religion*, Vol. 2, No. 5 (Sept.), Pp. 525-537.

Woodburne, A.S. (1923). The Present Religious Situation in India. *The Journal of Religion*, Vol. 3, No. 4 (July), Pp. 387-397.

Chapter - 9

A Case of MRPS Movement in Andhra Pradesh and Telangana

— Dr. Chandraiah Gopani

Abstract

There have been a series of democratic movements within Dalits for greater recognition and redistribution from the mid 1990s in India. These movements critically interrogated the Scheduled Castes (SC) category in particular and Dalit movement in general. Although Scheduled Castes (SC) and Dalit (oppressed) categories are to some extent able to homogenize all untouchable castes and consolidate their experience and politics in challenging the hegemonic power structures. However in practice, these categories are increasingly showing limitations to address the diversities and differences of various castes within the Dalits. Hence, the critical interrogation of these categories is an important intellectual discourse in contemporary Dalit movement and politics.

Introduction

For long time there is feeling among some Scheduled Castes that SC reservations are cornered by few castes, hence the most marginalised demand the justice to them. In this direction the Madiga Reservation Porata Samiti (MRPS) movement in Telugu region questioned the homogeneity of Scheduled Castes and demands the equity in SC reservation for the benefit of the lowest among low. The Dandora movement by Madigas and its satellite castes was started on July 7, 1994 in Edumudi village (Prakasham district) under the leadership of Manda Krishna Madiga for dignified identity and categorization of SC reservation; this soon created a nation-wide debate and raised many questions for public discussion. The issues include: (i) Is the SC category divisible? (ii) Can the Dalit category accommodate the differences and diversities among Dalits? (iii) Can the struggles for recognition and redistribution of the lowest Dalits divide the Dalit unity? These questions have come up for a wider discussion in public. The demand for SC categorization by MRPS got more support across the various sections of society. However, Mala Mahanadu emerged to oppose SC categorisation.[1]

The protests against positive discrimination have been frequent occurrences since implementation of the reservation policy in India. The demand for further inclusion of castes into reserved categories by some castes is not uncommon either. However, the phenomenon of caste groups in reserved categories complaining about the preponderance of some other castes in the same categories and consequently demanding some kind of rearrangement of reservation policies; to be more specific, the classification of caste into separate enclosures, with each group entitled to a fixed percentage of quotas within the broader category is unique and a relatively new one for Dalit and Adivasi discourse.[2] On the SC reservation categorization issue, there are contested views among scholars and activists who work on Dalits question. Some argue that struggles for recognition and redistribution by the lowest of the low within Dalits have greater ability to deepen Dalit movement and politics. So, it is suggested that the unity of the Dalits has to be built by recognizing the lowest among the low and their just demands.[3] The other group argues that this kind of move and demand for categorization would lead to division of Dalits and political manipulation by mainstream political parties.[4] At this critical juncture, there is a need to deeply engage and explore the complexity of the problem, its historical roots and its implications.

The contemporary Dalit movement is in an ambiguous stage, both at the moral and political levels, to address the emerging internal problems of this kind which has an all India nature. The struggles for recognition and redistribution of the Arundhatiya movement in Tamil Naidu, Madigas movement in Andhra Pradesh and Karnataka, Valmikis movement in Haryana, Punjab and Mangs' movement in Maharashtra, and Maha Dalit in Bihar are cases in point.[5] As already mentioned, the Dandora or MRPS movement, spread all over the state within a short period of time has been able to bring together the employees, students and masses from the Madiga community. Lakhs of people attended a number of dharnas, rastarokos, public meetings, Padayatras.[6] The movement explored multiple marginalization processes of Madiga subgroups within Dalits and outside Dalits. With strong organizational structure and continuous activities, it is able to get support and sympathy from all section of society, particularly progressive writers, and activists. It has succeeded in convincing the political parties to include the demand in their manifestos. To counter the classification movement, Malas and sub groups have consolidated themselves under the "Malamahanadu" (The great congregation of Malas) which brought the rhetorical argument of merit against the demand which is often put forth by the upper castes whenever there is a debate on reservation. Further, it is argued that the classification would divide Dalits.[7] In the early days of Dandora movement, a majority of Mala leaders, writers and activists did not respond positively to the categorisation demand. In this context, Madigas also started raising some socio, cultural questions on issues like: hierarchy of untouchability, cultural differences, occupational differences and historical experience of Madigas from their social location.[8] The consistent and continuous mobilisation of Madiga sub-groups made them a powerful negotiating force both in politics and civil society in erstwhile Andhra Pradesh. Now let us discuss the heterogeneity (After 2014 Andhra Pradesh and Telangana).

Scheduled Castes (SC) Category: Beyond homogeneity

Today, the category Dalit has become part of the local to global academic and activist agenda across different socio-cultural situations.[9] The word 'Dalit' often emerges in public discourse and most people refer to it in their writings, speeches, debates, discussions and analysis. Etymologically, Dalit (depressed or broken people) originates from the root word *Dal;* the adjective form of *Dal* is *"Dalit"*.[10] In Moles Worth's Marathi-English dictionary (1975 reprint of 1831 edition), the meaning of Dalit is generally given as "ground", "broken" or "reduced to pieces".[11] These English terms sum up the locations of a segment of Indian people who are discriminated, excluded, exploited and humiliated in the name of caste and religion. People (SC, Scheduled Tribes and Shudras (OBCs) and all women), who are crushed and cramped and discriminated by the Hindu religion and its caste hierarchy thereby positively asserted and declared themselves as Dalits. This identity was popularized with the emergence of the Dalit Panther movement in Maharashtra during the middle of the 1970s. The movement advocated that Dalits be proud of their culture and history.[12] The earlier nomenclatures of Dalits, i.e., "Untouchables", "Outcaste", "Panchamas", "Atisudras", "Avarnas", "Antyajas", "Namasudras", "Chandalas", "Pariahs", etc. basically referred to an entire people as un-seeable and unapproachable. Chandalas were in use during different phases of Indian history and in different parts of the country. The British used the terms Depressed Classes and Exterior Classes to refer to Dalits, thereby referring to the fact that they were kept away from Hindu society.[13] Gandhi preferred to call them

"Harijan", which literally means 'Children of God' a term, that he borrowed from a Gujarati Brahmin saint, Narasi Mehta. Ambedkar had objections against calling them *"Harijans"* because he found its implications to be derogatory and insulting (Harijan meant fatherless people).[14]

Dalit as a category in fact was used in the 1930s as a Hindi and Marathi translation of the Depressed Classes. It was used to refer to the SCs during the British period. In the 1930s, a Depressed Classes newspaper titled "Dalit *Bandhu*" (friend of Dalit) was in circulation. The term was also used by Ambedkar in his Marathi speeches.[15] References to it are also found during the Nizam period between 1940-55, for instance, in the name of an organisation called the Dalit Jatiya Sangh and Dalit Sarsvat Parishat (a literary organization) that was working for the upliftment of the untouchables. Ambedkar broadly described the term Dalit in his fortnightly "*Bahishkrut Bharat*" as an experience and condition of life that is characterized by exploitation, suppression and marginalization of untouchables by the social, economic, cultural and political domination of the caste Hindu Brahminical order. Ambedkar often deployed similar categories depending on the context; for instance, with the colonial state, he used the category of Depressed Classes, with caste Hindus he used the category "*Bahishkrut*" meaning totally outcaste. In the domain of politics he used the term Scheduled Caste. Ambedkar in an effort to politically radicalize and effectively mobilise untouchables used the term "*Pad Dalit*", thereby referring to those who were crushed under the feet of the Hindu social order.[16]

Scholars have also referred to Dalits differently. Those using class analysis associated Dalits with categories such as peasants, agricultural labor, factory workers etc. This kind of understanding one could see in the writings of subaltern historiography and in movements such as the Dalit Panthers. Those who use the framework of religion have considered Dalits to be a part of the Hindu religious[17] order. In order to differentiate caste specificities scholars also use the term "sub-subaltern" to refer to Dalits while anti-caste thinkers are described as caste radicals.[18] The Dalit Panthers manifesto defined the term in a broader sense. It included SCs, STs, neo-Buddhists, the working classes, the landless and poor peasants, women and all those who were being exploited politically and economically and in the name of religion.[19] Similarly, the Dalit Mahasabha of Andhra Pradesh (Manifesto, 1986) has defined Dalit as the people who have been exploited and discriminated across castes and are represented in the spheres of culture, economy and politics by their caste and religious locations within the Indian society.[20] In Babu Rao Bagul's view "Dalit" is a revolutionary category for its hermeneutic ability to recover the emancipatory potential of the historical past of Dalit cultures and values. He argues that this category has a greater capacity to reach out to a larger section of people. In Bagul's view, this category is based on a materialist epistemology and is not a mere linguistic construction. It is a category that is historically constructed through the revolutionary struggle of the Dalit.[21]

Gopal Guru argues that the category "Dalit" is not a metaphysical construction. It derives its epistemic and political strength from the material and social experiences of the community. The category Dalit takes ideological assistance from the philosophies of Buddha, Marx, Phule and Ambedkar and in the process becomes man-centered rather than God centered unlike what is implicit in the Gandhian connotation of Harijan.[22] He further elaborated that the category Dalit chose to radically distance itself from state constituted categories such as the SC, ST and Other Backward Castes (OBCs).[23] However, in practice the identity 'Dalit-Bahujan' is also widely used in scholarly writings and public discourse, in which Dalit refers to SCs and Bahujan refers to Shudras or the OBCs.[24] Although these categories appeal towards a unity and work towards a unified political goal, the existing historical and socio-economic disparities and heterogeneity inevitably place limitations on the realization of the identity in the everyday relationships between people. In order to recognize the lowest of the low within Dalits and taking their deprivation into consideration, the Bihar Government created a category called 'Mahadalit'[25] for whom the government created special provisions. Scholars have also called the lowest of the low as "Ati-Dalit"[26] by differentiating the smaller SC castes from the dominant SC castes.

However, the Dalit identity and the meaning it generates and the meanings people attach to it lie in the very objective condition in which the Dalit category operates. In the recent past the debates in academic writings and political discourse have equated it only to SC. As a result, the validity of Dalit becomes dependent on to what extent it can universally represent the realities of other identities that exist within it. There are many castes within SC such as Madiga, Mala, Adi-Andhra (A.P), Adi-Kannada, Holayas, Madigas (Karnataka), Pallars, Parayas (Tamil Naidu) Chamar (UP, Bihar), Mahar, Mathangs (Maharashtra) Valmiki/Bhangi (Punjab) and so on. These identities too exist at the grass root level and represent different degrees of socio-economic inequalities. The assertion of those identities can challenge the hierarchy and democratize the social relations at various levels.[27] It is articulated at many levels among the Dalits. This existence of multiple identities, both of the individual and the collective, certainly questions the validity and inadequacy of the top down identities and categories.

The contemporary SC sub categorization movements by Madigas in Andhra Pradesh, and Telangana, Arundhatiyars in Tamil Nadu, Mangs in Maharashtra, and Valmikis in Punjab raises historical challenges to the Dalit movement. These movements argue that different heterogeneous castes were legally clubbed into the SC category for administrative purposes that remained oblivious to sub-categories. The category SC is used by the government for all welfare schemes and implementation of reservation benefits. In practice, this category is available only to a section of dominant and educationally mobile castes within Dalits. The demand therefore is that the SC categorisation should benefit the lowest among the low. Further, they ask how the SC category can be homogenous when there are heterogeneous castes with specific socio-economic conditions. They argue that the Dalit category may outwardly represent some historical and political commonality, but the problematic has to be addressed. The socio-political visibility of Mahars, Malas and Chamars etc tends to hegemonise the Dalit identity but the diverse socio cultural aspects of other Dalit groups below them are never focused upon. If untouchability is an important demarcation to distinguish Savarnas[28] and avarnas (Dalits), the 'hierarchy of untouchability' among the untouched (Dalit) makes the Dalit category more ambiguous. Therefore, one has to understand the Dalit category in its multiple senses and in ever changing conditions. The ability to stimulate transformative politics of Dalits depends on the recognition of the lowest of the low among Dalits and the willingness to address the question of recognition and redistribution from its roots in order to consolidate untouchables (oppressed) to fight against caste and class oppressions. The following section deals with hierarchies and inequalities among Dalits.

MRPS (Dandora) Movement: The Struggle for Social Justice

Although the demand for SC reservation categorisation movement took a militant form in the mid-1990s, the demand was there much before MRPS, but in a different form. A Telugu Madiga, L.C Guruswamy, established the "Arundathiya Mahasabha" in 1920 in the Madras Presidency to initiate struggle for identity and social justice to Madigas. To counter the partisan attitude of Bagya Reddy Varma towards Malas, the excommunicated leader established "Arundhateeya Mahasabha in 1931 for Madigas in Hyderabad. Later on, 'Adijambava Arundhatiya Bandhuseva Mandali' was established in 1981 by first generation Madiga employees under the presidentship of Kishan Lal. For the first time, Madhava Rao who was a former president of

Bandu Seva Mandali used Madiga as a suffix and was the only activist known as Madava Rao Madiga.[29] In 1982, the Mandali published a document of socio, economic and representational status of Arunthatiyas in united Andhra Pradesh with detailed statistics. Through this document, the Mandali demanded SC categorisation into A, B, C, and D, according to population proportion of each caste. In the 1982 Assembly elections, the TDP promised categorization.[30] After that, employees and some civil society organisations started to agitate through 'Andhra Pradesh Madiga Sangam', which was the first Dalit association established with Madiga sub-caste name. In the year 1982, the Sangam activists enter the Assembly while Assembly was in session and threw pamphlets, titled "separate reservation for Madigas," from the visitor's gallery. Consequently, twelve activists of Madiga Sangam were convicted by the state Assembly for violating the rules. After that, the Karamchedu massacre took place in 1985. The post-Karamchedu agitations changed the terms of discourse among activists and social movements and the autonomous Dalit movement began until 1994, the categorisation issue was neglected, or deliberately excluded. On 2nd May 1994, in Nizam College ground in Hyderabad, the Congress Party and government encouraged caste wise public meetings. After this meeting, the Madiga, Koneru Ranga Rao, was appointed as deputy Chief Minister of A.P. with the purpose of consolidating Madigas. Whoever attended the meeting was disappointed with the Madiga leaders for their failure to assert the SC reservation categorisation issue. It was in this context MRPS grew under Manda Krishna Madiga.[31] He contacted Madiga employees in the regions where he was working, got basic information on the issue and discussed with many people. Then, he published a pamphlet with statistics in order to sensitise Madigas with Edumudi Madiga youth since they were active the Dalits movement. Then onwards, the struggle for categorisation and mobilisation was growing among employees and youths, especially in Coastal Andhra. According to P. Muthaiah, the MRPS movement used three identities: (i) Arundhatiya, Jambavantha, (ii) Madiga, and (iii) Dandora to mobilise people to struggle for a respectable identity and to demand SC categorisation. The leader took a pledge to make the derogatory term 'Madiga' as a respectable identity. For this, they propagated etymological meaning of Madigas. The Madiga means Maha (very) + Adi (from the beginning) +ga (moving). That means original inhabitants of India moving and living on earth from very beginning.[32] K. Balagopal observes:

> "The movement took the state by storm in a matter of months. The first and most audacious thing the Madigas did was to suffix the caste tag to their names. Krishna became Krishna Madiga, Krupakar became

a Krupakar Madiga, and so on down the line. In a society that addresses any number of Krishna shastries and Krishna Reddys respectfully, the discomfort this caused was most amusing to watch. As "Madiga" has served as term of abuse, whether directed against a Madiga or otherwise, it was most discomforting to be confronted by someone who wanted you to address him as "Krishna Madiga" and when people confessed to themselves that they found it embarrassingly absurd to think of someone as Krishna Shastri, Krishna Reddy or Krishna Naidu. Since true victory over an oppressor lies not in putting a bullet through his head but in making him turn a self-critical eye towards his own pretensions to superiority, it must be said that this deliberately chosen tactic of the Madiga was done to puncture upper caste arrogance".[33]

With this cultural and historical background, the M.R.P.S leaders and activist started to mobilise and sensitise Madigas and its sub-castes under the Dandora banner. Madigas started to form the district, mandal and village committees. They also used Ambedkar, Mother Teresa and Babu Jagjeevan Ram on their banners and pamphlets as their inspirations. They asserted that social justice means equal distribution and used white cloth flag with the symbol of man beating a drum in the middle of flag with in blue colour. Soon, it became a people's movement. In every corner of the villages, Madigas started to see the differences and hegemony within Dalits. They critically started to interrogate Dalit, and Scheduled Caste categories. After many long hunger strikes, marches, public meetings, the then TDP government under Chandrababu government appointed Justice Ramachandra Raju Commission to study the disparities among the Scheduled Castes examines demand for categorisation and some remedies. After six months of the Commission's appointment, Madigas felt that the categorisation was getting delayed intentionally. Then Dandora activists decided to pressurise the government and took a course of action to mobilise people on the delay. As part of that, hundreds of meetings, dharnas, rasta rokos, and protests were organised at various levels. There were separate demonstrations in order to attract more Madigas and make them to be involved in the movement particularly, Madiga children, (Bala Dandora), Madiga women (Madiga Mahila Dandora), Madiga Employees (Madiga employees Dandora) and Madiga students and youth Dandora were organised to show the strength. In this vibrant movement, one boy committed suicide, leaving the suicide note stating "SC categorization is the last wish', two more Madigas got killed in the conflict with Malas.[34] In order to put pressure on the government, Madiga Dandora members decided to launch a Mahapadayatra to mount pressure on the government. It began on 14th April in Chief Minister N Chandrababu Naidu's village "Naravarepally" in Chittoor district by presenting their demands to the Chief Minister's mother. The grand mobilisation and impact of the Padayatra was reported in the English daily The Hindu (May 7, 1997) as:

> "On Sunday, a group of youths wearing the anklets of dancers and beating drums started the walk, announcing the 'waging war against the government's indifference to the Madigas' problem'. This proclamation is the "Dandora', the traditional form of announcement in the villages, and the movement has to be called the 'Madiga Dandora'. The group holds wayside meetings at the Madiga hamlets situated on the outskirts of every village early in the day. The network of Madiga Yuva (youth) Sena is so extensive that they work as the courier system conveying the information about where the group would stop for lunch or halt for the night. The host villagers organise lunch and dinner.... about 500 people march together but about 300 of them are people of one village, who escort the group to the next village, when people of the next village take over.... their legs have swollen and have blisters. Yet, they walk with determination, about 20 to 30 kilometres a day, in order to awaken the Madigas. A jeep with their clothes and foodstuffs and trailer carrying a drum of drinking water follows them. M. Manda Krishna, who has taken the suffix "Madiga', leads this group on a journey by foot from Naaravaripalle, the native place of the Chief Minister Mr. N Chandrababu Naidu, in Chittoor district to his official residence in Jubilee Hills in Hyderabad".[35]

The Padayatra was depicted as equivalent to Dandi March of Gandhi and Mao's long march, for social justice to Madigas.[36] The movement began with some advantages like Malas; the Madigas are spread across the state. If not every village, certainly every second or third village in every corner of the state would have at least a few Madiga families. Secondly, though the reality of hierarchy within the outcastes and unequal access to reservations was known, felt and even mildly articulated for a long time, it was being expressed as a mass upsurge for the first time. It is a matter of common experience that a mass expression of a genuine public grievance for the first time attracts the most innocent and also disinterested from rest of the society. It is in course of second and third round that the expression and the sympathy are contaminated by what passes in the meantime and by self–serving afterthoughts. Thirdly, the demand Madigas raised was plain, simple and easily understood: "divide the SC reservation quota and give us our due". It was felt to be unproblematic since backward class reservation in the state have long been subdivided into four subgroups, which subdivision has been upheld by the Supreme Court. Fourthly, former Madigas found a dynamic and charismatic leader in Manda Krishna. However there was a opposition from the Mala groups against sub-categorization.

The Mala Mahanadu Opposition and its counter arguments against Sub-categorization

The Mala Mahahanadu was started by P.V Rao, a Govt. employee who resigned his job and started mobilising Malas, particularly employees and youth. It organised many public meetings against the categorisation movement. Leaders like Jupudi Prabhakar, Karem Shivaji and others organised Malas under various Malamahanadu factions. Interestingly, they organised meetings under Malamahanadu and invoked Dalit identity. Some of them went to the extent of saying that Ambedkar was born in a Mahar family and that Mahar is equivalent to Mala. It was also said that Mala bureaucrats lobby worked at various levels in approaching courts and stopping the GO in the Supreme Court. However, Malamahanadu brought the problematic arguments against the rationalisation of SC reservation, broadly the arguments were:

- SC (Scheduled Caste) or Dalits are homogeneous. Hence, there should not be any division among them
- Rationalisation of SC reservation is unconstitutional, it divides Dalits.
- Instead of SC categorisation, Madigas' should fight for SC reservations in the private sector.
- Those who have merit among Dalits will get the opportunity, so, Madigas lack merit.
- Madigas have caste occupation, whereas Malas don't have the caste occupation. So Malas got early education and employment through Christian missionaries enabling social mobility
- If Madigas are backward, they may get some special package- not SC reservation categorisation.
- By demanding SC categorization, they are fighting against Ambedkar spirit and by using Madiga as suffix promoting casteist ideology and humiliating entire Dalit community.

Organisations like 'Rajyanga Parirakshana Committee' headed by Malas 'Bahujana Vigyana Vedika' public meetings and published small booklets. Hence, most of the time, Malamahanadu activities were reactive to the MRPS activities. K. Balagopal, in his article, observes:

> "In any case, the Mahanadu plea is the kind of argument made first by the Brahmins and later by the other upper castes against reservations as such; give them help for economic uplift meant and we too will learn to honour the dignity of labour, but do not branch our preserve of expanding knowledge and the status and opportunities it carries. The argument, as well as the answer to it, will become clearer if one goes below the Madigas to castes such as the Rellies, who have as their exclusive vocation scavenging in which they face no threat of competition. Nor do the Rellies have any scope for advancement, if they remain scavengers. It was also argued that, instead of fighting among themselves for sub-dividing their common quota, Dalits should jointly fight for increasing the SC quota, commensurate with the proportionate increase in Dalit population and for a proper implementation of reservations, including the backlog of unfilled vacancies. There is no reason, however, why the desire for justice inter se should wait upon the later task or tasks. The desire and the tasks can proceed together, provided both sides -particularly the more privileged side- makes sure that the struggle for subdivision and the response to it do not vitiate the atmosphere to the extent of making the united struggle for the common goals impossible. In any case, this is again no different in principle from the argument offered by the upper caste anti-reservationists; let us fight not over division of the existing job opportunities, but for the creation of more, the two struggles can well go together and the onus of making this possible lies on the more privileged and not the less privileged. To ask the disadvantaged to give up their just demand of equal opportunity in order to pave the way for the unity required for a common fight for greater opportunities is plainly unethical".[37]

Here, K. Balagopal raised the ethical dimension of the just demand of Madigas and the unethical attitude of the Malas who oppose the rationalisation of SC reservation in the name of "Dalit unity". The Dalit leadership and organisation also did not initiate any method and negotiation to address the problem. So, it is argued that most of the so-called Dalits leaders belonged to the Mala community. This also made Madiga youth and employees lose their trust in Dalit leadership. According to Muthaiah (2000), Malas and Madigas historically are not united culturally and there are practical and ritualistic differences among these communities. There are 59 castes, among which Mala and Madigas are two numerically major castes. The social anthropological study conducted by T.R Singh and Muthaiah clearly shows the cultural world of these castes.

> "It can be seen that the Mitha Ayyalwar caste is at the top of Dalit hierarchy, while Dakkal at the bottom. The superiority in Dalit hierarchy flows from upward to downwards, while inferiority from downwards to upwards. In the Mala hierarchy, Mitha Ayyalwar is considered to be superior, standing at the top of the ladder. Mala Jangam and Mala Dasaries come from the priestly class and function as spiritual advisors to Mala satellite castes; they are also called Mala gurus. They consider Malas and Madigas inferior to them. In the Mala satellite castes, Mala Jangam/Dasaries (in some cases) is at the top of the Mala hierarchy. Next to them are Malas, Pambala, Masti and Gurram Malas in the descending order in the hierarchy? Syed Sirjul recorded that "Gurram Malas are regarded as the lowest of all the Mala sub castes. It is considered to be a degraded branch of Mala satellite castes.
>
> Madiga rank next to Malas in the Dalit hierarchy. In the Madiga satellite castes, the superiority flows from the Madiga guru, the Sangari to Dakkal and inferiority from Dakkal to Sangari. In the hierarchy of Madigas satellite castes, the Sangarie's position is the highest. All satellite castes, except Sangari, are inferior to Madigas. In the Madiga hierarchy, T.R Singh states that, in some villages, however, the Bindla and Verpula not only claimed, but also maintained, superiority over the Madigas. It is seen in villages, the Madiga, Bindla Mastu and Dakkal are inferior to Sangari in a descending order. All the castes, including the Madigas, treat a Dakkal as untouchable. Here, it is pertinent to mention that the Brahmanic innovation of superiority, inferiority and untouchable has percolated down to the Dakkal, the last man in homo hierarchy are the untouchables of the untouchables.[38]

In the hierarchy of untouchability one has to see critically in order to understand the everyday relations among the Scheduled Castes. In the layer of social status, Malas feel superior to other castes, therefore Malas also practice some sort of untouchability and discrimination on Madigas. Inter-caste marriages hardly taken place between them, even if this takes place, most of the time, these have led to conflict as it happen with upper caste people. Therefore, the cultural differences and historical roots of inequality indicate that the myth of Mala-Madiga unity did not exist even before emergence of the Dandora movement. However, both castes suffer untouchability; carry common experience of suffering. For the upper castes, both castes are untouchable. These historical visible inequalities made Madigas mobilize on large scale. After continuous struggles and agitations, Justice Ramachandra Raju Commission recommended SC categorization in 1997. The government passed a resolution on rationalization of SC reservation 2000. All political parties are unanimously agree for this act. According to act the listed Scheduled Caste are divided into four groups A.B.C.D. The following tables show the representatives castes. The percentage of reservation is allocated to this is 1% for group A, 7% for

Table 9.1: Group-A

Sl.No.	*Name of the caste*	*Traditional Occupation*	*Total of Sub Caste*
1.	Bavuri	Basket makers	756
2.	Chachathi	Fruit selling and scavenging	5, 244
3.	Chandala	NA	184
4.	Danadasi	Village watchman	5,410
5.	Dom, Combara, Paidi	Weavers, Musicians, drum beaters	23,214
6.	Chasi, Haddi Relli Chachandi	Fruit and vegetable sellers sweeping and scavenging	1872
7.	Godagali	Basket Making and Baboo Making	2,212
8.	Mehtar	Scavenging	4,553
9.	Paki, Moti, Thoti	Scavenging	7,876
10.	Pamidi	NA	5,647
11.	Relli	Scavenging, Fruits sellers	76,329
12.	Sapru	Scavengers and Fruit sellers	592
		Total	1,33,689 1.68%

Table 9.2: Group-B

Sl.No.	*Name of the caste*	*Traditional Occupation*	*Total of Sub-Caste*
1.	Arundatheeya	NA	78, 496
2.	Beda Jangam, Budgajangam	Hunting, Flowers and cultivators	12,024
3.	Bindla	Priest of Madigas, Appears of Goddesses	13, 589
4.	Chamar, Mochi	Shoe makers and leathers	12, 881
5.	Chambar	Shoe makers and leather workers	519
6.	Dakkal Madiga , Dakkal War	Mendicants, Bards of Madigas, Leather workers	1598
7.	Dhor	Leather and tanning works	2,452
8.	Godari	Leather and shoe makers	834
9.	Jaggali	Leather workers and agriculture laboureres	983
10.	Jambavulu	Agricultural laborers	22,335
11.	Kolupula Vandlu	Fore telling, appeaser of Goddesses	961
12.	Madiga	Leather tanning, Chappal making	35,72,622
13.	Madiga Dasu, Masteen	Spiritual advisers, acrobatics story tellers to Madigas	5,450
14.	Mang	Drum beaters, Basket, Mat making, Tanning, Jugglers snake charmers	8,007
15.	Mang Garodi	Snake charming, Buffellows shaving, Acrobats, Jugglers	107
16.	Matangi	Begging, singing, Tanning	323
17.	Samagara	Leather and tanning works	1845
18.	Sindhollu, Chinlollu	Drama, Dancing and prostitution	2,583
		Total	37,37,609 46.94%

group B, 6 % for group C, 15, for group-D 1% out of 15 percentage of total reservation to Scheduled Caste. The following tables are presenting the castes in each group included and their traditional occupation.

Table 9.3: Group-C

Sl.No.	*Name of the caste*	*Traditional Occupation*	*Total of the Sub-Caste*
1.	Adi-Dravida	NA	1,00,382
2.	Anamukh	NA	76
3.	Arya Mala	NA	1395
4.	Arvamala	NA	22,937
5.	Baniki	Village watchman, Palanquin beabers, watchmen	11,844
6.	Byagara	Watchmen of graveyards, weaving	14,120
7.	Chalvadi	Village watchman, weaving course cloth	1740
8.	Ellamalwaru, Yallmmalwandlu	Vagrant caste	358
9.	Gosangi	Mendicants	7,653
10.	Holeya	Agriculture labour , serfs, weaving course cloth	620
11.	Holeya Dasari	Begging	620
12.	Madasi Kuruva	Sheep and goat rearing	3,550
13.	Mahar	Weaving course cloth, village watch laborers	11,486
14.	Mala	Watchman, laboureres	28,94,643
15.	Mala Dasari	Spiritual laborers to Malas , agriculture laborers	18,416
16.	Malas dasu	Spiritual advisers, acrobatics story tellers	8,335
17.	Mala hannai	Vagarent caste	120
18.	Malajangam	Agriculture laborers	4,895
19.	Mala Masthi	Acrobatics	474
20.	Mala Sale, Nethakani	Weavers, Agricultural Laborers	18,272
21.	Malasanyai	N.A	300
22.	Manne	Village watch Man agricultures	64,668
23.	Mandala	Agricultural Laboureres	840
24.	Pambada, Pambanda	Devil Dancers and Musicians to Malas	2333
25.	Samban	NA	3233
		Total	32,63,675 40.99%

Table 9.4: Group-D

Sl. No.	*Name of the caste*	*Traditional Occupation*	*Total of sub-Caste*
1.	Adi-Andhra (Mala's and Madigas)	NA	6, 98,860
2.	Masthi	Dancers, Acrobatics Carpenters	2,922
3.	Mitha Ayyalwar	Priests and spiritual advisors to Madigas and Malas	2777
4.	Panchama, Pariah	NA	9,265
5.	Unclassified in Census	NA	1.12,933
		Total	8,26,757 10.39%

Source: P. Muthaiah, 2004, pp. 197-199, (Note the population numbers are old).[39]

From 2000 to 2004, the SC categorization policy was implemented. Manda Krishna[40] claims that during this period, the Madiga got more than 20,000 jobs. The Usha Mehara commission brought the facts that the result of SC reservation classification, the following table is an illustration to establish the fact that sub-categorization created equality and absence of categorization created inequality among scheduled castes during the academic year 2003-04 and 2004-05.

Table 9.5: The Inequality among Different Castes with and without Classification

Name of the Department/University	*Castes*	*Relli (A)*	*Madiga (B)*	*Mala (C)*	*Adi – Andhra (D)*	*Total*
Medicine	Without Classification	0	82 (16.87%)	345 (70.98%)	59 (12.14%)	486 (100%)
All Universities	With Classification	32 (6.58%)	227 (46.70%)	195 (40.12%)	32 (6.58%)	
Engineering Two Universities	Without Classification	0	70 (28.11%)	163 (65.46%)	16 (6.43%)	249 (100%)
	With Classification	16 (6.43%)	117 (46.98%)	100 (40.16%)	16 (6.43%)	
M.Sc Science Courses Three Universities	Without Classification	0 (0)	183 (36.30%)	314 (62.30%)	7 (1.40%)	504 (100%)
	With Classification	33 (6.54%)	236 (46.82%)	202 (40.04%)	33 (6.54%)	

Source: Usha Mehara Commission, 2008, pp. 79.

The above table clearly indicates the differences among scheduled caste and need of categorization in order to reach the lowest among low within Dalits or Scheduled caste. Although there are movements for SC categosation in various states, the central Govt. yet to take a proper policy level decision. After reviewing the available literature and preparing the brief profile of Madigas and its satellite caste in Andhra Pradesh. The pilot study has done for the selection of field site. However in 2004, the Supreme Court set aside categorizations GO in the case of petitioner E.V Chinnaiah Vs Andhra Pradesh Govt.,[41] and suggested Constitutional Amendment for SC reservations categorization. After the Supreme Court judgment, on three occasions, all political parties unanimously passed a resolution for amendment of SC categorization in the State Assembly, under Chief Minister Rajashekar Reddy all party delegation also the Prime Minister. After delegation and agitation, the then UPA Govt. appointed a single person commission, Justice Usha Mehra Commission. This Commission visited the three regions of the then Andhra Pradesh, consulted many organisations and individuals and finally recommended SC categorisation. However, the state and central Governments are yet to initiate the Constitutional Amendment.

After the TDP Government passed a resolution to bring rationalisation of SC reservation Act, 2000, the MRPS' attention changed from reservation to greater alliance of the oppressed communities for political power. With more than 20 social organisations with the encouragement of Maroju Veerana with the slogan of "Anagarina Kulala Ikya Dandora," the Mahajana Sangharshana Samithi" was formed under Manda Krishna Madiga's leadership. Under this banner, many activities were undertaken against violence on minorities, struggle for reservations in the private sector and agitation for land reforms. Although the Samithi contested in the election, it could not succeed. The MRPS succeeded in getting scholarship amounts increased and organised many conferences and protests for their rights through "Vikalangula Hakula Porata Samithi", child heart patients issue and was able to get public attention. The strong protests against the government influenced policy initiatives like "Arogya Sri," which benefitted many families across caste and religion. Most of the time, in academics works, it is theorized that the Dalits communities build movements around their identity, but MRPS creatively took issues and organised movements going beyond its community. Further it took up the differently abled, old age people, widows and 'Samajika Telangana' etc issues which expanded the MRPS horizons, both in theory and practice.[42]

Conclusion

After one decade of Karamchedu Dalit movement in erstwhile Andhra Pradesh, the Dandora or MRPS Movement emerged for the equitable distribution of SC reservation to all Scheduled Castes. The Dandora movement is a result of the failure of Dalit movement's leadership in addressing internal contradictions like socioeconomic inequalities among Dalits. The Dandora movement questioned the hegemonic attitude of Malas over the Dalit movement and disproportionate representation in employment and education. The Dandora movement as a 'New Dalit Movement argued that deepening of anti caste spirit lies in the very recognition of the lowest of the low and their just demands. The sooner the Dalit movement resolves these internal problems, the better will be the future of Dalit movement and politics.

Notes

1. Muthaiah, P. (2000). *Dandora: the Madiga Movement for Equal Identity and Social Justice in A.P.* Working paper, submitted to Anveshi, Hyderabad, p. 2.
2. See Shekar K and V.Sremanarayana Murthy. (2012). *The 'Drum Beat' heralds Schism in Dalit Movement.* In Brij Raj Chauhan and A.Satyanarayana. (Ed), (2012). *Changing Village India*. Rawat Publications, New Delhi.

3. See Muthaiah, P. (2004). Dandora: The Madiga Movement for Equal Identity and Social Justice in AP. *Social Action*, Vo-54, and April-June.pp.184-209. And See Balagopal, K. (2000). A Tangled Web; Subdivision of SC Reservations in Andhra Pradesh. *EPW,* Vo-XXXV, No-13, March 25.
4. See Gopal Guru. (2010). *Social Justice*. In Niraja Gopal Jayal and Pratap Bhanu Mehta. (2010). *The Oxford Companion to Politics in India*. Oxford University Press, New Delhi. And see Gopal Guru. (2010). *Struggle for the Margin or from the Margin*. In Gurpreet Mahajan and Surinder S. Jodhka, (Ed.), (2010), *Religion, Community and Development*. New Delhi, Routledge Publications.
5. See Yaganti, Chinna Rao. (Ed.), (2009). *Dividing Dalits*. New Delhi, Rawat Publications
6. See Gundimeda, Sambaiah. (2000). *The Emergence of Sub-Caste Identity and Consciousness among the Dalits in Andhra Pradesh; A case study of the Madigas*. Unpublished M.Phil Dissertation, Department of Political Science, University of Hyderabad.
7. Jangam Chinnaiah. (2009). *Sub-Caste Consciousness; Challenges before Dalit Intellectuals*. pp.100-105, in Yaganti China Rao. (Ed.), (2009). Dividing Dalits, New Delhi, Rawat Publication.
8. Illaiah,Kancha. (2009). *Post-Hindu India: a discourse on Dalit Bahujan, socio-spiritual and scientific revolution*. Sage publications, New Delhi and Darla Venkateswara Rao. (2008). *Dalitha Sahityam: Madiga Drukpadtham* (Essays on literary criticism). Society & Education Trust, Hyderabad, India.
9. Guru, Gopal. (Ed.), (2005). *Atrophy in Dalit Politics,* Mumbai, Vikas Adhyayan Kendra, Mumbai, p. 66.
10. See Williams, Sir Monier, (1964). *Oxford Sanskrit English Dictionary,* UK, Oxford. pp. 471.
11. Zelliot, Eleanor. (2005). *From Untouchable to Dalit*. New Delhi, Manohar Publishers, p. 267.
12. Louis, Prakash. (2003). *Political Sociology of Dalit Assertion*. New Delhi, Gyan Publishing House, p. 145.
13. *Ibid,* p. 135.
14. *Ibid,* p. 140.
15. John C.B. Webster. (2007). *Who is a Dalit.* In S.M. Michal (Ed.), (2007), *Dalits in Modern India*, New Delhi, Sage Publication, p. 76.
16. Guru, Gopal. (1998). The Politics of Naming, *Seminar* - 471, November, p. 16.
17. Generally if Dalits convert into Christianity they are legally considered into OBC (C) category in Telugu region. This means that to claim the status of Scheduled Caste (SC) they are forced to remain entangled as Hindus. So, this legal category culturally bound the Dalits into Hindu fold.
18. Illaiah. Kancha. (1995). *Caste or Class or Caste -Class: A Study in Dalit Bahujan Consciousness and Struggles in Andhra Pradesh in 1980s*. working paper Paper Submitted to the Centre for Contemporary Studies. Nehru Memorial Museum Library, Teen Murti House, New Delhi.And also see Rao, Anupama. (2010). *The Caste Question*. Permanent Black, New Delhi. pp. 39-80.
19. Omvedt, Gail. (2008). *Dalit Visions.* New Delhi, Orient Longman, p. 72.

20. Sambashiva Rao, U. (Complied, 2005). *Dalita Rnanninadam,* Idireeta Publications, Hyderabad, p. 11.
21. *Ibid,* p. 15.
22. Guru, Gopal. (Ed.), (2005). *Atrophy in Dalit Politics.* Mumbai, Vikas Adhyayan Kendra, pp. 69-71.
23. *Ibid,* pp. 72.
24. See Illaiah, Kancha. (2007). *Why I am not a Hindu*. Samya Publication, Kolkatha pp. vii-ix.
25. See Kunnath, George. (2013). Compliance or Defiance? The case of Dalits and Mahadalits. *Journal of the Anthropological Society of Oxford* 5(1): pp. 36-59.
26. See Narayan, Badri. (2015). Democracy and Identity Politics in India: Is it a Snake or a Rope. *EPW*, Vol: L, No:16, April 18. pp. 61-65.
27. See Ratnam, K.Y. (2008). *The Dalit Movement and Democratisation in Andhra Pradesh,* working paper No. 13, published by East-West Center Washington. Washington D.C.
28. Savarnas are broadly defined as other than outcaste or untouchables. Sudra castes are also included in this group who live in mainstream village along with upper caste Hindus.
29. Opt, cit, Muthaiah, P. (2000). pp. 5-6.
30. TDP newly emerged under the leadership of N.T Rama Rao thought that Malas were with the Congress, in order to attract Madigas into TDP, he focused the ABCD issue, people also say that Sada Laxmi also had more influential on the issue.
31. Manda Krishna Madiga interview open heart with R.K in ABN news channel, *https://www.youtube.com/watch?v=IZp09seXnBs*
32. Opt, cit, Muthaiah, P. (2000). p. 4.
33. Balagopal, K. (2010). *Reservations: A Socio-Legal Perspective*. New Delhi, Critical Quest, p. 36.
34. *Ibid.*
35. Daily English new paper 'The Hindu' on May 7, 1997.
36. Akhileshwari, Sunday Spotlight, Deccan Herald, on 8-6-1997.
37. Opt, cit, Balagopal, K. (2010). p. 41.
38. Muthaiah, P. (2006). "*Sub Caste Conflict and Dalit Movement in Andhra Pradesh"*. Working Paper, submitted to Anveshi, Hyderabad, p. 4.
39. Muthaiah, P. (2004), *"Dandora: The Madiga Movement for Equal Identity and Social Justice in AP",* Social Action, Vol. 54, April-June, pp. 197-199.
40. Manda Krishna Madiga interview 25th February, 2015, Hyderabad.
41. The Supreme Court judgment on 5th November 2004, Bench comprised of: N. Santosh Hegde, S.N Variava, B.P Singh, H.R Sema, and S.B Sinha.
42. Manda Krishna Madiga interview in 2014 general election, when Manda Krishna Madiga contested in Wardhanapeta for MLA constituency, he got merely 20,000 votes out of more than 2 lakhs votes. In the campaign, he focused on the issues related to differently able, the aged and widows' issues. Before election, he started MSP (Mahajana Socialist Party) on Louie Braille's birthday anniversary in the Differently-Able People State Level Convention at Hyderabad.

Chapter - 10

Secularism in India and Dalits

— *Dr. B. Balaswamy & Dr. K. Rajesh*

Abstract

The Preamble of Indian constitution describes India as a secular state. Right to religious freedom is a fundamental right under article 25 of the Indian constitution. This is available to all sections of Indian society except to Dalits as they have to profess only Hinduism to be considered as Scheduled Castes under Presidential Order 1950. Dalits are one of the most backward sections in the society. They belong to different faiths and practices including Christianity and Atheism. This chapter analyses the nature of secularism in India and the position of Dalits.

Key words: *Secularism, Dalits, Right to Religion and Discrimination*

Introduction

The Mandal and Masjid issues in the beginning of 1990s gave rise to two prominent slogans-secularism and social justice, which are playing an important role in Indian polity and with which Dalits are inseparably connected. While the priority of latter has slowly subsided, the former continuous to be a deciding factor for power capturing in Indian politics. In the name of secularism the parties are fighting for the power, the alliances are made; the governments are formed and governments are toppled. The United Progressive Alliance government with different parties having contradicting interests and ideologies could come into power with one single common super ideology-secularism. In this context, it is pertinent to examine the meaning of secularism, the prevailing nature of secularism in India, achievements and setbacks in providing the fruits of this great institution to the weakest among the weak and still voiceless sections, like Dalits who were denied for century's together entry into Hindu temples and have been subjected to religious discrimination.

The Preamble of India describes India as a sovereign, socialist, secular, democratic republic. Besides, it also says that securing liberty of thought, expression, belief and faith as one of the objectives of the constitution. While some of our neighboring countries are theocratic states, India opted to be a secular state. In the preamble of our constitution, it is expressed explicitly. Articles 25-28 of our constitution reflect the secular character of India. A country like India having different faiths doesn't have any other option, but the secularism is the best solution. Though majority of the people are Hindus in India, they are not majority in all the states. While Muslims constitute majority in Kashmir, Sikhs are majority in Punjab .In northeastern states-Nagaland, Meghalaya, Mizoram Christians occupy the majority position.

Concept of Secularism

Secularism champions universal human rights above religious demands. The separation of religion and state is the foundation of secularism. It ensures religious groups don't interfere in affairs of state, and the state doesn't interfere in religious affairs. In a secular democracy all citizens are equal before the law and parliament. No religious or political affiliation gives advantages or disadvantages and religious believers are citizens with the same rights and obligations as anyone else. It upholds equality laws that protect women, LGBT people and minorities from religious discrimination. These equality laws ensure that non-believers have the same rights as those who identify with a religious or philosophical belief (secularism.org.uk). Secularism seeks to defend the absolute freedom of religious and other belief, and protect the right to manifest religious belief insofar as it does not impinge on the rights and freedoms of others. Secularism ensures that the right of individuals to freedom of religion is always balanced by the right to be free from religion.

The unity and fraternity of the people of India, professing numerous faiths, has been sought to be achieved by enshrining the idea of a 'secular State', which means that the State protects all religions equally and does not itself uphold any religion as the She question of Secularism is not one of sentiments, but one of law. The secular objective of the state has been specifically expressed by inserting the word 'secular' in the Preamble by the Constitution(42nd Amendment) Act,1976. The orginal framers of the constitution adopted articles 25,26 and 27 so as to further secularism. It was verymuch embedded in their constitutional philosophy. The forty second constitutional amendment made it only 'explicit', which was already 'implicit'.The Secularism is a part of the basic structure of the constitution (Basu, 2015)

K.N. Panikkar argues that there are three characteristics of the kind of secular state that India claims to be: Firstly, the secular state postulates that political institutions must be based on the economic and social interests of the entire community, without reference to religion, race or seat; that all must enjoy equal rights and no privileges, prescriptive rights or special claims should be allowed for any group on the basis of religion. Secondly, it eliminates from the body politic ideas of division between individuals and groups on the basis of their faith and racial origin. In the third place, It is obvious that a composite secular state must accept as the basis of its policy what Aristotle termed as 'distributive justice', the idea that all communities must have power, as they must share the duties and responsibilities of being citizens(Fatima, 2017).

Dalits

Dalits constitute about 16.2 per cent of Indian population. Their population is more than the total population of some developed countries like England, Canada and Australia. Historically they were discriminated and occupied a low position in Hindu social structure. The word "Dalit" may be derived from Sanskrit, and means "ground", "suppressed", "crushed", or "broken to pieces". It was perhaps first used by Jyotirao Phule in the nineteenth century, in the context of the oppression faced by the erstwhile "untouchable" castes of the twice-born Hindus. (Mendelsohn, Oliver; Vicziany, Marika, 1998). According to Victor Premasagar, the term expresses the Dalits' "weakness, poverty and humiliation at the hands of the upper castes in the Indian society."Although many use the term in lieu of more derogatory terms, including "Untouchable", the term *Dalit* has become a political identity, similar to the way African Americans in the United States moved away from the use of the term "Negro", to the use of "Black" or "African-American." Dalits today use the term "Dalit" as they believe the term is more than being broken and is in fact an identity born of struggle and assertion.

Dalits are the poor and the downtrodden. Generally, Dalit includes those termed in administrative parlance scheduled castes (SCs), scheduled tribes (STs) and other backward classes (OBCs). However, in day-to-day usage in political discourse, the term is so for mainly confined to SCs. They are the castes identified by the President of India under Article 341 and put under Schedule. The term 'SC' was first used by the British in the

Government of India Act, 1935. Prior to this, some of these castes were included among the depressed classes- a category used for the first time at the beginning of twentieth century. Traditionally, in the Hindu Social order they are placed at the bottom of the hierarchy, considered Athi-Sudhras or Avarna, and are treated as untouchables. However, all ex-untouchables do not find a place in this Schedule, and all castes under the Schedule did not experience untouchability to an equal degree in the recent or distant past(GanshyamShah,2001). In the Hindu caste system, Dalit status is associated with occupations regarded as ritually impure, such as leatherwork, butchering or removal of rubbish, animal carcasses and human waste. Dalits work as manual labourers cleaning streets, latrines and sewers. These activities were considered to be polluting to the individual and this pollution was considered contagious(Singh,2015). Dalits were commonly banned from full participation in Indian social life. They were physically segregated from the surrounding community. For example, they could not enter a temple or a school and were required to stay outside villages. Other castes took elaborate precautions to prevent incidental contact with Dalits.

Though Dalits make up **16.2% of the total Indian population,** their control over resources of the country is marginal—less than 5%. Close to half of the Dalit population lives under the Poverty Line, and even more (62%) are illiterate. Among the Dalits, most of those engaged in agricultural work are landless or nearly landless agricultural laborers. The average household income for Dalits was of Rs. 17,465 in 1998, just 68% of the national average. Less than 10% of Dalit households can afford safe drinking water, electricity and toilets, which is indicative of their deplorable social condition. Moreover, Dalits are daily victims of the worst crimes and atrocities, far outnumbering other sections of society in that respect as well(navsarjantrust.org). The vast majority of these crimes remain unreported due to omnipresent fear, and those that are reported are often ignored by police or end up languishing in the backlogged court system. Between 1992 and 2000, a total of 334,459 cases were registered nationwide with the police as cognisable crimes against SCs(Saikia,2014).Traditionally, Scheduled Castes have been denied property rights. The caste hierarchy, as a system of occupational and social assignment, has relegated SCs to the periphery of the occupational realm and, therefore, economic mobility(Thorat,2009).

Religious position of Dalits

The present Dalits were treated as untouchables for long time. Dr.B.R.Ambedkar noted that Under the rule of the Peshwas in the Maratha country, the untouchable was not allowed to use the public streets if a Hindu was coming along, lest he should pollute the Hindu by his shadow. The untouchable was required to have a black thread either on his wrist or around his neck, as a sign or a mark to prevent the Hindus from getting themselves polluted by his touch by mistake. In Poona, the capital of the Peshwa, the untouchable was required to carry, strung from his waist, a broom to sweep away from behind himself the dust he trod on, lest a Hindu walking on the same dust should be polluted. In Poona, the untouchable was required to carry an earthen pot hung around his neck wherever he went—for holding his spit, lest his spit falling on the earth should pollute a Hindu who might unknowingly happen to tread on it(Ambedkar, B.R, 2018). The Telugu poet Gurram Jashua's book, "Gabbilam (Bat)' reflects how Dalits were not allowed to see and pray the Gods in temples. In spite of the denial of entry into temples, Dalits followed Hinduism in their own style. Daliths follow all major faiths-Budhism Sikhism, Christianity and Islam. There are also Daliths who are atheists.

Denial of a fundamental right to Dalits

Fundamental rights command heavy weight in the constitution. According to Article 13 of the constitution, (1) All laws in force in the territory of India immediately before the commencement of this Constitution, in so far as they are inconsistent with the provisions of this Part, shall, to the extent of such inconsistency, be void. (2) The State shall not make any law which takes away or abridges the rights conferred by this Part and any law made in contravention of this clause shall, to the extent of the contravention, be void .But,while article 25 of the constitution is guaranteeing all citizens of India, the freedom of conscience and the right freely to profess, practice and propagate any religion, in case of Dalits, such right is denied by introducing a Scheduled Caste Order 1950 appended to Article 341 of the Indian Constitution. The Order provides the list of Scheduled Castes (SCs) and serves as a precursor to a series of robust entitlements to India's 'untouchable castes' by guaranteeing political representation, share in public employment, access to educational institutions and assuring allocations in development schemes. The incorporation of Article 341 and constitutional support to the policy of positive discrimination was certainly a recognition of the long-drawn struggle of caste groups placed below the pollution line of the Hindu caste system(Fazal,2017). But the third paragraph of this order considers only the dalit Hindus as SC and provided them with the privileges and rights bestowed to the scheduled castes by the Constitution. Shocked by the draconian clause in the Presidential Order, innumerable demonstrations and protests were held in different parts of the country to end this discrimination, particularly for the inclusion of Scheduled Castes following Sikhism, Buddhism and Christianity. As a result, Para 3 was amended to include the Scheduled Castes following Sikhism and Buddhism in 1956 and 1990 respectively, promising inclusion of the Scheduled Castes following the Christian Faith as soon as possible. But still it remained to be a distant dream.

Caste is a reality in Indian society

One dogmatic argument that is brought forth about considering even those Dalits who follow Christian faith, as scheduled caste is that there is no caste system among Christians. This argument does not reflect the reality. Either those who are ignorant of social reality or having vested interest of denying what is due to Dalits brings this argument forward. The stark reality is caste is existing in Indian society among Christians, in the same manner as it is existing among Hindus. There are Christian Malas, Christian Madigas, Christian Reddies, Christian Kammas,etc. In fact, the domination of upper caste people continues even among Christians. Historical data abound with caste segregation and discrimination within the church right from its inception. The cathedral at Tiruchirappalli, built between 1839 and 1841 was provided with the customary caste bar. In some places, the dalits had their own churches, in other places they attended the services standing outside the church. In common churches they were seated in the side or at the back and could take communion only after the caste Christians (Louis, 2007). This is the reason why some influential and popular preachers could not show any concern for the fundamental right of these people though they have access to all prominent political leaders including the Prime Ministers and Chief Ministers. According to an estimation most of the crowds who attend gospel or healing meetings are Dalits only who have faith in Christ, but cannot claim them selves as Christians as they will forfeit their scheduled caste status. Thus one can see caste factor influencing various dynamics in religion. In reality Dalits don't have freedom to have a name of their choice. Many people do have two names-one for family and church and another for school. If Dalits go to revenue department for caste certificate, it is not issued so easily. The concerned officer asks the names of all family members including grand parents. The applicant should satisfy that none in their family have any Christian or western names. Interestingly, many Dalit families do have both Hindu and Christian names and they follow both the traditions. They celebrate both Hindu fesivals and Chrian festivals. There are number of instances where wife and husband belong to same dalit caste like *Mala* or *Madiga*, and they experience the same social status, including the descrimination, but while one is having SC status another one gets BC status just based on the difference in their faith. In their socio-economic status or treatment there is no difference at all in the society. Both are equally looked down upon by the upper caste people. Indeed Christian Dalits, whether they are officially Christians or unofficially Christians, face more discrimination in the society as their names themselves are likely to give an impression that they belong to lower castes.

The people belonging to Dalit communities raise several questions, such as, why right to religious freedom of Dalits should be restricted to Hinduism only, when even their great leader Dr. Ambedkar did not like to be in its fold because of its discriminatory nature? Why should Dalits be theists at all having a religion? There are so many people who do not believe in God. Many Dalits who follow leftist ideology do not follow any religion. They prefer to remain as atheists. Yet they are identified by their caste. Like caste in Christianity, there is also caste in leftist parties of India. How can the state impose Hinduism on them for giving benefits of scheduled caste? If it does so, how can India be called as a secular state, at least as far as Dalits are concerned?

In Search of Equality

In India, people belonging to all castes have religious freedom except to Dalits. A forward caste person can take any religion-Hinduism, Christianity, Buddism or any religion. It will not make any difference in his caste status. Rather, by taking religions like Christianity he will also enjoy some benefits under the category minority. A person belonging to backward class may follow any faith including Christianity. His backward class status is not determined by his religion but only by caste. A person belonging to a Scheduled Tribe also may follow any faith including Christianity, it will not have any effect on his Scheduled Tribe Status. His Scheduled Tribe status is determined not by his connection with any religion, but only based on the tribe to which, he belongs to. There is considerable tribal population in North-east India officially following the Christianity. But in case of Dalits, their caste status is determined not only based on their caste, but by linking it to their religion. This is where the religious freedom of Dalits is curtailed. According to the initial position of the presidential order 1950, only Dalits who claim to profess Hinduism were given Scheduled Caste. Dr. Baba Saheb Ambedkar, whom Dalits consider as a redeemer and who deeply analyzed the injustice and discrimination that was perpetuated by Hinduism on Dalits, publicly proclaimed In 1935, "I was born a Hindu because I had no control over this but I shall not die a Hindu." (Imam, 2017) He kept his word and shortly before his death in 1956, he embraced Buddhism along with thousands of his followers in Nagpur. His followers, who embraced Buddhism also suffered till 1990. It implies that Presidential order is not only contrary to the fundamental right thr right to religious freedom, even to the philosophy of Dr. B.R. Ambedkar.

Whether faith can be substitute to development

An argument that is put forward sometimes is Dalits who follow Christianity are more developed and they receive aid from the foreign countries. If one observes the ground reality, in dwellings of Dalits in coastal areas of Andhra Pradesh, they live in utter poor conditions. They face double discrimination being the Dalits and being the Christians. The victims of atrocities in Karamchedu and Tsunduru are the examples of this deplorable condition. It misleading to speculate about the development of people based on faith. If the faith can be seen as the development or substitute to development, the Governments need not to spend billions of rupees for development, the spreading of the Christian faith itself would have been a miraculous solution. A reality that should be recognized is that faith cannot be equated as development or status. It is arbitrary and deliberate attempt to keep Dalits only within the fold of a religious practice.

Religion as a criterion for reservations

During British Government reservation was provided to different religious groups like Muslims and Indian Christians. In independent India reservation is provided largely based on the caste. Some sections of people argue that reservations should not be provided based on the religion. Going by the same logic religion also should not be a criterion for denial of reservation to the deserving people. As religion is linked to determine the caste, Dalits are not in a position to freely exercise their right to freedom. One can change the religion easily as it is the matter of faith and practice. But one's caste does not change. Indeed some people practice multiple religions. Some people also do not follow any religion and they incline to be non-religious or atheists.

Conclusion

As Vijay Nambiar(1964) observed, Indian secularism has a peculiar quality: it is and yet is not. Though right to religious freedom is fundamental right, it is still not enjoyed fully by some sections of the people belonging to the Scheduled Castes .The Universal Declaration of Human Rights 1948 and its two International Covenants of 1966 declare that "all human beings are equal in dignity and rights" and prohibit all kinds of discrimination – racial, religious etc. The UN Declaration against all Forms of Religious Discrimination and Intolerance 1981 outlaws all kinds of religion-based discrimination. Caste system is an all-pervading social phenomenon of India shared by almost all Indian communities irrespective of religious persuasions. As recommended by National Commission for Religious and Linguistic Minorities(2007) the Para 3 of the Constitution (Scheduled Castes) Order 1950 – which originally restricted the Scheduled Caste net to the Hindus and later opened it to Sikhs and Buddhists, thus still excluding from its purview the Muslims, Christians, Jains and Parsis, etc. – should be wholly deleted by appropriate action so as to completely de-link the Scheduled Caste status from religion and make the Scheduled Castes net fully religion-neutral like that of the Scheduled Tribes. Justice delayed is considered as the justice denied. Providing complete religious freedom to Dalits does not involve any expenditure. It requires only political will and commitment. Just the caste and religion canbe seen separately and provision can be made to issue the Scheduled Caste certificates only based on caste and not by religion. This will solve the problem and creates some meaning of secularism to Dalits.

References

Ambedkar, B.R (2018), *Annihilation of Caste*, New Delhi, Rupa, pp. 27-28.

Basu, Durga Das (2015), *Introduction to the Constitution of India*, Gurgaon, Lexis Nexis, p. 28.

Fatima Sumbul (2017), Secularism in India: A Myth or Reality? *IOSR Journal Of Humanities and Social Science (IOSR-JHSS)* Volume 22, Issue 7, Ver. 11 (July. 2017) pp. 49-53.

Fazal Tanweer (2017) Scheduled Castes, reservations and religion: Revisiting a juridical debate, *Contributions to Indian Sociology* 51, 1.

Ganshyamshah (2001) Dalit identity and politics in Ghanshyam shah *(Ed)*), *Introduction: Dalit politics,* Vol. 2, New Delhi, Sage Publications. p. 19.

Imam Mujahid (2017), In 1935, he publicly proclaimed, "I was born a Hindu because I had no control over this but I shall not die a Hindu." Retrieved on 25.12.2019 from https://thecompanion.in/born-hindu-shall-not-die-hindu-struggle-equality-dr-b-r-ambedkar/

Louis Prakash (2007) Dalit Christians: Betrayed by State and Church*, Economic and Political Weekly,* April21, p. 1405.

Mendelsohn, Oliver; Vicziany, Marika, (1998), *The Untouchables: Subordination, Poverty and the State in Modern India*. Cambridge University Press. p. 4. https://navsarjantrust.org/who-are-dalits/

Report of the National Commission for Religious and Linguistic Minorities (2007) published by the Ministry of Minority Affairs, New Delhi. p. 154.

Saikia Sailajananda (2014) Discrimination of Fundamental Rights: A Critical Review on the Present Caste Based Status of Dalit's in India, *Journal of Social Welfare and Human Rights* March, Vol. 2, No. 1, pp. 41-52.

https://www.secularism.org.uk/what-is-secularism.html

Singh Lajwant (2015), Movement for the Changing Social Status of Untouchables in India: A Sociological Study, *International Journal of Humanities Social Sciences and Education* (IJHSSE) Volume 2, Issue 1, January, pp. 138-143, .arcjournals.org

Thorat Sukadeo (2009), *Dalits in India: Search for a Common Destiny*, New Delhi, Sage, p. 46.

Vijay Nambiar, (1964) India: How Secular? Book Review (India as a Secular State by D E Smith), *Economic and Political Weekly*, p. 947.

Chapter - 11

Nomadic, Semi-Nomadic and Denotified Tribe Reservations in Telangana State: Prospects and Possibilities

— Dr. Bheenaveni Ram Shepherd

Abstract

All societies face serious challenges on the account of birth-based-discrimination and inequality, whether those are Afro-Americans or aboriginal Americans in United States, on-Han minority in China or aborigines in Australia. But, nowhere in the world the inequality and discrimination is as so deep-rooted in string of all shades of a society as in the case of India. The orthodoxical varna *system is profound in Indian society from ancient time to till date. The ascribed status of an individual narrow-downs opportunities and widens the nexus between caste and poverty. This kind of trend is more prevalent in rural areas. To offer an immediate solution for birth-based-discrimination, certain special rights and privileges have been given for the suppressed communities on the lines of affirmative action is popularly known as 'Reservations' according to Indian Constitution.*

Reservation is not as simple and straightforward as people think of it as it is very complicated and cumbersome process. It has been one of the most controversial topics of all times in the social and political spheres of our country. It continues to be a hot potato among various sections of our society with no clear-cut answer. Also post-Mandal era, things have never been the same with continuous riots, protests, demonstrations against this system over the last 30 years. Thus, one cannot really think about it in the binary terms and should look the picture as a whole. At present there are lots of new reservation agitations and movements have come into limelight namely Patidar (Patel), Jat, Kapu, Gujjar at pan-India level and Mudiraj, Vaddera, Rajaka, Gollakuruma, Boya are visible in newly formed Telangana state. These movements are specific in nature but the discourse or its genesis is rooted in nomadic, semi-nomadic and denotified tribe reservations which were in force at one point of time. Keeping this is in view and the enforcement of newly up-came 'Economically Weaker Section (EWS)' reservation, the prospects and possibilities of nomadic, semi-nomadic and denotified tribe reservations have been thoroughly discussed in this paper.

Keywords: *Nomadic Tribe Reservation, Caste Reservation, Denotified Tribe Reservation*

Introduction Historical Account of Reservations

In fact, we have a misconception on reservation as most of us felt the reservation system has been introduced aftermath of enforcement of Indian Constitution that is 26th January, 1950. But we hardly knew that the quota system was introduced and implemented before independence. When British were ruling India, they used to bring all the administrators who are vital in implementing the policies and those have been chosen through The Indian Civil Service (ICS) examination, it was, for part of the 19th century, officially known as the Imperial Civil Service. However, it was the elite higher civil service of the British Empire in British India during British rule in the period between 1858 and 1947. All the Indian Civil Servants (Civilians) were appointed under Section XXXII (32) of the Government of India Act-1858 enacted by the Parliament of the United Kingdom[1]. The ICS was headed by the Secretary of State for India, a member of the British cabinet. They were ultimately responsible for overseeing all government activity in the 250 districts that comprised British India. At first almost all the top thousand members of the ICS, known as 'Civilians', were British, and had been from well-known British schools. There was no place for the Indians either to appear the Indian Civil Service (ICS) examination for direct appointment as a office or no promotion was sought for the lower grade office staff having Indian origin. As the position is highly reputed and having most influence over the bureaucracy, many Indians were willing to join in this service but the legal technicality was not permitted Indian to be in the part of ICS, thereby, this discrimination was articulated in different platforms. Eventually, British Indian Government had reserved several vacancies for Indian citizens and 14 had been selected as ICS administrators. Out of which, 13 were Brahmins and one was from Kshatriya background[2]. This was the first incident where the administrators had been selected under quota system. This was merely nominating system as the nomination system was prevailed upto 1853. In 1861, the nomination system was abolished by the Parliament in England and it was decided that the induction would be through competitive examinations of all British subjects, without distinction of race.

In 1882, the Hunter Commission was set-up, Jyotirao Phule, a social reformer from the lower caste made a demand for free and compulsory education as well as a proportionate representation in all government jobs. This was first demand of reservation came from backward sudra and athisudra communities. This argument was upheld by Shahu Maharaj, Kind of the Princely State of Kolhapur located in present Maharashtra in the year of 1901. The main intention to introduce this reservation provision was merely to favour the *sudra* and *atisudra* communities. Finally, in the year of 1902, Shahu Maharaj in the capacity of king gave a notification comprising 50% of reservations for backward classes/communities in all services of the State of Kolhapur. In 1908 reservations were introduced by the British Movement in the name of **Indian Councils Act 1909**, it was also known as **Morley-Minto Reforms wherein religion affiliation was critical to offer reservation. This is why, it had received lot of criticism that these reservations** aimed to divide the Indian society on the religious lines rather than offering real upliftment to the marginalized sections.

The Communal Award was introduced in 1933 on the basis of separate representations submitted by the Muslims, Sikhs, Christians, Anglo-Indians, Europeans, and *Dalit* for reservations. The most surpassing fact here to be noted that in case a seat was reserved for a community, the members belonging to that community only were entitled to vote. This was the reason why, the Communal Award was out-rightly opposed by prominent leaders of India but it had received strong support from the leaders belonging to minority community. Later, the Government of India Act of 1935 came into force and the term 'Scheduled Caste' was used for the first time to secure the reservations for communities mentioned in the schedule. However, this Act facilitated a constant way for the sustenance of reservations upto Indian independence.

After Independence, several provisions were given in the Indian Constitution to cherish certain privileges to offer social development on the lines of social equality, liberty, fraternity employment and so forth. The Articles 14, 15(1), 16(1), 16(2) and 16(4) vouch for this affirmative action. The system of reservation in India consists of a series of measures, such as reserving access to seats in the various legislatures, to government jobs, and to enrollment in higher educational institutions. The reservation is undertaken to address the historic oppression, inequality, and discrimination faced by those communities and to give these communities a place. It is intended to realize the promise of equality enshrined in the Constitution.

The Constitution laid down 15% and 7.5% of vacancies to government aided educational institutes and for jobs in the government/public sector, as reserved quota for the SC and ST candidates. That means only the communities included to the list of Scheduled Castes (SC) and Scheduled Tribes (ST) have secured the entitlements of affirmative action but the major chunk of sudra backward communities were not given any provision of reservation in the Indian Constitution due to various reasons. As a result, an agitation took place in the state of Kerala in 1951 and in order to resolve the issue, EMS Namboothiripad, the first CM of Kerala, who introduced the very idea of economic criteria for reservation in the capacity of the Head of Administrative Reforms Committee. Ramachandran Pillai, a Politburo member of CPIM, affirms that "*It was the Administrative Reforms Committee headed by EMS Namboodiripad which proposed for the first time in India, the exclusion of a well-to-do section from the backward communities from enjoying the benefits of reservation. The present practice of exclusion of "creamy layer" actually originated from this recommendation. Both the "forward" and the "backward" communities came against the recommendations of the committee and particularly against EMS Namboodiripad. The "forward" communities attacked the report as it recommended the continuation of the reservation system. The "backward" communities attacked the report for introducing economic criteria for exclusion*"[3].

Keeping the EMS Namboodiripad's idea of recommendation in view, Jawaharlal Nehru constituted the First Backward Classes Commission on 29th January, 1953 by adhering to Article 340 of the Constitution of India and it was set-up by a presidential order under the chairmanship of Kaka Kalelkar. He submitted report in two volumes with so many suggestions. Eventually, the Central Government took a decision that no all India lists of Backward Classes should be drawn up, nor any reservation made in the Central Government service for any group of Backward Classes other than the Scheduled Castes and Scheduled Tribes. Consequently, on August 14th, 1961, the Ministry of Home Affairs addressed all the State Governments stating, "while the State Governments have the discretion to choose their own criteria for defining backwardness, in the view of the Government of India it would be better to apply economic tests than to go by caste"[4].

In fact, the Union Government strategically used a trick to surpass the mess and burden contained over the issues of reservations (expect Scheduled Castes and Scheduled Tribes) and handing the reservations expect SCs and STs to the State Government created a confusion among the masses in understanding the core idea of reservation as an affirmative action. Now and then onwards, the State Governments had set-up different commission to look into the issue of reservation within their own contextual framework and have come-up with their own reservation policies which are vary one state to another. However, the state commissions meant for Backward, Nomadic, Semi-nomadic and Denotified communities did not inculcated the pan-Indian framework of understanding in terms of reservations like SCs and STs. Consequently, those backward communities, particularly, Nomadic, Semi-nomadic and Denotified were alienated and parochialized in terms of identity, inclusion and development. In certain states, these Nomadic, Semi-nomadic and Denotified communities were deliberately included either to the Backward Classes List or Most Backward Classes List due to lack of scientific and methodological understanding of nature various communities. For instance, in erstwhile Andhra Pradesh state, Anantharaman Commission (1965) has classified Vaddera/Odde and Boya communities (who were earlier listed in Criminal Tribe Acts) under BC-A category which also includes many other castes and the history of discrimination and deprivation of which is entirely different from denotified tribes (DNTs). It is strange to believe that this kind of reservation is still in enforcement in the States Talangana and Andhra Pradesh.

Nomadic, Semi-nomadic and Denotified Tribes: A Retrospective

The Criminal Tribes Act was firstly enacted by British Government in 1871 as the Criminal Tribes Act (CTA) and enforced mostly in North India. Later, the Act was extended to Bengal Presidency and Madras Presidency in 1876 and 1911 respectively. Under the act, several Indian ethnic groups were defined as "addicted to the systematic commission of non-bailable offences"[5] such as thefts, were systematically registered by the government. Since they were described as 'habitually criminal' who were prone to several restrictions on their movements and adult male members of these groups were invariably forced to report weekly to the respective local police station.

At the time of Indian independence in 1947, thirteen million people belonging to 127 communities were faced searching and arrest if any member of the group was found outside the prescribed area[6]. After India achieved independence in 1947, the Criminal Tribes Act, 1871 was reviewed and eventually repealed in 1952. This Act, however, was replaced by a series of Habitual Offenders Acts that asked police to investigate a "suspect's", "criminal tendencies" and whether their occupation is "conducive to settled way of life". The denotified tribes were reclassified as "habitual offenders" in 1959. As a result, all the castes and communities which were notified under the Criminal Tribes Act, 1871 were denotified.

The Committee Ananthsayanam Ayyangar Committee (1949) conducted a study across India vis-à-vis the Criminal Tribes Act and recommended for the repeal of the Act by offering suitable explanations for this. The Committee also emphasized the need for allocation of adequate funds for their welfare and rehabilitation. Aftermath, the Government of India repealed the Criminal Tribes Act with effect from 31 August 1952 by the Criminal Tribes (Repeal) Act, 1952 (Act No XXIV of 1952). But, to keep effective control over the so-called hardened criminals, Habitual Offenders Act was placed in the statute book.

Paragraph No. 48 of Kaka Kalelkar Commission Report (1955) suggested that the erstwhile 'Criminal Tribes' should not be called 'Tribes' nor should the names 'Criminal' or 'Ex-Criminal' be attached to them. They could be called 'Denotified Communities'. The Kalelkar Commission further recommended that *"these groups may be distributed in small groups in towns and villages where they would come in contact with other people, and get an opportunity for turning a new leaf. This would help in their eventual assimilation in society"*[7].

Paragraph No. 41 clears that that there were as many as 127 groups aggregating 22.68 lakhs in 1949 and 24.64 lakhs in 1951 described in official records as Ex-Criminal Tribes. These groups could be divided into two sections, i.e., (i) Nomadic; and (ii) Settled. Paragraph no. 135 states that "*there are a large number of small communities who eke out a precarious existence in the countryside. They have no fixed place of residence and they move from place to place in search of food or employment. They often rear pigs and poultry, hunt wild animals to satisfy their hunger and collect forest produce to make a living. They live in thatched sheds or gunny tents, and move in groups. They believe in witchcraft. Because of the insecurity of their life, some of these communities are given to crime. It should be the special responsibility of Government to give them a settled life*"[8].

Lokur Committee (1965) was aware of the anomalous situation of the communities being listed as SC in one State and as ST in another and states that "*this anomalous classification appears to have had its origin in the fact that members of the denotified and nomadic communities possess a complex combination of tribal characteristics, traditional untouchability, nomadic traits, and anti-social heritage*"[9]. Further, it also emphasized, in order to avail the development schemes specially designed to suit the dominant characteristics of Nomadic and Denotified tribes, that '*the present anomalous position regarding the denotified and nomadic tribes, who could more properly be identified as communities rather than tribes, should be rectified as soon as possible after a detailed investigation*'[10].

Mandal Commission (1980) expressed its concern over 'Depressed Backward Classes' whose mélange with the mainstream Indian society was either historically denied, socially prohibited and even segregated visibly on account of stigma of nomadism, resulting in their abysmally low social status. Those who are, generally, are ex-criminal tribes, nomadic and wandering tribes, earth diggers, fishermen, boatmen and palanquin bearers, salt makers, washermen, shepherds, barbers, scavengers, basket makers, furriers and tanners, landless agricultural labourers, watermen, toddy tapers, camel-herdsmen, pig-keepers, pack bullock carriers, collectors of forest produce, hunters and fowlers, corn parchers, primitive tribes (not specified as Scheduled Tribes), exterior classes (not specified as Scheduled Castes), and begging communities etc[11].

50% Cap on Reservations

In Indra Sawhney vs Union of India, 1992, the Supreme Court of India capped caste-based reservation at 50%, ruling that "no provision of reservation or preference can be so vigorously pursued as to destroy the very concept of equality", Since this Court has consistently held that the reservation under Articles 15(4) and 16(4) should not exceed 50% and the States and the Union have by and large accepted this as correct it should be held as constitutional prohibition and any reservation beyond 50% would liable to be struck down[12]. It is noteworthy to state here that the Apex Court has never explained why 50% is "reasonable". The number refers neither to a law, the Indian Constitution nor, for that matter, population of the country[13].

Even today, Tamil Nadu and Maharashtra states are giving more than 50 percent reservation. The reservation being implemented in Tamil Nadu state is up to 69 percent (SC-18%, ST-1%, BC-30%, MBC-20%), and was included in the Ninth Schedule. Laws under this schedule are beyond the purview of judicial review, even though they violate fundamental rights enshrined under Part-III of the Constitution. However, a nine-judge bench of the Supreme Court in the I.R. Coelho case (2007) upheld the authority of judiciary to review any law, including those put in the Ninth Schedule but the reservations beyond 50% have been continuing in the state of Tamil Nadu. The State Government of Maharashtra has been implementing 52% of reservations since long back. Similarly, the States of Karnataka, Haryana, Telangana, Andhra Pradesh, Gujarat and Rajasthan are continuously arguing for the removal of 50% cap in all kinds of reservations. For example: Karnataka wants to hike reservations to 70 percent, Andhra Pradesh to

55 percent and Telangana to 62 percent. And, these states have these quotas in the pipeline, waiting for nods from the Centre or the judiciary.

While introducing the bill for Economic Reservation in 2019, Arun Jaitley, in the capacity of Union Finance Minister, contended that the 50% cap on reservations imposed by the Supreme Court was only for caste-based reservations, and the Economically Weaker Section (EWS) reservation won't be impacted by it. Nevertheless, everyone has demystified about the 50% cap as it is notional and not essentially followed either by the States or by the Union.

Nomadic and Denotified Tribe Reservations: A Unique Case of Maharashtra

It is important to note that Maharashtra had broken the 50% cap of reservation long ago by bringing State Reservation Act-2001 and reserved 52% reservations in educational institutions and government jobs. The quota meant for various sections namely: SC-13%, ST-7%, OBC-19%, SBC-2%, Denotified Tribes (DNT)-3, Nomadic Tribes (NT-A, B, C)-7% and altogether it reaches 52%. This pattern of reservation system was in force from 2001 to 2018.

Table - 1: Social Category-wise Reservation in Maharashtra

Reservation Category	*Before 2018* %	*After 2018* %	*Number of Castes/ Tribes*
Scheduled Castes (SC)	13.0	13.0	59 Castes
Scheduled Tribes (ST)	07.0	07.0	47 Tribes
Other Backward Classes (OBC)	19.0	19.0	346 Castes
Special Backward Classes (SBC)	02.0	02.0	07 Castes
Denotified Tribes - A (Vimukta Jati)	03.0	03.0	14 Tribes
Nomadic Tribes - B (Banjara)	02.5	02.5	35 Tribes
Nomadic Tribes - C (Dhangar)	03.5	03.5	01 Caste
Nomadic Tribes - D (Vanjari)	02.0	02.0	01 Caste
Socially and Economically Backward Class (SEBC)	----	16.0	01 Caste
Total Percentage of Reservation	**52.0**	**68.0**	

The state of Maharashtra has evolved a unique kind of policy of reservations as Special Backward Class (SBC) category meant for extremely backward castes, Denotified Tribes (DNT) category meant for *vimukta jati* castes which are generally considered as Ex-Criminal Tribes and the Nomadic Tribes (NT) reservation category classified into 3 components namely B, C and D. Under NT-B category 35 tribes related to Banjara communities were identified. Surpassingly, under NT-C and NT-D, Dhangar and Vanjari communities were kept exclusively. However, it is strange as these categories were exclusively allocated for only one community. These are due to the Kelkar Observation Reports which convey that "......, given a list of backward classes and put a star (*) against those communities which are extremely backward and are leading a sub-human existence (e.g. The Class of Shepherd Community i.e. Dhangar/Hatkar/Hatgar/Gadri/Gadaria/Kurmar/Mirdha/Bharwad (Sr.No.27, Vol-II, p.66) (Their condition is far from satisfactory (Vol-I, pp.76-77) [(Found in Bombay, Hyderabad, Madhya Pradesh) (Now Maharashtra, Telangana, Madhya Pradesh, Gujarat)]. Those communities generally live in rural areas, and are mostly victims of the domination of the privileged and dominant communities. It should be an irony and a mockery of justice to allow such dominant communities to claim to be the natural leaders of these starred communities who are the victims of their domination.

However, no state in India has identified Denotified (DNT) and Nomadic Tribes (NT) as separate entities but Maharashtra state has identified and allocated substantial amount of reservations for the following communities/tribes under DNT and NT categories.

Denotified Tribes[14]: 1. Berad, 2. Bestar, 3. Bhatma, 4. Kaikadi, 5. Kankarbhat, 6. Katabu, 7. Lamani, 8. Phase-Pardhi, 9. Raj-Pardhi, 10. Rajput-Bhatma, 11. Ramoshi, 12. Vadar, 13. Waghari and 14. Chhapparbandh

Nomadic Tribes[15]: 1. Bawa, 2. Beldar, 3. Bharadi, 4. Bhute, 5. Chalwadi, 6. Chitrakathi, 7. Garudi, 8. Ghisadi, 9. Golla, 10. Gondhali, 11. Gopal, 12. Helwe, 13. Joshi, 14. Kasi-Kapadi, 15. Kolhati, 16. Mairal, 17. Masan-Jogi, 18. Nandi-Wale, 19. Pangul, 20. Raval, 21. Shikalgar, 22. Thakar, 23. Vaidu, 24. Vasudeo.

On 25 June 2014, the erstwhile Congress-NCP government had approved 16 percent reservation for Marathas and 5 percent for Muslims in government jobs and educational institutions. But the Bombay High Court put it on hold, saying the reservation ceiling cannot exceed 50 per cent, except in extraordinary situations and for extraordinary reasons.

The Maratha community which comprises over 30% of the Maharashtra State's population and has been consistently demanding for special reservations in government employment and education institutions for a longtime. Giving in to the demands of the Maratha protesters, the Devendra Fadnavis-led Maharashtra government has paved the way for providing quota in government jobs and educational institutions. While the proposal has been cleared by the cabinet, a legislation for the same is yet to be passed in the state assembly. In 2018, Maharashtra high court allowed 16% Maratha caste reservation in November 2018[16]. After the Union Cabinet approved the 10% reservation for the Economically Weaker Section (EWS),' the reservation has been estimated to increase upto 68% making Maharashtra the state with the highest percentage of reservation in the country.

NT/SNT/DNT Reservations in Telangana State Context and Prospects

A viable number of communities of Telangana engage begging, narration of folklore, medicinal preparation, faith healing, stone craving, animal play, cattle herding and so on entitled for Nomadic Tribe (NT), Semi-Nomadic Tribe (SNT), and Denotified Tribe (DNT) reservations in erstwhile Hyderabad State from 1955 to 1970. Later, the erstwhile Andhra Pradesh state was formed on the recommendation of first State Reorganization Commission (SRC) in 1956. In the mean time, the Kaka Kalerkar Commission (1955) had also mentioned and recommended those extremely backward nomadic and half nomadic communities in erstwhile Hyderabad, Bombay and Madhya Pradesh States. However, prior to the implementation of Anantaraman Commission Report (1970), those communities enjoyed the NT/SNT/DNT Reservations in erstwhile Andhra Pradesh State and those kinds of reservations are still in force in the state of Maharashtra.

Table – 2: Category-wise Reservations in Telangana State

Group		*No. of Castes*	*Reservation Recommended*	*Reservation in force*	*Present Demands for increase*
BC-A	Aboriginal Tribes, Vimukthi Jaties, Nomadic, Semi Nomadic etc	38	07%	07%	
BC-B	Vocational Groups	21	13%	10%	
BC-C	SCs converted into Christianity	1	01%	01%	
BC-D	Other Classes	33	09%	07%	
	Sub-Total	93	30%	25%	
BC-E	Backward Muslims	15		4%	12%
	Sub-Total				
SC	Scheduled Castes			15%	18%
ST	Scheduled Tribes			6%	10%

After enforcement of the Anantaraman Commission (after 1970 onwards), the state of erstwhile Andhra Pradesh has implemented reservation like 15% for Scheduled Castes, 6% for Scheduled Tribes, 27% for Backward Classes and the Backward Classes category was classified into A, B, C and

D. BC-A category is meant for Aboriginal, Denotified (Vimukti Jaties), Nomadic and Semi-Nomadic Communities, BC-B category is meant for vocational castes, BC-C is meant for Scheduled Castes converted into Christianity and BC-D is meant for other backward castes. Besides this, Scheduled Castes (SCs) are given 15% quota and Scheduled Tribes (STs) were given 6%.

The Congress party in its election manifesto before 2004 poll had promised 5% reservations to the Muslim community in government jobs and educational institutions. But two attempts of Y.S. Rajasekhara Reddy-led congress government in 2004 and 2005 failed as the high court and Supreme Court quashed its orders and legislation on the issue[17]. However, the Supreme Court has allowed Andhra Pradesh state government to give admission to students under BC-E category with 4% of reservation in professional colleges including medical and engineering colleges[18].

It is also pertinent to recall the promise of increase of the backward classes' reservation; NT. Rama Rao had announced increase in the reservations from 25% to 44 % in 1986. But the High Court of Andhra Pradesh rejected the Government decision. Neither the Government of Andhra Pradesh nor the Backward Classes Associations preferred an appeal the Supreme Court. Therefore the increased reservations were not implemented[19].

However, there is a relentless agitations have been taking place in terms of reservations in the states of Andhra Pradesh and Telangana for the last three decades and the demands are (1) inclusion caste in the list of scheduled castes (SCs) – this demand is very popular among Chakali/Rajaka community which traditionally engages in washing clothes and its similar caste called 'Dhobi' is listed in scheduled caste (SC) in many states of North India[20]. Vaddera community who historically stone-workers demanding for Schedule Tribe Status[21], in fact, they were earlier notified under Denotified Tribes and which present deserves for DNT status, (2) Change of category from BC-D to BC-A – the demand is so widespread among Mudiraj community. In fact, KCR led TRS government has moved the Mudiraj community from BC-D to BC-A but the High Court of the State objected the change[22]. Gollakurumas who traditionally engage in sheep rearing occupation are also demanding for Semi-Nomadic Tribe (SNT) status[23]. Gollakuruma community has enjoyed SNT status from 1955 t0 1970 and its similar community called Dhangar in Maharashtra is enjoying Nomadic Tribe reservation from 2001. Dhommara, traditional folklorist community is demanding for Nomadic Tribe (NT) reservation. Boya community has been fighting for the Scheduled Tribe (ST) status[24] and which was also listed in Denotified Tribes earlier.

It is true that Vaddera, Gollakuruma, Boya, Valmiki and many other communities had availed NT/SNT/DNT Reservations from 1955 to 1970, later it was removed for unknown reasons. In 2003, Vajpayee headed BJP Government has set-up the Balakrishna Renke Commission to identify the Nomadic Communities across India and it identified several communities as NTs/SNTs/DNTs in 2008.

In 2008, the National Commission for Denotified, Nomadic and Semi-Nomadic Tribes (NCDNSNT) of Ministry of Social Justice and Empowerment recommended equal reservations, as available to Scheduled Castes and Scheduled Tribes, for around 110 million people belonging to the denotified tribes, nomadic or semi-nomadic tribes in India. Along with the tribes designated as, "Nomadic" or "Semi-Nomadic", the denotified tribes are eligible for reservation.

Based on the Renke Commission, Bilku Ramji Idate, the present Chairman for "National Commission for De-notified, Nomadic and Semi-Nomadic Tribe" has prepared a draft list which also recommended those communities for such entitlements but those stakeholders do not any idea of what these are reservations? What kind of benefits to be avail by them? How to get them? etc..

The draft list of the National Commission for Denotified, Nomadic and Semi-Nomadic Tribes (NCDNSNT) listed Denotified Tribes and Nomadic reside in erstwhile Andhra Pradesh are as follows:

Denofited Tribes: 1. Telaga Pamular 2. Dandasis 3. Kondadoras 4. Rellies 5. Paidies 6. Kintili 7. Kalinga 8. Nakkalas 9. Parili Mukkalas 10. Donga Yathas 11. Vedurupaka Malas 12. Boyas 13. Nedetti Kothalas 14. Reddikas 15. Yanadis 16. Dommaras 17. Yerukulas 18. Anipi Malas 19. Vaddi Upparas 20. Budabukkalas 21. Lambadis 22. Vaddaras 23. Komparis 24. Pamula Buda Bukkalas 25. Reddi Yanadis 26. Jarugu Malli Madigas 27. Donga Dasari 28. Bandas 29. Donga Yanadis 30. Donga Yerukulas 31. Donga Waddars 32. Donga Dommaras 33. Jogulas 34. Yoyalpad 35. Annaboina Malas 36. Mutharachas 37. Pichiguntalas 38. Sugalis 39. Korchas 40. Donga Malas 41. Amagunta Palegars 42. Paryas 43. Thota Naicks 44. Bhattu 45. Turakas 46. Pedda Boyas 47. Dobbala Korchas 48. Donga Korchas 49. Dasari 50. Sakalas 51. Peddigollas 52. Mondi Vagulas 53. Nir Shikaris 54. Donga Ura Korchas 55. Iranis 56. Kayyar Bhatta 57. Jatur Mixed Gang 58. Todnapur Maharatras 59. Donga

Boyas Source: *Renke commission -2008 60. Lodha/ Lodhi 61. Copakapu 62. Oddar 63. Kaikadi 64. Charuka

Nomadic Tribes: 1. Are Bondhili 2. Balasanthu, Bahurupi 3. Banda, Mondivaru, Mondibanda 4. Bavuri 5. Budga Jangam 6. Borewale (Muslims) 7. Budabukkala 8. Chenchu 9. Dakkal 10. Dasari, Donga Dasari 11. Devara 12. Dom, Dombara, Pano 13. Dommara 14. Gandla 15. Gangiredlavaru 16. Ganta Sayebulu 17. Ghasi, Haddi, Relli Chachandi 18. Godagali 19. Golla, Pedditi 20. Golla, Yerra 21. Goudu 22. Guddi Eluguvallu 23. Hatkar 24. Holeya Dasari 25. Irani 26. Irla 27. Jalakaduguvallu 28. Jalari 29. Jogi 30. Kachi 31. Kaikadi 32. Kanjara-Bhat 33. Katipapala 34. Kattunayakan 35. Kepmare or Reddika 36. Kolam 37. Kommula 38. Donga Ura Korchas 39. Konarlu 40. Kuruma 41. Madaari 42. Madiga Dasu, Mashteen 43. Mala Dasari 44. Malajangam 45. Mandula 46. Mang Garodi 47. Medari or Mahendra 48. Nokkar 49. Odde 50. Pamula 51. Pardhi (Mirshikari, Nirshikari) 52. Peddammavandlu 53. Poosala 54. Rajannalu 55. Sakala Budbudike 56. Sakunapakshollu 57. Samayavallu 58. Sikligar 59. Sindhollu, Chindollu 60. Lambadis 61. Vanjara 62. Donga Yerukulas

Present Scenario of Reservation Movements in Telangana

The Telangana State Assembly passed a Bill on 16 April 2017, giving a 12% reservation quota for socially and economically backward classes among the Muslims in educational institutions and government jobs. The Bill hiked the quota for Muslims from 4% to 12%, and the Scheduled Tribes quota from 6% to 10%, thereby taking the quantum of reservations in the state to 62%[25]. Chief Minister K. Chandrasekhar Rao has emphasized in many public meetings and TV interviews that the 50% cap on reservation is merely trash and no legal or constitutional measure confine to exceed 50% reservations. Further, he also asserted that state governments have to be given utmost freedom to formulate their own legislations to implement appropriate quotas with regard to their local context[26].

So far most of the communities or community leaders do not aware of Nomadic, Semi-Nomadic and Denotifed Tribe reservations. With the spur of Economically Weaker Sections (EWS) reservation, Socially and Educational Backward Community (SEBC) reservations for Maratha community and relax over 50% cap over caste-based reservations, certain caste based organizations have started their agitation for the demand of these unknown reservations. It is so visible with Dommara, Sagara, Uppari, Gandireddula, Gollakuruma, Vaddera, Boya and so on. However, in coming future, these demands will be articulated by the political parties to create their own caste-reservation vote banks. One can assume that the EWS quota should face serious threat by these NT/SNT/DNT reservations as these were in enforcement once and many commissions have recommended them and more of, those communities are historically deprived and are in dire need of affirmative action.

References

1. Dewey, Clive, 1993. Anglo-Indian Attitudes: Mind of the Indian Civil Service. London: A&C Black.
2. A Booklet on Reservations published by Nava Telangana Publishing House, Hyderabad.
3. S. Ramachandran Pillai, EMS Namboodiripad and the Communist Government of Kerala, The Marxist XXV, 3-4 July-September 2009.
4. Omprakash Sharma (2005). Reservation Identification and Determination of Backward Classes in India, Unpublished PhD thesis, University of North Bengal, available at: http://hdl.handle.net/10603/33131.
5. Bates, Crispin (1995). Race, Caste and Tribe in Central India: the early origins of Indian anthropometry. In Robb, Peter (ed.). The Concept of Race in South Asia. Delhi: Oxford University Press. p. 227.
6. Motiraj Rathod (2000). Denotified and Nomadic Tribes in Maharashtra, available at: http://sickle.bwh.harvard.edu/india_tribes.html
7. Report of Kaka Kalelkar Commission or First Backward Classes Commission (1955)
8. *Ibid.*
9. Report of Lokur Commission.
10 *Ibid.*
11. Report of Mandal Commission or Second Backward Classes Commission (1980)
12. Shoaib Daniyal (2018). Explainer: Why is caste-based reservation in India capped at 50%?, https://scroll.in/article/890512/explainer-why-is-caste-based-reservation-in-india-capped-at-50
13. Shoaib Daniyal (2017). What justifies an arbitrary 50% cap on reservations – when upper caste numbers are much smaller?, https://scroll.in/article/856462/what-justifies-an-arbitrary-50-cap-on-reservations-when-upper-caste-numbers-are-much-smaller
14. Motiraj Rathod (2014). "Denotified and Nomadic Tribes In Maharashtra", Anarchy India, November 7, 2014.
15. *Ibid.*
16. https://bombayhighcourt.nic.in/libweb/acts/Stateact/2018acts/2018.62.pdf
17. https://economictimes.indiatimes.com/news/politics-and-nation/andhra-pradesh-high-court-rejects-centres-4-5-minority-sub-quota/articleshow/13621380.cms?from=mdr
18. P.S. Krishnan (2010). Understanding the Backward Classes of Muslim Society, Economic and Political Weekly, Vol. 45, No. 34 (August 21-27, 2010), pp. 46-56.

19. E. Venkatesu (2006). State Policies towards the Empowerment of Backward Castes in Andhra Pradesh, The Indian Journal of Political Science, Vol. 67, No. 3 (July-September, 2006), pp. 443-454.

20. http://www.uniindia.com/apcc-appeals-govt-to-accord-sc-status-to-rajaka-community/states/news/813902.html

21. https://timesofindia.indiatimes.com/city/hyderabad/st-quota-hike-may-fail-statute-test-govt-includes-new-castes-in-the-list/articleshow/58216793.cms

22. https://www.thehindu.com/news/states/Mudiraj-community-case-no-stay-atthis-stage-says-Supreme-Court/article16300557.ece

23. http://www.newindianexpress.com/states/telangana/2018/feb/07/golla-kurumas-to-exert-pressure-on-govt-to-include-them-under-semi-nomadic-tribe-1769488.html

24. https://www.thehansindia.com/posts/index/Andhra-Pradesh/2017-12-03/Centre-urged-to-include-Valmiki-Boyas-in-ST-list/342744.

25. Telengana Legislative Assembly: Telangana Backward Classes Scheduled Castes and Scheduled Tribes Act 2017, http://14.139.40.216//handle/123456789/12699.

26. https://www.indiatoday.in/india-today-conclave-south-2018/story/kcr-demands-removal-of-50-per-cent-reservation-cap-1149146-2018-01-18.

Chapter - 12

Affirmative Action: Reservations and Quotas in India: Other Backward Classes (OBCs)

— Dr. Chalamalla Venkateshwarlu

Abstract

About half the population of India belongs to the so-called socially and Educationally Backward Classes. The reason is that Socially and Educationally Backward Classes are eligible for affirmative action. The central government reserves 27 percent of all government jobs and places in institutions of higher education exclusively for the backward classes. Most states follow this policy, though some have even higher reservation percentages. Besides the backward classes' quota, there is affirmative action for other social segments as well. However, the socially and Educationally Backward Classes were never a clearly. Reservation in India is the process of facilitating the person in education, scholarship, jobs, and in promotion who have category certificates. Reservation is a form of quota-based affirmative action. Reservation is governed by constitutional laws, statutory laws, and local rules and regulations.

Reservations in favour of Backward Classes (BCs) were introduced long before independence in a large area, comprising the Presidency areas and the Princely states south of the Vindhyas. In 1882, Hunter Commission was appointed. Jyotirao Phule made a demand of free and compulsory education for marginalised sections along with proportionate representation in government jobs. In 1891, there was a demand for reservation of government jobs with an agitation (in the princely State of Travancore) against the recruitment of non-natives *into public service overlooking qualified* native *people. In 1901, reservations were introduced in Maharashtra (in the Princely State of Kolhapur) by Shahu Maharaj. Chatrapati Sahuji Maharaj, Maharaja of Kolhapur in Maharashtra introduced reservation in favour of non-Brahmin and backward classes as early as 1902. In 1908, reservations were introduced in favour of a number of castes and communities that had little share in the administration by the British. There were many other reforms in favour of and against reservations before the Indian Independence itself. Under Article 340 of the Indian Constitution, it is obligatory for the government to promote the welfare of the Other Backward Classes (OBC). The Mandal Commission which was set up for the purpose recommended 27 percent job reservations in government services for the OBCs. Presently the Reservation Quota In India Total is 50%(OBC –27.5%, SC –15%, ST 7.5%)*

Problems of this kind are manifold in the case of other backward classes, as in each state there are dominant groups, usually with economic and political clout, who reap the benefits of reservations. There are Lodhs and Koeris in Central India, Jats and Gujjars in Rajasthan, Kapus in Andhra Pradesh, Patels, Gujjars in Gujarat which, despite their dominant status, have been clubbed as backward classes eligible for benefits under reservations. For these reasons, reservation has become a contentious issue today, more so when it is applied to other backward classes.

The 93rd Constitutional Amendment (2005) *allows the government to make special provisions for "advancement of any socially and educationally backward classes of citizens", including their admission in aided or unaided private educational institutions. When the then HRD ministry introduced 27.5% reservation for OBC in centrally funded educational institutes including IIMs and IITs. Impact of reservation policy on employment and education. However, their accessible share in employment and educational institutions still falls short of the target in certain categories of jobs and higher education. However, as All India Services and central services for which employment is made through the Union Public Service Commission, representation of other backward classes is very meager to their share.*

The present paper is an attempt to Affirmative Action: Reservations and Quotas In India: Other Backward Classes (OBCs), it also understanding its emergence and growth. Explains the existing educational institutions and job reservation policies for the OBCs and Impact of reservation policy on employment and education. Besides, the Indian caste system, politics and its relation to reservation policy. It also explores the welfare policies for the OBCs in the light of Backward Classes Commissions and Mandal Commission Report have been discussed.

Key Words: *Reservation, Caste, Identities, Quotas, Affirmative Action, OBCs.*

Introduction

Reservation in India is the process of facilitating the person in education, scholarship, jobs, and in promotion who have category certificates. Reservation is a form of quota-based affirmative action. Reservation is governed by constitutional laws, statutory laws, and local rules and regulations. Scheduled Castes (SC), Scheduled Tribes (ST) and Other Backward Classes (OBC), and in some states Backward Classes among Muslims under a category called BC(M), are the primary beneficiaries of the reservation policies under the Constitution – with the object of ensuring a level playing field.

Reservations in favour of Backward Classes (BCs) were introduced long before independence in a large area, comprising the Presidency areas and the Princely states south of the Vindhyas. In 1882, Hunter Commission was appointed. Jyotirao Phule made a demand of free and compulsory education for marginalised sections along with proportionate representation in government jobs.

In 1891, there was a demand for reservation of government jobs with an agitation (in the princely State of Travancore) against the recruitment of *non-natives* into public service overlooking qualified *native* people. In 1901,reservations were introduced in Maharashtra (in the Princely State of Kolhapur) by Shahu Maharaj. Chatrapati Sahuji Maharaj, Maharaja of Kolhapur in Maharashtra introduced reservation in favour of non-Brahmin and backward classes as early as 1902.

In 1908, reservations were introduced in favour of a number of castes and communities that had little share in the administration by the British. There were many other reforms in favour of and against reservations before the Indian Independence itself.

The Rise of the Other Backward Classes (OBCs)

The rise of the Other Backward Classes (OBCs) in the political arena since the mid-1980s has been heralded as India's \silent revolution" (Jafferelot, 2003). This political ascendancy has also been viewed as representing a large enough ux in the traditional hierarchies of the caste system, such that we now have \a plethora of assertive caste identities... [that] articulate alternative hierarchies" leading to a scenario where \there is hardly any unanimity on ranking between jatis" (Gupta, 2009). Indeed, there is no doubt, especially since the 73rd and 74th constitutional amendments in the early 1990s, that the so-called lower castes have become an important force in Indian politics at all levels - local, state and national. Has this change in the political arena been accompanied by a corresponding reshuffling of the traditional economic hierarchies, such as The nature and degree of change in the economic ranking between castes, or broad caste groups, is a matter of empirical verification.

While there is a large and growing body of work documenting the changes in the standard of living indicators of the Scheduled Castes and Tribes (SCs and STs), as well as the economic discrimination faced by these groups, (see Deshpande 2011, for a review of the recent research), the discussion about the material conditions or the economic dominance of the group of castes and communities classified as the \Other Backward Classes” (OBCs) in India is prompted more by beliefs, or localized case studies, rather than by an empirical analysis of the macro evidence. Part of the reason for this lacuna is the lack of hard data: until the 2001 census, OBCs were not counted as a separate category, while affirmative action (quotas in India) was targeted towards OBCs at the national level since 1991, and at the state level since much earlier. This would be the only instance of an affirmative action program in the world, where the targeted beneficiaries are not counted as a separate category in the country's census.

Researchers have, therefore, had to rely on data from large sample surveys, such as the National Sample Survey (NSS) or the National Family and Health Survey (NFHS), in order to get estimates about the material conditions of the OBCs. The use of this data has generated research which undertakes a broader analysis of various caste groups, OBCs being one of the groups in the analysis, along with the SC- STs and \Others”, the residual group comprising the non-SC-ST-OBC population \Others” include the Hindu upper castes and could be considered a loose approximation for the latter, but data constraints do not allow us to isolate the upper castes exclusively. Existing evidence suggests that OBCs lie somewhere in between the SC-STs and the Others, but, very little is known about their relative distance from the two other categories, and second, in order to make a meaningful intervention about the possible links between their political ascendancy and their economic conditions, it is important to trace how their relative economic position has changed vis-a -vis the other two groups over time. Here again, the economic researcher is stymied by the lack of good longitudinal data.

The caste system is a system of graded inequalities, with the so-called upper castes conventionally at the top of the socio-economic hierarchy, and the ex-untouchable castes, now clubbed together in the social category of Scheduled Castes are at the bottom. This allows us to gauge the relative generational shifts between the major caste groups. Our analysis focuses particularly on the OBCs, and compares how the evolution of the different OBC cohorts (in relation to the Others) compares with the evolution of the corresponding SC-ST cohorts to the Others.

Who are the Other Backward Classes (OBCs)

Parts of British India enacted preferential policies for the \Depressed Classes”, which included communities that were classified as \backward”, as well as for the untouchables, tribals and some non-Hindu communities. Even though there were preferential policies for the \Backward Classes", their exact definition had not been clearly articulated and details of the various definitions employed during the British period are spelt out in Galanter (1984).

The constitution of independent India did not de ne Other Backward Classes (OBCs) in a specific way either. However, after the Scheduled Castes were listed as a separate category, the term Backward Classes started to be used in two senses: one, as the group of all communities that needed preferential treatment, and two, as castes low in the socio-economic hierarchy, but not as low as the untouchables. We should note that the two usages overlap considerably. However, the exact identification of groups and communities to be counted as OBCs has been fraught with a great deal of controversy. Even before the constitution of independent India came into effect in 1950, several states formed the category of OBCs for the first time (e.g. Bihar in 1947; Uttar Pradesh in 1948) and conferred benefits on them, while those states which already had benefits for the backward castes from before independence, expanded the existing range of benefits. Thus, in 1978, without any central reservations for OBCs, at least 13 states reserved seats for Backward Classes, other than SCs and STs. These reservations were found throughout southern India, in Maharashtra and Gujarat and in parts of north India, with the heaviest representation in the south (Galanter 1984, 87).

The first Backward Classes Commission (with Kaka Kalelkar as its chairman) was established in 1953, which was directed to first ascertain the criteria that should be adopted to determine whether any section of the population could be considered backward (other than the SC and ST), and then according to these criteria, prepare a list of such classes. The Commission prepared a list of 2399 groups, which were roughly 32 percent of the population. It was generally understood that the groups identified by the commission would be castes or communities. This meant that backwardness was defined or understood in terms of the \social hierarchy based on caste".

Thus, the commission listed as criteria of backwardness - trade and occupation, security of employment, educational attainment, representation in government service and position in the social hierarchy. Much like the contemporary experience, there was a rush among communities wanting to be classified as backward due to the potential bene ts that this status would confer upon them. However, in deciding on the validity of these multiple claims, the commission was stymied by the lack of data. Despite the lack of data, the commission made wide-ranging recommendations for benefits to be conferred to the backward classes, often relying on just the names of the caste to make its case. However, at the last minute, the 5 chairman repudiated the report of the commission by stating that he found the use of caste as antithetical to democracy and to the eventual creation of a casteless and classless society.

Due to several factors (the rush of communities wanting to be classified as backward, the unreliability of data, the extensive recommendations of the commission), the work of the commission was widely criticized. The basic point of contention was the use of caste or community as one of the principal criteria to determine backwardness. There was a forceful plea made to use economic criteria alone to determine backwardness, and hence decide which individuals should be considered backward on the basis of objective economic indicators, rather than social criteria such as castes or communities. In 1965, when the report was finally tabled in parliament, the central government firrmly opposed the definition of backwardness on the basis of communal criteria (i.e. communities or castes),arguing that the use of caste was administratively unworkable and was contrary to the \rst principles of social justice" in their exclusion of other poor.

The centre decided not to impose a uniform criterion on the states, but persuaded them to use economic criteria, rather than community based ones, to identify the backward. Various state governments set up backward classes commissions, and some followed the economic criteria endorsed by the Centre. However, most states continued to place a greater emphasis on the caste criterion. The second Backward Classes commission was set up in 1978 under the chairmanship of B.P. Mandal to examine the entire issue of backwardness, starting again with ascertaining the criteria that should be used to identify the backward.

The Mandal Commission used 11 criteria to determine eligibility, which were grouped under three heads: social, educational and economic. These were combined using weights (social criteria were given a weight of three, educational got two and economic criteria were given a weight of one). This was done for all the Hindu communities. For the non-Hindus, the commission used another set of criteria: all untouchables who had converted to other religions but were still identi able by their traditional occupations, for which the Hindu counterparts were included in the list of backward classes, also got enlisted.

Based on this, the commission identified 3743 caste groups as backward, which were 52 percent of the population (as against 32 percent identified by the Kalelkar commission and the roughly identified 40 percent from the NSS data). The 52 percent gure was arrived at after subtracting from 100 percent the share of the SC-ST population, the non-Hindu population based on the 1971 census, and the share of the Hindu upper castes extrapolated from the 1931 census. The residual was actually 43.7, to which was added half of the non-Hindu population share. Since the identification of OBCs is done at the state-level, there are communities identified as OBCs in one state, but not in another, e.g. Jats are classified as OBCs in Rajasthan, but not in Haryana. Several of the communities classified as OBCs are \occupation castes" e.g. darzi (tailor), teli (oil presser), julaha (weaver), sonar (goldsmith), kanbi (agricultural caste), madari (juggle 6 and/or monkey-minder, someone who earns money by showing tricks to a crowd), rangrez (painter), halwai (sweetmeats and snacks maker) etc. It is clear that seen at the national level, the OBC category is an omnibus one, which includes a diverse set of communities. In some states, groups classied as OBCs are dominant landowning castes, such as Kammas and Reddys in Andhra Pradesh, or Vokkaligas and Lingayats in Karnataka.

These groups are not necessarily backward in terms of their socio-economic status, but are included in the legal OBC category. Our estimates cannot distinguish between dominant OBC castes and those that are truly backward, as the OBC count with NSS data includes all the legal OBCs. We should note that in states where (legal) OBCs are also dominant (in terms of status), the aggregate outcomes of OBCs would be pulled up, as the dominant OBCs are also the landowning castes. This heterogeneity also characterizes the comparison social category of \Others' (and to a smaller extent, SCs and STs), such that the inclusion of poorer Others pulls the averages for the Others category down. As a result, a comparison between these omnibus categories would understate the actual gap between the top end of the \Others', and those who are genuinely backward among the OBCs. While the use of these broad categories limits a nuanced understanding of inter-community dierences within the category, the advantage is that it enables us to identify the \macro" picture, which smaller, case- study-based comparisons do not allow, especially given that the number of communities runs into thousands.

Even after the Indian Independence there were some major changes in favour of the STs, SCs and OBCs. One of the most important occurred in 1979 when the Mandal Commission was established to assess the situation of the socially and educationally backward classes. The commission did not have exact figures for a sub-caste, known as the Other Backward Class(OBC), and used the 1930 census data, further classifying 1,257 communities as backward, to estimate the OBC population at 52%. In 1980 the commission submitted a report, and recommended changes to the existing quotas, increasing them from 22% to 49.5%. As of 2006 number of castes in Backward class list went up to 2297 which is the increase of 60% from community list prepared by Mandal commission. But it wasn't until the 1990s that the recommendations of the Mandal Commission were implemented in Government Jobs by Vishwanath Pratap Singh.

Census has been conducted in India since 1872 and 2011first time after 80 years since 1931, to find the exact population of Other Backward Class (OBCs) in India, which was later accepted and Socio Economic Caste Census 2011 was conducted whose first findings were revealed on 3 July 2015 by Union Finance Minister Arun Jaitley. Mandal Commission report of 1980 quoted OBC population at 52%, though National Sample Survey Organisation (NSSO) survey of 2006 quoted OBC population at 41%. A survey by the National Sample Survey Organisation (NSSO) put the OBC population in the country at 40.94%, the SC population at 19.59%, ST population at 8.63% and the rest at 30.80%.

Caste system in India: different opinions

The Indian caste system is a system of social stratification and social restriction in India in which communities are defined by thousands of endogamous hereditary groups called Jatis.

The study of caste system in India and Reservation policy for marginalised sections has become extremely important ever since. Louis Dumont calls the Hindu homo hierarchicus on the basis of it characteristics. G.S.Ghurye in his book Caste and race in india made a significant analysis of caste system., he says that caste is strictly limited to the Hindus. J.H.Hutton defined caste as the internal endogamous caste as a whole.

H.H. Risely defines caste as a collection of families or groups. Edmund R. Leach considers caste as a cultural or a structural phenomenon. Max Weber regards caste as a fundamental institution of the Hindus. EAH. Blunt characterizes caste in terms of hereditary.

There have been challenges to the caste system from the time of Buddha, till then several thinkers discussed and opposed This Jatis /Varna system.

Social Reformers-Annihilation of caste system

However Mahatma JotiRao Phule, Periyar, Narayana Guru, and Ambedkar made a monumental contribution in this direction.in India. There have been challenges to the caste system from the time of Buddha, till then several thinkers discussed and opposed this Jatis/Varna system.

Jyotiba Phule was one of the prominent social reformers of the nineteenth century India. He led the movement against the prevailing caste-restrictions in India. Gandhi's contribution toward the emancipation of the untouchables is still debated, especially in the commentary of his contemporary Dr. B.R. Ambedkar, who frequently saw Gandhi's activities as detrimental to the cause of upliftment of his people. Ambedkar the caste system in India has been a divisive instrument from the very beginning . He had a firm view that till this caste system continues, the outcastes liberation is not possible. This was the reason that he started a strong movement against caste system.

Since then may writers have been attracted towards this important field of study like western writers are also active in India. Therefore many Indian writers along with foreign writers have been making strenuous efforts to study carefully the caste system . There is no universally accepted theory about the origins of the Indian caste system.

Constitutional protections of OBCs

Preamble of the Constitution

Every Constitution has philosophy of its own. The Preamble of our Constitution proclaims the resolution of PEOPLE OF INDIA to constitute India into a SOVEREIGN, SOCIALIST, SECULAR AND DEMOCRATIC REPUBLIC and to secure to all its citizens:

JUSTICE, social, economic and political;

LIBERTY of thought, expression, belief, faith and worship;

EQUALITY of status and opportunity; and to promote among them all;

FRATERNITY assuring the dignity of the individual and the unity and integrity of the Nation.

The ward 'social justice' in the Preamble implies recognition of greater good to a larger number without deprivation of legal rights of anybody.

The concept of equality, enshrined in the Preamble has also found expression as a fundamental right in Article 14 to 16,

Reservations for OBCs

Reservations for OBCs began even before Independence. In 1880, a century before the Mandal Commission, the Public Instruction Department of the British government observed: "The small number of children of the lowest castes reading in schools is deplorable. The classes who are taking advantage of schools, public and private, throughout the country are the well-to-do and not the masses of the labouring population." The provisions available in the Constitution of India, based on which orders relating to reservations in services for Scheduled Castes (SCs), Scheduled Tribes (STs) and other Backward Classes (OBCs) have been issued by Department of Personnel & Training and Ministries of Social Justice of Government of India.

The provisions made in the Articles 16, 335, 338, 340, 341 & 342 of the Constitution relate to reservation, protection and safeguards, in public employment in respect of the persons belonging to the SCs/STs and other backward classes to recommend steps to be taken for the advancement of the socially and educationally backward classes of citizens so identified; to examine the desirability or otherwise of making provision for the reservation of appointments or posts in favor of such backward classes of citizens which are not adequately represented in the public service and posts in connection with the affairs of the union or any State; and present to the President a report setting out the facts as found by them and making such recommendations as they think proper.

The Commission submitted its report on 31.12.1980. identify the backward classes (other than SCs and STs) the Second Backward Classes Commission (Mandal Commission) was constituted by an order made by the President of India in 1979 under Article 340 of the Constitution with the following terms of reference: to determine the criteria for defining the socially and educationally backward classes; Constitutional Provision for Reservation in Services. The entire gamut of the constitutional provisions pertaining to reservations was addressed by the Supreme Court in writ Petition (Civil)No.930 of 1990 {Indira Sawhney Vs UOI-AIR 1993-SC 477}. The Supreme Court upheld the reservation for 'other backward classes' (OBC) in the services. The aforesaid case came as the order issued by the Constitutional Provision for Reservation in Services *Institute of Secretariat Training & Management*

Government of India on 1990 reserving 27% of posts for Other Backward Classes was challenged before the Hon'ble Supreme Court to understand fully the Article 16(4), four of the following terms which appear in the said Article needs to be fully understood:-

(a) State
(b) Backward Class of Citizens
(c) Opinion
(d) Not adequately represented.

The Supreme Court held in the case of Indra Sawhney that "indeed, even without clause (4), it would have been permissible for the State to have evolved such a classification and made a provision for reservation of appointment/posts in their (Backward Classes) favour. Clause (4) merely puts the matter beyond any doubt in specific terms".

Educational (2 points for each of the three indicator- total 6 points)

Castes/ classes where the number of children in the age group 5-15 years who never attended school is at least 25% above the State average; Castes/ classes where the rate of student drop out in the age group of

- 5-15 years is at least 25% above the State average; Castes/ classes amongst whom the proportion of matriculation is at least 25% below the State average.
- Economic (1 point for each of 4 indicators- total 4 points) Castes/ classes where the average value of family assets is at least 25% below the State average.
- Castes/ classes where the number of families living in kuccha houses is at least 25% above the State average;
- Castes/ classes where the source of drinking water is beyond half a kilometer for more than 50% of the households; Castes/ classes where the number of households, having taken consumption loan in at least 25% above the State average.

Reservation Quota: In India

Total–50%(OBC –27.5%, SC –15%, ST 7.5%)

Tamilnadu

—69% (BC -30%, MBC –20%, SC -18% (15% + 3% EXCLUSIVELY FOR ARUNDHATHIYAR COMMUNITY) AND ST –1%

Telangana

Reservation given to SC, ST & BC in a recruitment notified by TSPSC -BC(A)- 07%; BC(B)-10%; BC(C)- 01%; BC(D)-07%; BC(E)-04%, ST- 06%; SC-15%.

Impact of reservation policy on employment and education

The 93rd *Constitutional Amendment (2005)* allows the government to make special provisions for "advancement of any socially and educationally backward classes of citizens", including their admission in aided or unaided private educational institutions. Gradually this reservation policy is to be implemented in private institutions and companies as well.

When the then HRD minister Mr. Arjun Singh introduced 27.5% reservation for OBC in centrally funded educational institutes including IIMs and IITs

Impact of reservation policy on employment and education. As may be evident from the particulars in the earlier paragraphs, the strategy of reservation had a helpful effect in conditions of induction of scheduled castes, scheduled tribes and other backward classes into public sector employment and in educational institutions. However, their accessible share in employment and educational institutions still falls short of the target in certain categories of jobs and higher education.

The target in the case of Groups D and C are close to the population mark of 15 percent for scheduled castes and 7.5 % for scheduled tribes but fall short in Groups A and B. As against this, the true position regarding the representation of other backward classes in central services is not available.

However, as All India Services and central services for which employment is made through the Union Public Service Commission, representation of other backward classes is very meager to their share.

Conclusion

The data provided by the ministry of personnel indicates that in recent years the vacancies reserved for the scheduled castes, scheduled tribes and other backward classes are being filled fully even in the elite services at the centre. 8.3. Reservation did not provide equal opportunities within each group/community to all beneficiaries. Consequently, different castes and tribes within a group/community have not benefited from reservation equally. Almost in all categories of beneficiaries among scheduled castes, scheduled tribes or other backward classes and minorities, there is a growing sense of deprivation amongst different categories, which is leading to internal dissension.

For example, in Punjab, the Valmiki Samaj is asking for a separate quota of reservations on the ground that Ramadasis and Mazbis have cornered the benefits. Likewise, Chamars in Uttar Pradesh and Mahars in Maharashtra are said to have benefited from the reservations more than other castes identified in the schedule from these regions.

Similar accusations have been made against the Meena community by other scheduled tribes. Problems of this kind are manifold in the case of other backward classes, as in each state there are dominant groups, usually with economic and political clout, who reap the benefits of reservations.

There are Ezhavas in Kerala, Nadars and Thevars in Tamil Nadu, Vokkalligas and Lingayats in Karnataka, Lodhs and Koeris in Central India, Yadavs and Kurmis in Bihar and Uttar Pradesh and Jats in Rajasthan, Kapus in Andhra Pradesh, Gujjars in Gujarat which, despite their dominant status, have been clubbed as backward classes eligible for benefits under reservations. For these reasons, reservation has become a contentious issue today, more so when it is applied to other backward classes.

References

1. Basu, Durga Das. Introduction to the Constitution of India. Nagpur: Lexis Nexis Butter worths Wadhwa. (2008)
2. Bhattacharya, Amit. "Who are the OBCs?". Archived from the original on 27 June 2006. Retrieved 19 April 2006. Times of India, 8 April 2006.
3. Chalam, K.S. "Caste Reservation and Equality of Opportunity in Education" Economic and Political Weekly, Vol. 25, No. 41, October 13, 1990.
4. Chapter 3- An Assessment of Reservations (Pg. 32)". News. Dalit Bahujan Media. Retrieved 17 November 2011.
5. Das, Bhagwan "Moments in a History of Reservations" Economic and Political Weekly, Vol. 35, No. 43 and 44, October 28, 2000.
6. Education Safeguards". Department of Education. Government of India. Retrieved 27 November 2011. Indra Sawhney And Ors. vs Union Of India (UOI) And Ors. on 8 August 1991. New Delhi: Supreme Court of India. 1991.
7. Financial Support". University Grants Commission, India. Retrieved 20 October 2011.
8. Galanter, Marc, Competing equalities: law and the backward classes in India University of California Press Berkeley, 1984.
9. Ghose S.K., Reservation in Services (A manual for Government and Public Sector), Akshar Publication, New Delhi.
10. Government of India, Brochure on Reservation for SCs/ STs in Services, GOI Press, Department of Personnel and Training {EsttSCT}
11. Government of India, The Constitution of India, GOI Press New Delhi.
12. Gupta, Dipankar, Caste in question: identity or hierarchy?, Vol. 12, SAGE Publications India, 2009.

13. Jarelot, Christophe, India's silent revolution: the rise of the lower castes in North India, Orient Black-swan, 2003.
14. Kundu, Amitabh "Reservation, Anti-reservation and Democracy" Economic and Political Weekly, Vol. 25, No. 45, November 10, 1990.
15. Laskar, Mehbubul Hassan. "Rethinking Reservation in Higher Education in India". ILI Law Review.
16. Muthuswamy and Bindra, Swamy's Compilation on Reservation and Concessions for SCs/STs OBC, Swamy's Publishers (P) Ltd.Chennai and New Delhi.
17. Nigam, Aditya "In Search of a Bourgeoisie" Economic and Political Weekly, Vol. 37, No. 13, March 30, 2002.
18. Nigam, Aditya "Mandal Commission and the Left" Economic and Political Weekly, Vol. 25, No. 48,49, December 1-8, 1990.
19. Omvedt, Gail "Hinduism and Politics" Economic and Political Weekly, Vol. 25, No. 14, April 7, 1990.
20. Pandian M.S.S "One Step Outside Modernity" Economic and Political Weekly, Vol. 37, No. 18, May 4, 2002.
21. Pinto, Amrose "U.N. Conference Against Racism – Is Caste Race?" Economic and Political Weekly, Vol. 36, No. 30, July 28, 2001.
22. Radhakrishnan P. "Sensitizing Officials on Dalits and Reservations" Economic and Political Weekly, Vol. 37, No. 7, Feb. 16, 2002 Virginius "Protective Discrimination : Why Scheduled Tribes Lay Behind Scheduled Castes" Economic and Political Weekly, Vol. 36, No. 29, July 21, 2001.
23. Ramaiah, A (6 June 1992). "Identifying Other Backward Classes" (PDF). Economic and Political Weekly. pp. 1203–1207. Archived from the original on 30 December 2005. Retrieved 27 May 2006. Parliament of India. Retrieved 4 November 2011.
24. Supreme Court Judgement in Indra Sawhney Vs UOI Writ Petition (Civil) No. 930 of 1990.
25. The Politics of Backwardness: Reservation Policy in India Edited by VA Pai Panandiker.
26. The Untouchables of India". Praxis. Retrieved 20 October 2011.

Struggles for Sub-Categorization of Scheduled Castes (SC) Reservations

Chapter - 13

Governmentality towards the Implementation of the Reservations the Dynamics of Caste & Politics in Indian Democracy: A Reference to OBCs in Telangana

— Dr. Y. Prabhanjan Kumar Yadav

Abstract

The Reservations in favor of Backward Classes (BCs) in the country were first implemented by Sahu Maharaj in 1902to engulf the social discrimination and disparities, to abridge the social inequalities and to eradicate poverty from amongst them and to give them their due share in the State Administration. The notication of 1902 created 50% reservations in services for backward classes/communities in the State of Kolhapur. This is the rst Government Order providing reservations for the welfare of the depressed castes in India.

Later Dr. B.R. Ambedkar represented and due to his unrelenting efforts Backward Classes particularly Scheduled Castes and Scheduled Tribes reservations got approved. At that point of time, Dr. Ambedkar also lamented that Other Backward Classes (OBCs) did not join him in the fight for reservations. As the Other Backward Classes were not organized and could not wage a concerted fight, they could not get the reservations on par with Scheduled Castes and Scheduled tribes. However, Dr. Ambedkar with his foresight for the benefit of the OBCs has suggested that a commission need to be constituted to look into the reservation demands of the OBCs in the future.

The first OBC commission was constituted in 1953 under the chairmanship of Kaka Kalelkar, which described the plight of OBCs but did not recommend the reservations to the OBCs, instead recommended special measures for the benefit of OBCs. Even then the issue was not subsided and being continued.Later, the Janata Government constituted Second OBC Commission under the chairmanship of BP Mandal on 1st January 1979. It submitted its report on 31st December1980. The report was willfully not tabled till 1989 by the successive Governments.The VP Singh led Janata Dal government was forced to declare the implementation of Mandal Commission report for the OBCreservations in employment and educational sectors to the tune of 27 per centon August 7th, 1990.As per the Supreme Court directions, the Creamy Layer clause has been hampering the OBC reservations and only 9 percent of earmarked OBC posts were filled. The OBC reservations in the country remained on paper but the implementation lacked spirit at different levels.

In the erstwhile Andhra Pradesh too, in 1986 the then TDP government-led by NTR has constituted Muralidhar Rao commission that has recommended increased reservations to the BCs in the State. There was a lot of hue and cry against the implementation of the Muralidhar Rao Commission recommendations and there were agitations across the State.The Congress government led by Dr. YSR has also implemented the 4 percent quota for the Muslim minorities in the State. In the recent past, in newly formed Telangana State KCR led TRS government taking efforts to implement the sub quota for the Most Backward Classes (MBCs and Scheduled Tribes) in accordance with their population. But the BCs, who comprise more population in number and major chunk of vote bank, were neglected willfully.

In this backdrop, the implementation of the OBC reservations has lacked the real spirit and majority of the posts earmarked for the OBCs as part of the OBC quota remained vacant, under the pretext of "No suitable candidate found". But against the earmarked OBC reserved vacancies Upper caste candidates were filled with out-sourcing category. Even those posts which got filled under the OBC quota were that of lower cadre posts. The glaring example of the faulty implementation of the OBC reservation is visible in the universities and other higher educational institutions of the central government where less than 4 percent of the faculty belongs to the OBC category. Going by this way, the implementation of 27 percent OBC reservation to its full extent will take a very long time and it is clear that the governmentality is very much opposed to the genuine implementation of the OBC reservations.

This paper takes a critical perspective on the history and implementation of the OBC reservations, Creamy Layer clause directed by the Supreme Court and how the Governmentality is hampering the implementation of the OBC reservations.

Key Words: *Brahmanism, Divide and Rule, Varna and Caste System, Discrimination, Disparities, Democracy, Republic, Equality, Social Justice, Reservations, Backward Classes, Other Backward Classes (OBCs),Scheduled Castes and Scheduled tribes, Self-esteem and self-respect.*

Introduction

We take pride in reiterating that the Republic of India is the world's largest democracy. The social values- Freedom, Equality, Fraternity, Fundamental

Rights, Social Justice and Independence of Judiciary are the threadbare and basis for Indian democracy. These values provide opportunities to all, share responsibilities, free expression of opinions, respect the opinion of others, accept the opinion of majority, ensure peoples' participation and every one should be given his/her due share. But most of the times, in India, majority of the people are either spectators or the scapegoats. So far they did not enjoy their due share and own space in Indian democracy. It is because, in the guise of democracy, only the people of a few privileged castes are enjoying the power and the property of the nation. The peoples' participation can hardly be found in any of the activities of democracy in the post independent era. The role of people in Indian democracy is reduced to the level of franchising their votes with a regular interval of every ve years.

In the recent past, during the elections it was witnessed some incidents of deleting the names of the prospective voters from the voters list, tampering the EVMs, rigging the votes, booth capturing or alluring and bribing the voters. People are not free, at least to avail their right to vote. Indian democracy has been ridiculed by money, muscle, maûa and media, which are controlled by the privileged castes. Indeed, they are playing a prominent role in all sorts of manipulations. It is because some of the fundamental rights and directive principles of state policy, which are quite contradictory. At the same time both of them co-exist in the Constitution of India. When the Constitution guarantees the right to property, which was later shifted to directive principles of state policy, how can be equality found. In fact this dichotomy leads to many confusions and controversies. Further, it engulfed the gaps among different stake holders of Republic of India. The evil impact of the Hindu caste system on the life of downtrodden can be seen all over India even after 72 years of independence.

Caste politics in India

B. R. Ambedkar and Jawaharlal Nehru had radically different approaches to caste, especially concerning constitutional politics and the status of untouchables. After the formation of Bahujana Samaj Party (BSP) under the leadership of Kanshiram, who applied and put the theory of Phoole-Ambedkar into practice. Hence from 1980s, the caste has become a major and crucial issue in Indian politics. Many political parties in India have openly indulged in the politics for Social Justice. Parties such as Bahujan Samaj Party (BSP), the Samajwadi Party, the Rashtriya Janata Dal and the Janata Dal, the Lok Janashakti claim that they are representing the backward castes, and rely on OBC support, along with Scheduled Castes and Scheduled

Tribesand Muslim support, to win elections. Remarkably, in what is called a landmark election in the history of India's most populated state of Uttar Pradesh and Bihar, Samajwadi and the Bahujan Samaj and the Rashtriya Janata Dal parties were able to garner a majority in the respective state assembly elections and in the power for more than a decade.

Reservations in India

Reservations are intended to increase the social diversity in campuses, workplaces and legislatures by lowering the entry criteria for certain groups that are under-represented in proportion to their population. The Indian government follows a policy positive discrimination towards the Backward Classes. to eradicate poverty from amongst them and to give them their due share in the State administration.

In Pre-Independence era

Reservations in favor of Backward Classes(BCs) were introduced long before Independence in a large area, comprising the Presidency areas and the Princely States south of the Vindhyas. Chatrapati Sahuji Maharaj, Maharaja of Kolhapur in Maharashtra introduced reservation in favor of backward classes as early as 1902 to eradicate poverty from amongst them and to give them their due share in the State administration. The notication of 1902 created 50% reservations in services for backward classes/ communities in the State of Kolhapur. This notication is the rst Government Order providing for reservations for the welfare of the depressed castes in India.

In Post-Independence era

The framers of the Constitution understood that, due to the caste system, SCs and the STs were historically oppressed, denied respect and equal opportunities in Indian society and were thus underrepresented in nation-building activities. First the reservation policy is provided to the Scheduled Castes and the Scheduled Tribes for representation in Indian Legislature. In accordance to this policy, 15% for Scheduled Castes and 7.5% for Scheduled Tribes in education and employment along with political reservations to enter the legislature bodies.

Later, in 1953 the first BC Commission was established under the chairmanship of Kalelkar to assess the situation of the socially and educationally backward class. The report was accepted but the recommendations for OBCs were rejected. Later, the Janata Government constituted Second BC Commission under the chairmanship of B P Mandal on 1st January 1979. It submitted its report on 31st December1980. The report was willfully not tabled till 1989 by the successive Governments. The VP Singh led Janata Dal government was forced to declare the implementation of Mandal Commission report for the OBC reservations in employment and educational sectors to the tune of 27 percent on August 7th, 1990. As per the Supreme Court directions, the Creamy Layer clause has been hampering the OBC reservations and only 9 percent of earmarked OBC posts were filled. In this backdrop, the implementation of the OBC reservations has lacked the real spirit and majority of the posts earmarked for the OBCs as part of the OBC quota remained vacant, under the pretext of "No suitable candidate found". But against the earmarked OBC reserved vacancies Upper caste candidates were filled with out-sourcing category. Even those posts which got filled under the OBC quota were that of lower cadre posts. The glaring example of the faulty implementation of the OBC reservation is visible in the universities and other higher educational institutions of the central government where less than 4 percent of the faculty belongs to the OBC category. Going by this way, the implementation of 27 percent OBC reservation to its full extent will take a very long time and it is clear that the governmentality is very much opposed to the genuine implementation of the OBC reservations.

The OBC reservations in the country remained on paper but the implementation lacked spirit at different levels.The OBC leaders R Krishanaiah, president of Backward Classes Welfare Organization and V Hanumantha Rao, the former Convener of OBC MPs forum have been relentlessly waging the fight for the OBC reservations in the Legislatures and also giving the representations to the successive Prime Ministers. But thePrime Ministers are deaf and dumb to the political reservations for OBCs.

Vote Bank Politics

It has not been a very happy experience during the 72 years of independence. The Hindu caste hegemony and upper caste privileged social order in India did not want to lose the power. So they did not touch the basic issues; rather they conned to only to make the Scheduled Castes as their vote bank and providing a few benets. This has been the approach of various bourgeois landlord political parties on the caste issue. All political parties know that "divide and rule" policy based on castes and religion will make them rich, will always help them hide their corruption and bad deeds and they are following it religiously. But even today there is no much change in the plight of OBCs. Now it is under criticism that the reservations on the basis of caste and religion are being continued as vote bank politics. Our politics is largely governed by cash and caste vote banks. Selection of candidates for elections is not made of the numerical caste distribution in a constituency, but made on money power of the candidates who naturally belongs to higher castes since they possess the properties. The selected candidates buy the caste leaders because voters in most areas vote on caste lines. Even the so-called intellectuals tend to operate on caste lines. Thus, in the elections to teacher unions, bar associations and other unions tend to vote for candidates of their own castes. Even Muslims, Christians and Sikhs often have caste divisions, although their religions preach equality. The leaders and social reformers from productive and service castes have been demanding for the reservations in the legislature too. But it has been delayed by the upper caste rulers to deny them not to become a part of democracy. Once again, the upper castes turned its evil eye to exploit fellow beings in the guise of Women reservations in the legislature.

Phoole-Ambedkar thought and Kanshiram practice

The Hindu Caste hegemony still exists with expanding its evil antennas. It is clearly evident in the world's largest democracy even after six decades of independence. As long as the Brahmanical caste hegemony continues to exist there is no room for equality in Indian Democracy. So freedom without equality is a sham. The great anti-caste ghters and social reformers like Mahatma Jyotirao Phule, Periyar E V R and Shri Narayana Guru, Chatrapati Sahu ji Maharaj, Dr B R Ambedkar and Kanshiram bitterly attacked the caste system, its intrinsic inequalities and empowerment of dalits and other backward castes. With this inspiration of ghting for the lost rights several social reformers relentlessly strived for the due share of the productive and service castes in India. The socio-political thinkers of the school of Mahatma Jyotirao Phoole-Ambedkar are no more in dilemma. They are very clear in their thought, in understanding and analyzing the socio-political dynamics of Indian democracy in the post independent era. They are also persuading the social engineering cause. The self-respect movements and socio-political empowerment struggles to capture the political power are going on in different regions and states of India.

Self-respect movements in Telangana

With the entry of Bahujana Samaj Party in Telangana the morale of the downtrodden people was boosted. There was a great debate in all schools of political thoughts from extreme left to right. During 1980s and 1990s several self-respect and identity movements had come up in Telangana under the leadership and guidance of Maroju Veeranna who was under the inuence of Karl Marx-Mahatma Jyotirao Phoole and Dr B R Ambedkar. Indeed this was initiated by Koora Rajanna, Secretary of CPI-ML Janashakti. CPI-ML People's War former leader, KG Satya Murthy alias Siva Sagar, several Professors of various universities Kancha Ilaiah, S Simhadri, PL Vishweshwar Rao, Mural Manohar, Inukonda Tirumali, Bhuky Bangya, Srinivasulu, Md Ansari and Chakradhar Rao, political activists Maroju Veeranna, U Samba Siva Rao, Justice BSA Swamy, Bojja Tarakam, Senior Journalists Dr Ambati Surendra Raju, Y Prabhanjan Yadav and others initiated the Caste and Class conscious struggles in Telangana. As a result the struggles for the self-respect, the justied due share and the equal opportunities by Madiga Reservation Porata Samiti(MRPS)-Dandora, Golla-Kurma Hakkula Porata Samiti- Doludebba, Lambada Hakkula Porata Samiti and so on and so forth had come up. They are carrying message of the father of Indian Constitution Dr B R Ambedkar, "Political power is the master key for all the problems" to every heart and ever hut. As the ideology is spreading the movements are swelling like anything. Even they went to the extent of saying "Votes are ours, so as Seats", as rightly said by Kanshiram. So is the case with the people of Telangana(State).

In Erstwhile Andhra Pradesh

Formation of Andhra Pradesh is lust for power The Andhra leadership still smarting at the ill-treatment meted out to them by the Tamil ruling class in the old Madras Presidency. Another reason is also the lust for power and money of the feudal castes of the Andhra and Rayalaseema areas, Kammas, Reddys and Brahmans. In the erstwhile composite Andhra Pradesh OBCs were neglected till in 1982 by the successive governments and the Reddy dominated Congress party. Only Harijana-Girijana, Scheduled Castes and the Scheduled Tribes were lured and given priority in political sphere.

The power monger Kamma Community formed a new political party TDPled by NTR, a cine glamorous hero.Kammas with an eye to lure OBCs who consists of major population and large chunk of vote bank in the State. The prospective leaders of OBCs were considerably accommodated politically to grab the power from Reddys. Kamma a feudal caste, which has lust for power and money, polarized under the leadership of a ûlm Star NTR with an attractive slogan "Telugu Pride and Self-respect". Till then the Congress Party was in power lulled and lured only Harijans and Girijans (SCs & STs) and ignored the Backward Classes.

Telugu Desam Party realized that the Backward Classes comprise more than Fifty percent of the population wooed Backward Classes by offering majority of seats in the State Assemble elections. With the overwhelming support of OBCs Telugu Desham Party won the elections with bumper majority and formed Government in 1983. As a sign of gratitude the emotional leader and Chief Minister NTR constituted the Muralidhar Rao Backward Classes Commission in 1986, whichrecommended increased reservations to the BCs in the State. There was a serious opposition from Upper Castes like Reddy, Brahman, Kamma and so on and so forth. That led to Anti and Pro Reservation Movements. There was a lot of hue and cry against the implementation of the Muralidhar Rao Commission recommendations and there were agitations across the State. The Backward Classes movement also gathered momentum.

Backward Classes movement in Telangana

In Telangana, Konda Laxman Bapuji, Bala Goud and Siva Sanker are the leaders of Congress party remarkably contributed their best to the amelioration of Backward Classes.Then the student leaders R Krishnaiah, VGR Naragoni and Y Shanker, Y Prabhanjan Yadav and others relentlessly fought for the cause and advanced the Backward Classes movement in Telangana. For more than four decades R Krishnaih has been the Champion, who has been ghting with a single point i.e., the welfare and empowerment of Backward Classes under the Banner of AP BC Welfare Association. R Krishnaiah, has been demanding the successive governments both at the State and the Centre to provide 50% reservations for OBCs in the State legislatures and Parliament. Hence there are several uncompromised and relentless struggles are going on in Telangana to change the Hindu Brahmanical caste hegemonic system.

The Congress government led by Dr. YSR has also implemented the 4 percent quota for the Muslim minorities in the State. In the recent past, in newly formed Telangana State KCR led TRS government taking efforts to implement the sub quota for the Most Backward Classes (MBCs), Scheduled Tribesand the Muslim minorities in accordance with their population. But the BCs, who are more in number and major chunk of vote bank, were neglected willfully. Before the formation of Telangana State the composition of State Assembly from Telangana out of 119 seats OBCs were 24. In newly formed Telangana State only less number of candidates was given tickets by all the political parties and only 19 OBC MLAs were elected out of 119 seats. In the recent elections also Congress and TRS parties denied giving tickets according to OBC population in the State, so only 21 OBC MLAs were elected out of 119.

At the present, out of 119 there are about 42 MLAs from single Reddy community which consists of only 3% and 11 MLAs from Velama caste which comprises 0.4 %of population in Telangana. The composition of TRs government is still worse. Out of 11 minsters including CM 2 are Velama caste, Reddy are 5, rest are 3 OBCs- Yadava 1, Gouda 1, Mudiraj 1 and 1 SC-Mala-1. According to Justice Sri Krishna Commission the OBC population in Telangana State is 60% and SCs are about 17%.It shows that the power did not percolate to the bottom of all the sections of the society. All most all political parties and organizations, in Telangana, are headed by the upper castes. Is it a democratic process? This question is being raised by several leaders of OBC, SC and ST organizations.But during the first and second phases of Telangana Movement OBCs participated in large number, self-immolated and sacrificed their lives. This should not go in vain. OBCs must gear up and rise to the occasion to capture the power in Telangana State and that should be a path finder for the entire Nation.

Change for Equal Opportunities

The people, who have been exploited for centuries under the Brahmanical social order are aware of their rights and put their best foot forward to ght for their lost rights. With these developments and with constant and uncompromised sustained efforts of some of the social reformers and ghters, a few facilities were achieved. But the wealthy and strong upper castes have a tendency to establish their hegemony over productive and service castes. The Brahmanical social order particularly, made most of the productive and service castes inferior to the upper strata and ruled them for centuries together. For the smooth exploitation, these upper caste rulers provided some facilities to productive and service castes. With the awakening of intelligentsia from these castes which created awareness among the masses, many revolts are taking place bravely for the self-respect and self-rule. Change occurs out of necessity or compulsion. Now days, it became the buzzword of all. "One has to realize that the building of India on modern democratic and secular lines requires an uncompromising struggle against the caste biased Hindu society and its culture. There is no question of secular democracy, not to speak of socialism, unless the very citadel of India's 'age old' civilization and culture – the division of society into hierarchy of castes – is broken. In other words, the struggle for radical democracy and socialism cannot be separated from the struggle against caste and class society."

References

1. Prof Kancha Ilaiah. **Why I am not a Hindu**.
2. Prof P L Vishweshwar Rao & Prof Simhadri, **The Dynamics of Under development of Telangana**.
3. Dr B R Ambedkar Annihilation of Caste in India
4. Dr Y Prabhanjan Yadav, Beyond Challenges, Prabhanjana Patham Publications, Hyderabad.
5. Kanshi Ram Speeches and his biography

Chapter - 14

Right to Equality in India: Relevance of Reservations in Favour of Backward Classes

— Dr. Someshwar Bonakurthy

Abstract

The Constitution guarantees equality to all citizens and establishes a rule of nondiscrimination by the state in any manner. It ensures the state to treat all citizens equally and allows equality of status and opportunity to all and specifically provides that discrimination on the basis of religion, sex, colour, caste or race are impermissible. The high objective was to convert a society fragmented on the lines of religion, caste and economic status into a homogenous society. Reservation at the time of independence was meant to achieve the ultimate goal of development. But now it has resulted in further fragmentation and division of the society on caste lines which was never the objective with which special provisions for upliftment had been incorporated.

Therefore the Constitution accords to these weaker sections of society protective discrimination in various articles, including Article 15(4) and 16(4). This clause empowers the state to make special reservation for the advancement of any socially and educationally backward classes of citizens or for scheduled castes and scheduled tribes. This article aims to discuss equality and reservation given to us by the constitution and also deals with Mandal Commission and how it affected the reservation policies.

Key Worrds: *Constitution, Equality, Reservation, Article 15(4), Article 16 (4), Mandal Commission.*

Introduction

Equality affirms that all human beings are born free and equal. Equality presupposes that all individuals have the same rights and deserve the same level of respect. All people have the right to be treated equally. This means that laws, policies and programs should not be discriminatory, and also that public authorities should not apply or enforce laws, policies and programs in a discriminatory or arbitrary manner. Non-discrimination is an integral part of the principle of equality. It ensures that no one is denied their rights because of factors such as race, colour, sex, language, religion, political or other opinion, national or social origin, property or birth. In addition to those grounds, discrimination on certain other grounds may also be prohibited. These grounds include age, nationality, marital status, disability, place of residence within a country and sexual orientation. Sometimes it may be necessary to treat people differently to achieve equality. This is because differences between people may make it difficult for them to enjoy their rights without support. Different treatment may not amount to prohibited discrimination if the criteria for the differentiation are reasonable and objective and if the aim is to achieve a purpose which is legitimate under the International Covenant on Civil and Political Rights.

The right to equality and non-discrimination encompasses both positive and negative obligations - the obligation to refrain from discriminating or eroding equality and the obligation to protect and advance the fulfilment and enjoyment of the rights to equality and non-discrimination for all people.

Right to equality means the absence of legal discrimination against any one individual, group, class or race.

Equality in India is a relatively recent concept as enshrined in our Constitution. The Right to Equality is a Fundamental Right, and our Constitution gives all Indians the right to practice it, irrespective of caste, creed, economic status, race or gender. Ancient Indian civilization was steeped in inequalities, mostly of caste. With the advent of Buddhism and Jainism, the caste system received a jolt, as the common man started questioning its very basis. Later, Christianity and Islam too, spoke of the equality of all men in the eyes of God. The Bhakti movement in medieval India borrowed from these concepts and the majority of Indians became familiar with the concept of equality. With India achieving independence in 1947, equality became a matter of State authority. The framers of the Constitution made sure that future governments should be able to apply its principles to the social fabric of the nation.

This has resulted in all Indians being provided with equal opportunities to excel. The concept of reservation was enshrined in the Constitution to allow the so-called deprived classes to come at par with the so-called privileged ones. The Constitution of India allows this kind of positive discrimination in order to bring about equality of opportunity and status in the society. The founding fathers had never intended Reservation to be a temporary phenomenon. Reservations to the underprivileged were to be extended until they were uplifted socially and stabilized economically. Reservations with the view of helping the deprived classes to gain a better footing and avail equal benefits of an independent and free nation was introduced in the system.

Right to Equality

Foremost among the fundamental rights guaranteed by the constitution of India is the right to equality. Articles 14-18 constitute the Right to Equality in India. As such article 14 was considered generally a negative right of an individual not to be discriminated in access to public offices or places or in public offices generally. It did not take into account of existing inequalities arising even from the public policies and exercise of public power. The makers of Indian Constitution were not satisfied with that kind of undertaking of the right to equality. They knew that even though Buddha was one of the earliest proponents of equality in this land followed by many others, wide spread social and economic inequalities sanctioned by public policies and exercise of public power supported by religion and other social norms and practices existed. Such inequalities could not be removed, minimized or taken care of by a provision like Article 14 alone. But even though they could be so taken care of, it would have been a very slow process. Therefore, they expressly abolished and prohibited some of the existing inequalities practised not only by public power or state but even by private persons and expressly authorized the state to take necessary steps to minimize and remove them.

Articles 15 -18 clearly expresses such intention of the constitution makers. Thus the right to equality in India is not merely a negative right not to be discriminated against but also a positive right to be treated as an equal.

Article 14

Art 14 states that "*The state shall not deny to any person equality before the law or the equal protection of the laws within the territory of India.*"

The two phrases—(a) **equality before the law** and (b) **equal protection of the law** do not mean exactly the same thing. The former is negative in content implying absence of special privilege in favour of any section of the people or any individual. Equal protection of the law is positive in content. It implies equality of treatment in equal circumstances. Again "equality before the law" implies that all are equal in the eyes of law and from the highest to the humblest, all will be tried by the same law and will be given the same punishment for same crime. The phrase "equal protection of the laws" is borrowed from the 14th amendment of the U. S. constitution. It means that like should be treated alike, that none should be favoured and none should be discriminated, against. This allows the Parliament to classify persons for the various purposes. The classification should be reasonable.

Test of Reasonable Classification

While Article 14 forbids class legislation, it does not forbid reasonable classification of persons, objects and transactions by the legislature for the purpose of achieving specific ends. But classification must not be "arbitrary, artificial or evasive". A legislative classification to be valid must be reasonable. In order to pass the test of reasonable classification two conditions must be fulfilled, namely:

1. The classification must be founded on an intelligible differentia which distinguishes persons or things that are grouped together from others left out of the group
2. The differentia must have a rational relation to the object sought to be achieved by the statute in question

In ***E.V. Chinnaiah v. State of AP,*** the main question before the court was whether sub classification or micro-classification of Scheduled Castes for the purpose of reservation is volatile of Article 14 of the Constitution or not? The Supreme Court held that such sub classification is violative and liable to be struck down. The Court rightly pointed out that in *Indira Sahani*it was specifically held that sub-division of backward classes is not applicable to Scheduled Castes and Scheduled Tribes.

Article 15

Art 15 states that *"the state shall not discriminate against any citizen on grounds only of religion, race, caste sex, place of birth or any of them."* This article ordains that no citizen shall be denied

(a) "access to shops, public restaurants, hotels or places of public entertainment or

(b) the use of wells, tanks, bathing ghats, roads and places of public resorts maintained wholly or partly out of state funds."

his article however does not forbid the state from making special provisions for women and children. The state is equally free to make special provisions for socially and educationally backward classes and for the scheduled castes and tribes.

Supreme Court in *Nain Sukh Das v. State of* *UP5* invalidated an Act of State Legislature which provided for elections on the basis of separate electorates for members of different religious communities. In *D.P. Joshi v. State of M.B6,* the Supreme Court held that a law which discriminates on the ground of residence did not infringe Article 15. Place of birth in Article 5(1) is different from residence. In a significant judgement7, a five judge bench of the Supreme Court has held that a person belonging to Scheduled Caste or Scheduled Tribe, bearing the same nomenclature in two States is entitled to the rights, privileges and benefit only in the State of his origin but not entitled to those rights and benefits in other States where he immigrates.

Clause 5 was added by Constitution (93rdAmendment) Act, 2006. It has been enacted to nullify the effect of the three decisions of the Supreme Court, i.e., *T.M. Pai Foundationn v. State of Karnataka8* and *Islamic Academy v. State of Karnataka 9*. It provided provision for reservation of backward and SC & ST classes.

Article 16

Art. 16 guarantees equality of opportunity in matters of public employment. The article states that:

(i) There shall be equality of opportunity for all citizens in matters relating to employment or appointment to any office under the state. The article also forbids discrimination on grounds only of religion, race, caste, sex, descent, and place of birth or any of them in matters of public employment. There are five exceptions to prohibition of discrimination under Art. 16. (I) The Parliament may lay down residence qualification for some appointments in states.

(ii) The state may reserve some appointments for backward classes if they are not adequately represented in the state services.

(iii) Offices in the religious institutions may be kept reserved for the followers of the religion concerned.

(iv) Posts in the state services may be kept reserved for the scheduled castes and tribes.

(v) Finally Art. 16 forbid discrimination in matters of state employment only on the grounds

(vi) stated in the article itself. It does not forbid preferential treatment on other grounds such as efficiency or mercy.

Under Article 16 the guarantee against discrimination is limited to 'employment' and 'appointment' under State. Equality of opportunity in matters of employment can be predicated only as between persons who are either seeking the same employment or have obtained the same employment, and that "equality of opportunity in matters of employment under Article 16(1) means equality between members of the same class of employees and not equality between members of separate independent classes." Equality of opportunity in matters of appointment does not, however, prevent the State from prescribing the necessary qualifications and selective tests for recruitment for Government services.

Article 17

Art. 17 of the constitution says, "***Untouchability is abolished and its practice in any form is forbidden***." The position is further fortified by the Abolition of the Untouchability Act of 1955. Though the term untouchability has not been defined in either the constitution or the Act of 1955, practice of untouchability in any form is strictly forbidden. Refusing admission to public institutions like schools and hospitals on grounds of untouchability is a punishable crime.

Article 18

Art. 18 ***forbid titles*** except military or academic distinctions. Title from foreign governments such as knighthood is forbidden. However honours conferred by the government of India such as Bharat Ratna or Padmashri etc. are not titles but are only recognition of meritorious services. Right to equality in all its forms are available to Indian constitutional remedies against the violation of fundamental right to equality.

Reservation System in India

Reservations were introduced during the last decades of the 19th century at a time when the subcontinent could be broadly divided according to two main forms of governance British India and the 600 princely states. Some of these princely states were progressive and eager to modernize through the promotion of education and industry; and by maintaining unity among their own people, like Mysore in south India and Baroda and Kolhapur in western India. Thus, the very first records of implementing reservations policies are from these princely states. The question of reservations was also discussed in the *"Round Table Conferences"* and provisions were made in the *Communal Award of 1935* in spite of opposition by Mahatma Gandhi. Dr. B.R. Ambedkar was appointed member of the Viceroy's Executive Council and he submitted a memorandum titled, *'On the Grievances of the Scheduled Castes'*. The scheduled castes were allowed 8.5 percent reservation in central services and other facilities for the first time in the history of India in 1942.

Immediately after the adoption of the Constitution, the provision of reservation under Article 16 was challenged through a writ petition filed in the Madras High Court – "***State of Madras v ChampakamDorairajan,*** The case came before the Supreme Court of India. The Madras government's policy, which stipulated admission to medical and engineering colleges in a proportion, based upon caste and religion, was challenged, *inter alia*, under Article 15(1) [recall that 15(4) did not exist at the time]. The State made an argument that reservations in educational institutions were justified under Article 46, part of the Directive Principles of State policy, which required the State to *"promote with special care the educational and economic interests of the weaker sections of the people."* The Court rejected the argument on two grounds: *first*, obviously, that the Directive Principles were not enforceable. *Secondly*, however, it argued that if reservations could be justified under Article 46, this would make 16(4) redundant. It logically follows, then, that Article 16(4), which allows for reservations under the broader Article 16 scheme of equality of opportunity, is an exception to Article 16(1), and that 16(1) *itself*does not contemplate reservations in its guarantee of the equality of opportunity – because if it did, finding *another* source for the government's reservation-making power, in Article 46, would not make Article 16(4) redundant. In other words, the redundancy argument works only if we assume that Article 16(4) is the *source* of the government's power to make reservations, and from that it follows that Article 16(1) *cannot be.* This, precisely, is the ideal of colour-blindness that we discussed in the last post: even for remedial purposes, equality under the colour-blind theory does not permit classification on prohibited bases, and such classification can be justified only by carving out a specific constitutional exception (16(4)). Since Article 15 had no parallel 15(4), the Court struck down the Madras Government's policy.

Mandal Commission Report

The Mandal Commission was established in India in 1979 by the Janata Party government under Prime Minister Morarji Desai with a mandate to "identify the socially or educationally backward. It was headed by Indian parliamentarian *Bindheshwari Prasad Mandal* to consider the question of seat reservations and quotas for people to redress caste discrimination, and used eleven social, economic, and educational indicators to determine backwardness. In 1980, the commission's report affirmed the affirmative action practice under Indian law whereby members of lower castes (known as Other Backward Classes (OBC) and Scheduled Castes and Tribes) were given exclusive access to a certain portion of government jobs and slots in public universities, and recommended changes to these quotas, increasing them by 27% to 49.5%.

In **Mandal Commission II**, SC held that total number of reserved seats even after carrying forward of the unfilled seats by the candidates belonging to ST/SC/OBC group cannot be extended beyond 50%.

Suggestions given by Mandal Commission:

- Reservation of 27% jobs for backward classes
- Socially advanced layer i.e. creamy layer from the said backward class is to be excluded
- Reservations should confine to initial appointments and not to promotions
- Total reservation shall not exceed 50%

The **93rd Constitutional Amendment** allows the government to make special provisions for "advancement of any socially and educationally backward classes of citizens", including their admission in aided or unaided private educational institutions. Gradually this reservation policy is to be implemented in private institutions and companies as well. This move led to opposition from non-reserved category students, as the proposal reduced seats for the General (non-reserved) category from the existing 77.5% to less than 50.5% (since members of OBCs are also allowed to contest in the General category).

Scope of Article 15(4) and Article 16(4)

Article15(4) of our constitution empowers the government to make special provisions for advancement of backward classes. This was added by the Constitution (First Amendment) Act, 1951, as a result of the decision of the SC in ***State of Madras v.ChampakamDorairajan****13*. *"Nothing in this article or in clause (2) of Article 29 shall prevent the State from making any special provision for the advancement of any socially or educationally backward classes of citizens or for the Scheduled Castes and the Scheduled Tribes"*

The provision made in 15(4) is only an enabling provision and does not impose any obligation on the State to take any special action under it. It merely confers a discretion to act if necessary by way of making special provision for backward classes. A writ cannot be issued to the State to make reservation. The principle behind Article 15 (4) is that a preferential treatment can be given validly where socially and educationally backward classes need it. Article 15 (4) is not an exception but only makes a special application of the principle of reasonable classification.

Article 16(4)empowers the state to make special provision for the reservation of appointments of posts in favour of any backward class of citizens which in the opinion of the state are not adequately represented in the services under the State.

Thus two conditions have to be satisfied:

1. The class of citizens is backward
2. The said class is not adequately represented.

Clause (4-A) in Article 16 was added by **77th Amendment, 1955**. It empowers the state to make any provision for reservation in matters of promotions for SC and STs which, in the opinion of the State, are not adequately represented in the services under the State.

Legislature intended to nullify Supreme Court's decision in Mandal case by passing this amendment. The **Constitution (81st Amendment) Act, 2000** has added a new Clause (4-B) in Article 16 of the Constitution which seeks to end the 50% limit for SC and STs and other Backward Classes in backlog vacancies which could not be filled up due to the nonavailability of eligible candidates of these categories in the previous year or years. It has often been stated by various Indian Courts that Articles 15(4) and 16(4) do not guarantee a fundamental right to reservation and are merely enabling provisions. However, the march of aw includes a number of cases where views to the contrary have been expressed.

Equality and Reservation

Equality has been promised by State under Article 14 of the Indian Constitution and Article 14 is considered as the soul of the Indian Constitution because without equality no country can be considered as republic and it is the need of equality which have forced human beings to come under state so that they can get security, equal protection of law and equality in all aspects. In our Preamble, the word equality is derived from the *French Revolution* which itself shows the aims of our Constitution and Article 14 further is a step forward towards the accomplishment of that aim.

Equality itself means that like should be treated alike and not unlike should be treated like.That is why Article 14 permits reasonable classification between likes and unlike so that unlike should be given special treatment to bring them on the equal footing with the likes and in fact identical treatment in unequal circumstances would itself amount to inequality. Goal of equality will not be considered to be achieved till everyone will be on the equal footing. Thus idea to attain equality has given birth to the concept of reservation or affirmative action. Reservation is a special treatment given to the unlike till they come on the equal footing with the likes in the society. Reservation is a concept developed with a view to provide special help to the weak so that they can overcome their weakness and can compete with the strong.

In landmark judgments of ***D.V. Bakshi v. Union of India****28* and ***Air India v. NargeshMirza***, The Supreme Court's judgments have proved that inequality anywhere will never be tolerated and therefore Judgments of these cases have established new landmarks in the concept of Equality. Equality is a state of complete justice and in order to attain it reservation is a powerful remedy. Reservation have proved to be highly successful in many countries for e.g. United States has affirmative action for blacks and in various other countries reservation is playing major role in narrowing the gap between different classes. In the historic Mandal Commission case the Supreme Court by the 6-3 majority has held that the sub classification of the backward classes into more backward classes and backward classes can be done for the purpose of Article 16(4).**But as a result of sub classification the reservation cannot exceed more than 50 percent**. The distinction should be based on the degree of social backwardness. In fact such classification would be necessary to help the more backward classes otherwise those of the Backward Classes who are little more advanced than the more backward classes might take away all the seats.

> **"Thus reservation and equality are two sides of the same coin and if equality is the aim then reservation is the best possible way to reach that aim"**

Conclusion

If one takes a look at the issue objectively one will realize that the intention behind reservations is not faulty at all but it is the implication and the application of it that has proved ineffective. The way reservation has been implemented all these years has deepened and aggravated the caste distinctions in the society, marginalised the poor and the needy and has benefited only the topmost layer of the so called Backward classes. The benefit of reservation has failed to trickle down to the lowest section of the society. Moreover, it has killed the spirit of brotherhood and healthy competition, the desire to surge forward and to work hard. Reservations based on the narrow concept of caste are thus, fundamentally wrong and hence has proved to be a failure.

Thus, it is time to introspect, while keeping aside the greed of political mileage and think objectively about where things have gone wrong. It seems that nobody really cares about the welfare of the underdog but wants to gain a bit of the large chunk of political boost for the next elections. Reservation should not be forsaken because, in fact, everyone wants that society should develop as a whole and everyone should reap the benefits of development. But reservations instead of being caste-based to meet the political needs of our power hungry politicians should be based on a more acceptable criteria through which every section of the society is benefited. For instance, it can be based on economic status or anything else that can work truly for our society and state. We should take a lesson from the United States in this regard. It is the most market-oriented country and has a policy of affirmative action. US universities and the government give preference to Black and Hispanic applicants in admission as well as jobs. Yet the US economy remains among the most competitive in the world. The trick lies in undertaking affirmative action by providing incentives rather than quota-based restrictions.

References

1. *Sheth, D. L. (14 November 1987). "Reservations Policy Revisited". Economic and Political Weekly.* ***22*** *(46): 1957–1962. JSTOR 4377730.*
2. Laskar, Mehbubul Hassan. "Rethinking Reservation in Higher Education in India" (PDF). ILI Law Review. pp. 29–30. Archived from the original (PDF) on 25 April 2012.
3. *Menon, V. P. (1957). Transfer of Power in India (Reprinted ed.). Orient Blackswan. pp. 49–50. ISBN 978-81-250-0884-2.*
4. *"Human Development Report 2016" (PDF). UNDP. p. 119. Retrieved 21 March 2017.*
5. *Passin, Herbert (October 1955). "Untouchability in the Far East". Monumenta Nipponica.* ***11*** *(3): 247–267. doi:10.2307/2382914. JSTOR 2382914.*
6. *"Educational Safeguards" . Department of Education. Government of India. Archived from the original on 19 June 2009. Retrieved 27 November 2011.*

7. Bhattacharya, Amit (8 April 2006). "Who are the OBCs?" . The Times of India. Archived from the original on 27 June 2006. Retrieved 19 April 2006.

8. *Ramaiah, A. (6 June 1992). "Identifying Other Backward Classes" . Economic and Political Weekly. pp. 1203–1207. Archived from the original (PDF) on 30 December 2005. Retrieved 27 May 2006.*

9. *"Implementation of Recommendations of Mandal Commission". Parliament of India. Retrieved 4 November 2011.*

10. Article 15, Section 4 of the Constitution of India (1950)

Chapter - 15

Theme: Introductions 10% Reservation for EWS

— *Dr. Elisha Kolluri*

Abstract

Reservation is the process of facilitating people in education, scholarship, jobs etc. that were faced with historical injustice. It is the form of quota-based affirmative action. It is also governed by constitutional laws, statutory laws, local rules and regulations. The system of reservation in India constitutes a number of initiatives like reserving access to seats in the legislatures, to government jobs and to enrolment in higher educational institutions. The reservations is undertaken to resolve the historicoppression, inequality and discrimination suffered by those communities and to give them a place. It meant to achieve the promise of equality enshrined in the constitution. The main objective of the reservation system in India is to improve the social and educational status of underprivileged communities and thus improve their lives.This paper attempts to focus on social justice, social equality and social legitimacy of every unit of man in context of all men. Economically Weaker Sections (EWS) is a term used to refer to those citizens or households with income below a certain threshold level. Though there may be other economic factors in deciding on the economic weakness of the citizen/household, income is the dominant criterion. In public policy domain the term has to be appreciated in the context of the Preamble to India's Constitution which seeks Justice- social, economic and political. The Constitution (103rd Amendment) Act, 2019, which came into effect on January 14, 2019, has amended Articles 15 and 16 of the Constitution by adding two new clauses which empower the state to provide a maximum of 10 percent reservation for "economically weaker sections" (EWS) of citizens other than *the Scheduled Castes (SC), the Scheduled Tribes (ST) and the non-creamy layer of the Other Backward Classes (OBC-NCL).The proposed amendment Bill will define Economically Weaker Section (EWS) as one having:annual household income below Rs 8 lakh, agriculture land below 5 acres, residential house below 1000 sqft, residential plot below 100 yards in notified municipality, residential plot below 200 yards in non-notified municipality area.*

Key words:*Indian Constitution, Preamble, Reservations, Economically Weaker Section, Social and Educational status.*

Introduction

Meaning of Reservation

Reservation is the process of facilitating people in education, scholarship, jobs etc. that were faced with historical injustice. It is the form of quota-based affirmative action. It is also governed by constitutional laws, statutory laws, local rules and regulations. The system of reservation in India constitutes a number of initiatives like reserving access to seats in the legislatures, to government jobs and to enrolment in higher educational institutions.

Need of Reservation

The reservation is undertaken to resolve the historic oppression, inequality and discrimination suffered by those communities and to give them a place. It meant to achieve the promise of equality enshrined in the constitution. The main objective of the reservation system in India is to improve the social and educational status of underprivileged communities and thus improve their lives.

Historical background of Reservations

The system of reservation in India consists of a series of measures, such as reserving access to seats in the various legislatures, to government jobs, and to enrollment in higher educational institutions. The reservation nourishes the historically disadvantaged castes and tribes, listed as Scheduled Castes and Scheduled tribes (SCs and STs) by the Government of India, also those designated as Non-Creamy layer Other Backwards Classes (OBCs) and also the economically backward general. The reservation is undertaken to address the historic oppression, inequality, and discrimination faced by those communities and to give these communities a place. It is intended to realize the promise of equality enshrined in the Constitution.

The Constitution prohibits untouchability and obligates the state to make special provision for the betterment of the SCs and STs. Over the years, the categories for affirmative action, also known as positive discrimination, have been expanded beyond those to the OBCs.

Reservation is governed by the Constitution, statutory laws and local rules and regulations. The SCs, STs and OBCs, and in some states Backward Classes among Muslims under a category called BC(M), are the primary beneficiaries of the reservation policies. There have been protests from groups outside the system who feel that it is inequitable.

The primary objective of the reservation system in India is to enhance the social and educational status of underprivileged communities and thus improve their lives. The government of India believed that it was important to give benefits to people who have been historically denied access to social and economic resources so that they have a chance to establish a livelihood. The cost of these benefits would be paid by all taxpayers of India and international funding agencies such as World Bank, IMF and Asia development bank.

After the independence of India in 1947 there were some major initiatives in favour of the STs, SCs and after the 1980s in favour of OBCs.(Other Backward Castes)and in 2019 for poor general category. The country's affirmative action programme was launched in 1950 and is the oldest such programme in the world.

A common form of caste discrimination in India was the practice of untouchability. SCs were the primary targets of the practice, which was outlawed by the new Constitution of India.

In the year 1942, Dr. B.R Ambedkar established the all India depressed classes' federation to support the advancement of the scheduled castes. He demanded reservations for the Scheduled castes in government services as well as other sectors. However, in the year 1947, India obtained independence and Dr. B.R. Ambedkar was appointed chairman of the drafting committee for Indian Constitution. The India Constitution prohibits discrimination on the grounds only of religion, race, caste, sex and place of birth. While providing equality of opportunity for all citizens, the Constitution contains special clauses "for the advancement of any socially and educationally backward classes of citizens or for the Scheduled Castes and the Scheduled Tribes".

Separate constituencies allocated to scheduled castes and tribes to ensure their political representation for 10 years. It is significant to note that according to "the article 15(4) of constitution of India, which provides a constitutional basis for reservation in education, did not form part or the Constitution as it originally stood in 1950, although there was provision for reservation of appointments or posts in favour of any backward class of citizens under article 16(4). However, an equivalent of the current article 15(4) was the subject matter of considerable debate amongst the founding fathers of the constitution (Singh, S.N, 1996)".

In 1954, the Ministry of Education suggested that 20 percent of places should be reserved for the SCs and STs in educational institutions with a provision to relax minimum qualifying marks for admission by 5 percent wherever required. In 1982, it was specified that 15 percent and 7.5 percent of vacancies in public sector and government-aided educational institutes should be reserved for the SC and ST candidates, respectively.

A significant change began in 1978 when the Mandal Commission was established to assess the situation of the socially and educationally backward classes. The commission did not have exact population figures for the OBCs and so used data from the 1931 census, thus estimating the group's population at 52 percent. In 1980 the commission's report recommended that a reserved quota for OBCs of 27 percent should apply in respect of services and public sector bodies operated by the Union Government. It called for a similar change to admissions to institutes of higher education, except where states already had more generous requirements. It was not until the 1990s that the recommendations were implemented in Union Government jobs.In 2019 the government announces the 10% reservation in educational institutions and government jobs for economically weaker section of general category.

Reservations: The genesis and evolution

Even prior to India's independence and the provision of reservations in the Constitution, several princely states had in the 19th and early 20th century provided reservations in some form to lower castes.While the Scheduled Castes (SC) and Scheduled Tribes (ST) were able to avail reservations right after Independence; it took much longer for what was mandated in the Constitution to be implemented for the Other Backward Classes (OBCs).

Reservations for Scheduled Castes and Scheduled Tribes

Article 341 and Article 342 of the Constitution provides for the inclusion of groups under the SC and ST category. In 1956, lower castes from the Sikh community were included and considered as Scheduled Castes, whereas the neo Buddhists were included in 1990. Groups from the previously untouchable castes who converted to Islam and Christianity have not been included in the SC list.

Reservations in cases of promotions for SCs and STs

With a constitutional amendment in 1995, reservations were made available to SCs and STs in matters of promotion as well.The validity of this amendment was challenged in *M. Nagaraj vs Union of India 2006.* The court restricted the scope of the amendment by subjecting it to the concept of creamy layers. This was upheld in a 2018 Supreme Court judgement which upheld the application of creamy layer in matters of promotion.

Reservations for Other Backward Classes (OBC)

The first commission to investigate the possibility and details of providing reservations to OBCs was set up in 1953. They provided their report to the Central government in 1955, which didn't act on it, but asked several of the states to set up their lists of backward classes and fix quotas for them. Several states set up Backward Class Commissions, and provided reservations in public services and employment which varied in number from state to state.

The Second Backward commission was set up in 1978 which estimated the OBC population in the state to be around 52 percent and recommended 27 percent reservations for them. The report known as the Mandal Commission (headed by Bindeshwari Prasad Mandal) report was submitted to the government in 1980 but it wasn't until 1990 with the non-Congress Coalition government in place that the recommendations were implemented. Initially, reservations in public services of the central government came into force, whereas reservations in central higher educational institutions were implemented in 2006.Both the steps by the government were strongly resisted by the upper castes, with several mass protests, but got judicial backing. The courts while upholding 27 percent reservations put conditions and restricted the 'creamy layer' of OBCs from accessing reservation.

Reservations in private institutions

The 93rd Constitutional Amendment Act which came into force in 2006 paved the way for reservations in private institutions. The amendments insert a clause in Article 15 of the constitution and the clause states that special provisions can be made "for the advancement of socially and educationally backward classes of citizens or for the Scheduled Castes or the Scheduled Tribes in so far as such special provisions relate to the their admission to educational institutions including private educational institutions, whether aided or unaided by the State," except in minority institutions.While the provision is available in the Constitution, there has not been any legislative action taken by the Central government to mandate it. On January 15th, the government announced that reservations for SCs, STs, OBCs and EWS would be applicable for private institutions as well from the following academic year.

The percentage of reservations for various categories

15 percent and 7.5 percent of positions in central government services are reserved for SCs and STs respectively, while 27 percent are for OBCs. The same percentage also applies to seats in central educational institutions.

Economically Weaker Sections (EWS)

Economically Weaker Sections (EWS) is a term used to refer to those citizens or households with income below a certain threshold level. Though there may be other economic factors in deciding on the economic weakness of the citizen/household, income is the dominant criterion. In public policy domain the term has to be appreciated in the context of the Preamble to India's Constitution which seeks Justice- social, economic and political.

This categorization as EWS is distinct from other categories like "disadvantaged sections" which refer to those belonging to the Scheduled Caste/the Scheduled Tribe/other socially backward communities who may be having a disadvantage owing to social, cultural, geographical, linguistic, gender or such other factors.

There is no coherent single / unique definition for EWS in India. It is defined differently for different schemes run by the Government. Further, state and central (Union/Federal) governments may set different criteria for deciding on the EWS status. Governments periodically review and re-fix income ceiling levels for Economically Weaker Sections (EWS) to keep it relevant and contemporary.

Generally EWS status is confirmed based on the Income certificate issued by a Revenue Officer not below the rank of Tehsildar (Taluk office in-charge), BPL Ration card or Antodya Anna Yojna Ration Card (a ration card issued to the poorest of the poor) or Food Security Card issued by the state government concerned. In some places a legal affidavit is taken for the issue of EWS certificate.

The criterion of EWS is evoked while granting benefits under education or housing.

The proposed amendment Bill will define Economically Weaker Section (EWS) as one having:

- Annual household income below Rs 8 lakh.
- Agriculture land below 5 acres.
- Residential house below 1000 sqft.
- Residential plot below 100 yards in notified municipality.
- Residential plot below 200 yards in non-notified municipality area.

With the addition of 10 percent for EWS, as per the latest Constitutional Amendment Bill, the percentage of reservations in central government services and educational institutions will now be around 59.5 percentages.In reservation to services and educational institutions at the state level, the percentage for SCs, STs and OBCs vary from state to state based on the demographics. For example, in Arunachal Pradesh there is 45 percent reservation for STs, 1 percent reservation for SCs and no reservation for OBCs as there is no OBC population in the state. Most states in the north-eastern part of the country have higher reservation rates under STs. Himachal Pradesh and Punjab with 25 and 29 percent respectively are two of the state with comparatively higher reservations for SCs.

Following instructions are issued in consultation 'with' Ministry of Social Justice and Empowerment and Department of Legal Affairs regarding reservation for EWSs not covered under the reservation scheme for SCs/STs/OBCs in respect of direct recruitment in civil posts and services in' the Government of India.

Quantum of Reservation

The persons belonging to EWSs who, are not covered under the scheme of reservation for SCs, STs and OBCs shall get 10% reservation in direct recruitment in civil posts and services in the Government of India.

Exemption from Reservation

"Scientific and Technical" posts which satisfy the conditions mentioned shall be exempted.

Criteria for Income & Assets

Persons who are not covered under the scheme of reservation for SCs, STs and OBCs and whose family has a gross annual income below Rs 8 lakh (Rupees eight lakh only) are to be identified as EWSs for benefit of reservation. Income shall also include income from all sources i.e. salary, agriculture, business, profession, etc. for the financial year prior to the year of application.

Also, persons whose family owns or possesses any of the following assets shall be excluded from being identified as EWS, irrespective of the family income:-

1. 5 acres of agricultural land and above;
2. Residential at of 1000 sq ft. and above;
3. Residential plot of 100 sq. yards and above in notified municipalities;
4. Residential, plot of 200 sq. yards and above in areas other than the notified municipalities.

Income and Asset Certificate Issuing Authority and Verification of Certificate

Benefit of reservation under EWS can be availed upon production of an Income and Asset Certificate issued by a Competent Authority. The Income and Asset Certificate issued 'by any one of the following authorities in the prescribed format as given in Annexure-I shall only be accepted as proof of candidate's claim as 'belonging to EWS.

Effecting Reservation – Maintenance of Rosters

Department of Personnel and Training had circulated Office Memorandum No.36012/2/96-Estt (Res) dated July 2, 1997, regarding the implementation of post-based reservation roster. The general principles for making and operating post-based reservation roster would be as per the principles laid down in the said Office Memorandum.

Adjustment Against Unreserved Vacancies

A person belonging to EWS cannot be denied the right to compete for appointment against an unreserved vacancy. Persons belonging to EWS who are selected on the basis of merit and not on account of reservation are not to be counted towards the quota meant for reservation.

Fortnightly/Annual Reports Regarding Representation of EWS

The Ministries/Departments shall send single consolidated fortnightly report including their attached/subordinate offices beginning from 15.2.2019 as per format at Annexure-VL. From 01.01.2020, the Ministries/Departments shall upload data on the representation of EWSs in respect of posts/services under the Central Government on the URL i.e. www.rrcps.nic.inas on 1st January of every year. All Ministries/Departments have already been provided respective user code and password with guidelines for operating the URL.

Maintenance of Register of Complaints by the Government Establishment

Every Government establishment shall appoint a senior officer of the Department as the Grievance Redressal Officer.

Liaison Officer

Ministries/Departments/Attached and Subordinate Offices shall appoint Liaison Officer to monitor the implementation of reservation for EWSs.

The above scheme of the reservation will be effective in respect of all direct recruitment vacancies to be notified on or after 01.02.2019.

Reservations – Court Judgement

The Congress government under the leadership of P.V Narasimha Rao, which came to power in 1991, had added a notification for 10 percent Central reservation to sections of people who were economically backward and not covered under any existing schemes. However, the Supreme Court in the case of *Indra Sawnheyvs. Union of India 1992* struck this down while stating that economic criteria can't be the sole factor for backwardness, but it can be considered along with or in addition to social backwardness. In the same judgment, the apex court also said:

"Just as every power must be exercised reasonably and fairly, the power conferred by Clause (4) of Article 16 should also be exercised in a fair manner and within reasonably limits – and what is more reasonable than to say that reservation under Clause (4) shall not exceed 50% of the appointments or posts, barring certain extra-ordinary situations as explained hereinafter…

The provision under Article 16(4) – conceived in the interest of certain sections of society – should be balanced against the guarantee of equality enshrined in Clause (1) of Article 16 which is a guarantee held out to every citizen and to the entire society. It is relevant to point out that Dr. Ambedkar himself contemplated reservation being "confined to a minority of seats". No other member of the Constituent Assembly suggested otherwise. It is, thus clear that reservation of a majority of seats was never envisaged by the founding fathers. Nor are we satisfied that the present context requires us to depart from that concept."

However, the judgment also pointed out that while 50 percent shall be the rule, there could be certain extraordinary situations inherent in the diversity of India and its people that call for relaxation of the rule. But for that, extreme caution must be exercised and a special case made out.

Several groups including the Patidars in Gujarat, Jats in Haryana and Marathas in Maharashtra have in the recent past violently agitated for their inclusion in the state reservation quotas. Haryana had in 2016 passed a bill which created reservations for the Jats and five other groups by including them in a new category called 'backward classes'. This move was stayed by the High Court of Punjab and Haryana, which stated that reservations would then exceed the 50 percent limit set by the Supreme Court.

Recently in November 2018, the Maharashtra assembly unanimously passed a billwhich provided for 16 percent reservation in higher education and public services to the Maratha community. But similar reservation provided to the community in 2014 was stayed by the Bombay High Court, pointing to reservations exceeding 50 percent.

The Constitution of India states in article 15(4): "Nothing in [article 15] or in clause (2) of article 29 shall prevent the State from making any special provision for the advancement of any socially, educationally and economically backward classes of citizens of or for the Scheduled Castes and the Scheduled Tribes." Article 46 of the Constitution states that "The State shall promote with special care the educational and economic interests of the weaker sections of the people, and, in particular, of the Scheduled Castes and the Scheduled Tribes, and shall protect them from social injustice and all forms of exploitation."

The Supreme Court of India ruled in 1992 that reservations could not exceed 50 percent; anything above which it judged would violate equal access as guaranteed by the Constitution. It thus put a cap on reservations.However, the recent amendment of the constitution exceeds 50% and also there are state laws that exceed this 50 percent limit and these are under litigation in the Supreme Court.

The Constitution (103rd Amendment) Act, 2019, which came into effect on January 14, 2019, has amended Articles 15 and 16 of the Constitution by adding two new clauses which empower the state to provide a maximum of 10 percent reservation for "economically weaker sections" (EWS) of citizens *other than* the Scheduled Castes (SC), the Scheduled Tribes (ST) and the non-creamy layer of the Other Backward Classes (OBC-NCL).

The new clause (6) of Article 15 allows the state to make any "special provision" including reservation in admissions to educational institutions, whether aided or unaided, other than minority educational institutions under Article 30(1). The new clause (6) of Article 16 allows reservations in appointments or posts under the state.The reservation for the new category will be over and above the existing scheme of 15 per cent, 7.5 percent and 27 percent reservations respectively for the SC, ST and OBC-NCL, thus bringing the total reservations to 59.50 percent.

An 'Explanation' states that EWS shall be such as may be notified by the State from time to time based on family income and other indicators of economic disadvantage.In its Office Memorandum no. 20013/01/2018-BC-II dated January 17, 2019, the Ministry of Social Justice and Empowerment, Government of India has stipulated that only persons whose families have a gross annual income less than Rs.8 lakhs, or agricultural land less than 5 acres, or residential flat less than 1,000 sq. ft., or residential plots less than 100 sq. yards in notified Municipalities, or residential plots less than 200 sq. yards in areas other than notified Municipalities, are to be identified as EWS for the benefit of reservation.

It is true that the Supreme Court has repeatedly held that economic backwardness cannot be the sole criterion for reservation, and that reservation only provides a right of access for the under-represented classes and is not an anti-poverty programme. But those Supreme Court decisions involved testing legislation or an executive order against the Constitutional provisions as they existed then. They stand negated now that we have a Constitution amendment validating economic backwardness as the sole criterion for a new category of reservation.

It is also true that the Supreme Court has consistently ruled that for reservation to be reasonable and not defeat or nullify the main right to equality, the total reservations should not be greater than 50 percent. The Court has emphasized that this is not a mere rule of prudence but a binding rule. But this '50 percent ceiling' stands effectively breached by the latest Constitution amendment.

The fraught legal history of reservations in India shows that from 1951 onwards whenever the Supreme Court gave an adverse ruling on some aspect of reservations in education or public employment, the Parliament responded by amending the Constitution to reverse or overcome the inconvenient judicial pronouncements. The Constitution (103rd Amendment) Act, 2019, is the latest step in this direction to overcome the Supreme Court's bar on economic criteria for backwardness and the 50 per ceiling on total reservations.

The only possible legal challenge to the validity of the 103rd Amendment is a 'basic structure challenge'. In the landmark case of *Kesavananda Bharati vs State of Kerala* (1973), the Supreme Court ruled that the Parliament's power to amend the Constitution under Article 368 is not absolute and even a Constitutional amendment can be struck down if it has the effect of destroying or abrogating the 'basic structure' of the Constitution. The phrase is not to be found in the Constitution and is a judicial invention. The "doctrine of basic structure", also known as the "doctrine of constitutional identity", holds that there are certain systematic and structural principles such as the democratic form of government, republican form of government, federalism, equality, freedom, secularism, independence of the judiciary, power of judicial review and so on that form the core or the essence of the Constitution and give it a particular 'identity'. They are beyond the words of any particular Article, and underpin and connect several related Articles of the Constitution. They are part of the Constitutional law even if they are not expressly stated in the form of rules. They are beyond the amending power of the Parliament because amending them would amount to destroying the very identity of the Constitution.

In *Indira Nehru Gandhi v. Raj Narain* (1975), the Supreme Court ruled that the claim of any particular feature of the Constitution to be a 'basic feature' would be determined by the Court in each case that comes before it. So far, a multitude of features have been declared 'basic' by different Judges, individually, in different cases. However, this lack of unanimity has not stood in the way of the Supreme Court applying the basic structure doctrine in several cases.

It is pertinent to note that, out of the 72 Constitution Amendment Acts enacted since 1973 excluding the latest one, the Supreme Court has invoked the "basic structure" doctrine to strike down only seven of them, mostly in cases where the power of judicial review or the independence of the judiciary was threatened by a Constitutional amendment. While in six of these cases, only some parts of the Amendment Acts were struck down, the first time an entire Amendment Act was stuck down was the recent Constitution (99th Amendment) Act, 2015 relating to the replacement of the Collegiums' system by the National Judicial Appointments Commission. The Court has otherwise been loath to invalidate Constitutional amendments, especially those relating to reservations. For the legal challenge against the 103rd Amendment to succeed, one must therefore show that it has mangled the right to equality, which is part of the basic structure of the Constitution, beyond recognition.

The Constitution of India set out to redress the historic injustices and correct the manifest imbalance in matters of higher education and public employment by delineating an "equality code". Article 14 guarantees equality before the law and the equal protection of law for all persons. Article 15(1) prohibits discrimination of any citizen on grounds only of religion, race, caste, sex, or place of birth. Article 16(1) guarantees equality of opportunity for all citizens in matters of public employment. A related provision is Article 29(2) which prohibits denial of admission into any state-maintained or state -aided educational institution on grounds only of religion, race, caste or language.

On the other hand, clauses (3) to (5) of Article 15 and of Article 16, and Article 46 (which is part of the legally unenforceable Directive Principles of State Policy), are intended to promote substantive equality. They provide the basic framework for positive discrimination in favour of the grossly under-represented and pathetically neglected sections of the society. For instance, Article 15(4) provides for 'special provision' (which includes reservation) in admissions to educational institutions for "socially and educationally backward classes and for Scheduled Castes and Scheduled Tribes" while Article 16(4) provides for reservation in public employment for "backward classes" which are "not adequately represented in the services under the State". [The term "backward classes" in Article 16(4) includes SC and ST]. Article 46 urges the State to promote the educational and economic interests of the weaker sections, especially SC and ST, and protect them from social injustice and all forms of exploitation. All these Articles are group-centric because *in so far as individuals had suffered discrimination historically; it was because of their membership of certain groups* – as women, as lower castes and so on. There are two criticisms of such a group-based approach for reservations:

- It tends to reinforce and perpetuate group identities such as gender, caste or race instead of rendering them irrelevant. The counter-argument is that given the way discrimination has played out historically, a group-based approach is unavoidable and a necessary evil. You cannot remedy discrimination based on gender except by taking gender into account; ditto for caste and race. Even though the Constitution of India has used the word 'class' instead of 'caste' for defining a beneficiary group eligible for reservation, there is doctrinal disarray among different rulings of the Supreme Court which have held caste as a 'relevant criterion', 'sole criterion' or 'dominant criterion' for defining a class.

- While there is little dispute regarding the identification of SC and ST and the historic, institutionalized discrimination against these two groups, the conditions of victimization suffered by the various Shudra castes are matters of degree with a wide range of variation. Inclusion of a Shudra caste in the OBC category generates reasonable claims for inclusion of other caste(s) 'on the margin', and any cut-off is likely to be perceived as arbitrary and unfair. There is also the problem of dominant castes/individuals within the OBC cornering all or most of the benefits. This can be remedied by applying the concept of 'creamy layer' whereby persons having income or assets greater than specified limits are excluded from the benefits of reservation.

Conclusion

"With a view to fulfil the mandate of Article 46, and to ensure that economically weaker sections of citizens get a fair chance of receiving higher education and participation in employment in the services of the State, it has been decided to amend the Constitution of India," the statement of objects of the bill said.

References

1. Sheth, D. L. (14 November 1987). "Reservations Policy Revisited". Economic and Political Weekly. 22 (46): 1957–1962. JSTOR 4377730.
2. Jump up to: Laskar, Mehbubul Hassan. "Rethinking Reservation in Higher Education in India" (PDF). ILI Law Review. pp. 29–30. Archived from the original (PDF) on 25 April 2012.
3. Menon, V. P. (1957). Transfer of Power in India (Reprinted ed.). Orient Blackswan. pp. 49–50. ISBN 978-81-250-0884-2.
4. "Human Development Report 2016" (PDF). UNDP. p. 119. Retrieved 21 March 2017.
5. Passin, Herbert (October 1955). "Untouchability in the Far East". Monumenta Nipponica. 11 (3):247267.doi:10.2307/2382914. JSTOR 2382914. (Subscription required (help)).
5. "Educational Safeguards". Department of Education. Government of India. Archived from the original on 19 June 2009. Retrieved 2011-11-27.
6. Jump up to: Bhattacharya, Amit (8 April 2006). "Who are the OBCs?". The Times of India. Archived from the original on 27 June 2006. Retrieved 2006-04-19.

7. Ramaiah, A. (6 June 1992). "Identifying Other Backward Classes" (PDF). Economic and Political Weekly. pp. 1203–1207. Archived from the original (PDF) on 30 December 2005. Retrieved 2006-05-27.
8. "Implementation of Recommendations of Mandal Commission". Parliament of India. Retrieved 2011-11-04.
9. Article 15, Section 4 of the Constitution of India (1950)
10. Article 46, Section 0 of the Constitution of India (1950)
11. "BJP's OBC pitch: How stronger new backward classes panel will function".
12. "Seventy Seventh Amendment". *Indiacode.nic.in*. Retrieved 2011-11-19.
13. "Eighty Fifth Amendment". *Indiacode.nic.in. 4 January 2002*. Retrieved 2011-11-19.
14. "Eighty First Amendment". *Indiacode.nic.in. 29 August 1997*. Retrieved 2011-11-19.
15. "Eighty Second Amendment". *Indiacode.nic.in*. Retrieved 2011-11-19.
16. ET Explains: What is Constitution (One Hundred And Twenty-Fourth Amendment) Bill, 2019?, The Economic Times, 9 January 2019.
17. In-depth: Who is eligible for the new reservation quota for general category?, Business Today, 8 January 2019.
18. "Challenge to reservation for economically poor". *1, Law Street. 2019-02-11*. Retrieved 2019-02-20.
19. Office Memorandum, ncbc.nic.in, pp. 7–8.

Chapter - 16

Representation of Muslim Women in Urban Local Politics: A study of Greater Hyderabad Municipal Corporation

— *Dr. Pallavi Kabde*

Abstract

In the era of urbanisation, the role of Urban Local Government assumes a great importance in the proper management of urban areas. The core function of the Urban Government includes the provision of sufficient, affordable and quality basic services . Public services have an immense potential to create more equal societies and bridge the gap of social and economic inequalities. There are certain areas where women can play a catalytic role in promoting the causes of social development . But women in the politics of Urban Local bodies, always took a back seat. They have a very limited role in the urban governance.

The discriminatory practices, social norms and cultural perceptions limit women's involvement in politics. Family and child care responsibilities hamper the political aspirations of many women. Thus the reservation for women in the local bodies is aimed at securing their active involvement and support in socio-economic development. With the passing of 74th constitutional amendment act we witnessed, one-third of the seats were occupied by women in urban local bodies and now the wheel has turned, as this has been enhanced to fifty percent in most of the states including Telangana.

The present paper **"Women in Urban Governance: Em'POWER'ed or 'POWER' less**"?? *is an empirical study. It is an attempt to study the representation of muslim minority women in urban governance of Greater Hyderabad Municipal Corporation. Though fifty percent of the seats were reserved for the women in GHMC elections- 2016, more than fifty percent of the women were elected. This has definitely improved the numbers of the women in Governance but has it enhanced their role in Urban Governance and Decision Making is a question to be answered. Hence this study is made to examine whether reservation of women in urban local bodies is empowering them or making them powerless inspite of having the power in their hands.*

Introduction

The role of Urban Local Government assumes importance in the proper management of urban areas. But in the politics of Urban Local bodies, women always took a back seat. The discriminatory practices, social norms and cultural perceptions limit women's involvement in politics. Family and Child care responsibilities hampers the political aspirations of many women. With the passing of 74th constitutional amendment act we witnessed, one-third of the seats were occupied by women in urban local bodies and now the wheel has turned, as this has been enhanced to fifty percent in most of the states including Telangana.

The interesting consequence of this development is observed in the Greater Corporations of Hyderabad and Bangalore, where more than fifty percent of the seats are occupied by the women. If we take the case of BBMP i.e Bruhat Bengaluru Mahanagara Paalika out of 198 corporators, 101 are women and men corporators are only 97.

Greater Hyderabad Municipal Corporation (GHMC)

After the formation of the State of Andhra Pradesh In 1956, Hyderabad was designated as its Capital. Hyderabad Municipal Corporation is formed in 1955 for civic administration and infrastructure development in the city and collection of taxes. Its area was 173 sq.kms. The city was then divided into 4 zones and 7 circles. The Greater Hyderabad Municipal Corporation was formed on 16 April 2007 by merging 12 municipalities and 8 gram panchayats with the erstwhile Municipal Corporation of Hyderabad. The municipalities that were merged are: L. B. Nagar, Gaddi annaram, Uppal Kalan, Malkajgiri, Kapra, Alwal, Qutubullapur, Kukatpally, Serilingampalle, Rajendranagar, Ramachandrapuram and Patancheru. All these municipalities are in Rangareddy district. The merged panchayats are: Shamshabad, Satamarai, Jallapalli, Mamdipalli, Mankhal, Almasguda, Sardanagar and Ravirala.

The greater Hyderabad covers an area of 650 square kilometers and has a population of 6,809,970, making it the fourth largest city in India while the population of the urban agglomeration is 7,749,334. Greater Hyderabad Municipal Corporation is divided into five zones - East, West, North, South and Central. Further five zones are divided into 18 circles.

- East Zone: Kapra is Circle 1, Uppal 2; LB Nagar & Gaddiannaram are under Circle 3.

- South Zone: Erstwhile Circle 1 under MCH is Circle 4, old Circle 2 is Circle 5, and Rajendranagar is Circle 6.
- Central Zone: Old Circle 4 is Circle 7, old Circle 6 is Circle 8, old Circle 3 is Circle 9 & old Circle 5 is Circle 10.
- West Zone: Serilingampally (south) is Circle 11, Serilingampally (north) is Circle 12, Ramachandrapuram & Patancheru are under Circle 13 and Kukatpally is under Circle 14.
- North Zone: Qutbullapur is Circle 15, Alwal is Circle 16, Malkajgiri is Circle 17 & Secunderabad division comes under Circle 18.

As a result of 50% of reservation in the GHMC Elections, 50% the total 150 divisions of Greater Hyderabad were reserved for Women Candidates in the last GHMC Elections i.e 75 divisions. But the total number of Women Corporators in GHMC is 79 more than the Men Corporators. Though 75 women Corporators have won from the reserved divisions, 4 women have won from general category. Among 79 women corporators, 21 are Muslim women corporators.

The 21 divisions from where muslim women corporators have won are Azampura (GW), Allahpur (GW), Moulali (GW), Langerhouz (GW), Moghalpura (GW), Old Malakpet (BCW), Nawabsahebkunta (BCW), Erragadda (BCW), Chintal (BCW), Golconda (BCW), Toli Chowki (BCW), Sulemannagar (BCW), Asifnagar (BCW), Ahmednagar (BCW), Mallepalli (BCW), Vijayanagar Colony (BCW), Red Hills (BCW), Barkas (BCW), Kanchanbagh (BCW), Talab chanchal (BCW), Kurmaguda (BCW). If we observe the demography of these areas, they are mostly muslim populated areas.

In total 5 Muslim Corporators have won from General women reserved divisions, 16 Muslim Women Corporators have from BC Women Reserved Divisions. Three of them belong to Ruling Party and rest of the 18 Muslim women corporators belong to AIMIM.

The Muslim Women Corporators constitute 27% of the total Women Corporators and this number has gone up when compared to the last GHMC elections where only 10 Muslim women corporators were elected. The rise in number is obviously with the increase in reservation quota for women.

This study is an attempt to study the background of the elected Muslim women corporators of GHMC, their motivation for being into politics, their vision for development and their struggle.

For this purpose, the official contact numbers of these women corporators from GHMC Office were collected and an attempt was made to contact them.The telephonic interview of Muslim Women Corporators.

All the 21 muslim women corporators were contacted but depending upon the access to them few observations were made.

(i) Three of the corporators could come into direct contact .

(ii) Two of the corporators's phones were with husband but later they spoke through other number. One corporator's Phone was with husband and the other was with father.

(iii) Nine of the corporators's Phones were either with the with Husband/Brother/Father-in-law. They spoke on the behalf of their female family member who was corporator

(iv) Five Corporators's Phones were with husbands. I was asked to call later. Again and again but neither they spoke nor they let their wives speak

(v) Two of the corporators never answered.

It is observed that there is a relation between the corporator possessing mobile phone and answering the call and their political empowerment.

The first group of Corporators who responded over phone are three in number.

- The three corporators who had phone with them are highly self-motivated without any influence of other family members.
- They didn't have any family background in politics
- They are into higher education. One has done double PG,one in Social Work and other in English. She has applied for Ph.D as well in Osmania University.
- The other corporator has done LLB and now pursuing LLM. The third corporator is pursuing graduation from Dr.B.R.Ambedkar Open University.
- They are strong aspirants of politics, have vision for development and concern for the problems of the people in general and muslim women in particular.
- In fact the corporator who has done double PG has even developed Ward Development Plan and is looking forward for the association with the different learned people of the society.

Two corporators are categorised into second group

- They are well qualified. One is a graduate and other is pursuing post graduation in Pharmacy. Their phones were with husband and father.
- Husband and father were in politics since very long.
- The male family members are very actively involved in politics even now.
- Due to reservation of seat, they were made to contest.
- But these two corporators have political interest though it has been developed later.
- They have a clear understanding of the problems of their division and they are confident that they are going to solve the problems of people and especially musim women.

Nine corporators are grouped into third group, whose phones are with husbands.

- The husbands of respective corporators didn't feel it is important for their wife to speak
- They all are in politics. They let their wife to contest only because the seat is researved for women.

Some of the phrases which they used to express their agony are

- Madam.. voh house wife hain kya baat kareinge. (Madam ..She is house wife, what will she speak)
- Madam.. unhe kuch maloom nahi.. hum hi sab dekhte hai.. (she doesn't know anything madam, it is me who looks after all the affairs)
- Madam.. app ko kya puchna hai .. hame puchiye..(Whatever you want to ask, you ask. I will answer).
- Majboori.. Madam... Majboori.. Ladies reservation ki vajhe se unko bahar laana pada. (Since the seat is reserved for women, we are compelled to bring our women out)
- Hamare usme aurtan bahar nahi ate.. phir bhi reservation hai bolke..voh politics mein aye.. hum ko ana tha..asal mein.. (Women are not supposed to come out in our community but for reservation she is into politics. Otherwise I would have been into politics)

They confessed that it is they who take the decisions on behalf of their wife/daughter. It is astonishing to know that few women corporators go only to meetings and all the issues are dealt with their male family members.

Even the interaction withj the public is not done by the women corporators themselves. Except signing.

Fourth group comprise of five corporators whose phones are always with husbands. They asked me to call later, when called again the same answer. Later most of them stopped answering.

Finally Two of them are grouped into fifth group who never answered to the calls.

With this study it can be concluded that mere reservations will not empower women politically, though it is a beginning, it is a first step towards political empowerment. When they come out definitely, they have to interact with the people, know their problems, try to bring out possible solutions.

Women can play a positive and supportive role who would facilitate movement against discrimination and struggle to gain gender equality. Women urban leadership can play a very vital role in civic matters, development of the city and improving the quality of life of the citizens particularly the marginalised sections of the society .As many of the muslim women corporators are first time into the governance, a strong support system is required from all the levels of the governance. No doubt reservation of women increases the representation of the women in the governance but there is a need to create a suitable environment for the women political representatives to enable them to play their roles effectively. The participation and interference of their male counterparts must be checked and minismised to allow the women corporators to use their capacities to the fullest and discharge their duties to their best. It is the time to make them function responsively as public representatives, policy makers and change agents.

We need to remember that "***Hands which can rock the cradle .. can definitely rule the world***"

References

Prasad, D. Ravindra. "Women empowerment in urban governance in India." *Indian Journal of Public Administration* 60.3 (2014): 426-442.

https://www.ghmc.gov.in/Elections.aspx

Chapter - 17

Historical specificities of Reservation and 'Social Justice': A Hermeneutic Reading.

— *Reshma R.N*[1]

Abstract

In this paper an attempt has been made for an historical exploration and Hermeneutic reading of the text and contextuality of the concept of reservation. Can social and economic justice be reconciled with the contemporary democratic principles? This is what is attempted to delve into here. In recent decades, this question has been at the forefront of academic and political debate .Social Justice theories are yet to catch up with experience and social realities. The current understanding of social justice is that is a mandatory and progressive concept and the value of social justice can be taken as criterion for radical social change in public sphere. Given the current global condition, social justice must include an understanding of the interactions within and between a multitude of people.

This paper investigates whether and, if so, to what extent, state's policy of reservation and choice of social justice principles are related to the type of Globalized state regime they live under, as well as to relook the most crucial policy formulations across the span three phases in India. The first part deals with Pre-independent period - how the British government policies were working for the Compensatory Discrimination programmes and its implementation upon the Indian society. The second part studies the Post-independent period - in terms of specifying the impact and role of lower caste movements in 'colonial' India and the third phase analyses the emerging manifestations of reservation.

Key Words: *Compensatory Discrimination Lower Caste Movements, Social Justice, Constitutional Debates.*

Introduction

State and the state system are basic features of modern system. It is important to address the state system as an historical institution. It has been routed by certain people at a certain time. The state system has been a central institution of Indian politics for a very long time ,and still remains so. Even though the history of a policy is a part of world politics and state politics, states and the state system have always managed to adapt to significant historical change.

History therefore, is like the life sketch of society and knowledge about the relationship between social institutions. Life sketches are judged from the vantage point of internal and external development of a society. Indias colonial social past has been shaped by caste (Jatis) hierarchy and Varna system. Reservation in Ancient period saw the Hindu social structure divided into four Varna, or classes, a convention which had its origins in the Rig Veda, the first and most essential set of hymns in Hindu scripture which dates back to 1500-1000 B.C.3 At the top of the hierarchy are the Brahmins, or priests, followed by the Kshatriyas, or warriors. The Vaisya, the farmers and artisans, represent the third class. At the bottom are the Shudras, the class responsible for serving the three higher groups (Galanter 1984: 10). Finally, the Untouchables fall completely outside this system. Under the caste system the Brahmin occupied top of the hierarchy whereas the former untouchable occupied the lowest position in the society. The untouchables known as scheduled castes are the lowest ranked not only in term of social position but also in term of economy, education and so on. Apart from the scheduled castes and another community of Indian society which is considered as most deprived economically, educationally etc. are the Scheduled tribes. There are also many other backward castes or other backward classes who occupy the low positions in the society.

The first part looks at the 'historicality' of societal experiences on reservation, it is basically produced by human action. Three different actions in historical alphabets are practiced before pre-independent period, Post-independent period and contemporary arena such as:

1. Individual
2. Society
3. State

Going back to history, in the pre-colonial period historical consciousness led society in a new form of analysis. There are three levels of Action in the history of reservation and the first and foremost one is individual oriented actions. Every individual is abstracted from their personal, social, economic contexts. The first or so called stage is natural phenomena and is explained as the result of individual analogies. The individualistic postulates of history undermines its social content.

Secondly, society oriented actions. Society is the primary source of substance of human life. In providing a more graphical replica, society is a verticality, it means vertical relation between two axis. Multiple institutions intersects each other in grid line formation. These coherent, bounded intersecting zone creates zone of equality and social justice in Society when it comes to humans. Caste, Language, Religion, etc are the important source of their social actions or their existence. However, the has been many lower Caste movements throughout history that has continuously changed the society.

Thirdly, when understanding State oriented actions we can see that the state was given some amount of attention to accomplish the objectives of individual, and society within the parameters set trough the rulers in India. The social roles taken upon by the state is being increasingly abrogated. In the case of reservation the individual, society, and state are more dependent to each other. Instead of being an authority, state acts as an instrument of social, economic and political development.

Reservation is aims to taken by the state to remove persistent and continuous discrimination on a particular section of the society. Its aims to provide access to equal opportunities and thereby grants full participation in the governance of the country. It also helps to overcome the chronic under representation of a particular social group in the government machinery. Reservation start equal steps forward of these three segment of actions together.

In the 1950s Professor Alexandrowicz proposed 'protective discrimination' and later, Marc Galanter called it as 'compensatory discrimination' (Galanter Marc 1984 42). It has been adopted by the borrowed American term 'affirmative action' which began to be used in the early 1980s. In article 15 or article 29(2) of the India constitution states that, it shall prevent the state from making any special provisions for the advancement of any socially and educationally backward classes of citizens or for the scheduled castes and the scheduled tribes. But these, along with specific provisions for reservation of seats in legislative bodies are the core of the constitutional commitment to compensatory discrimination.

The principle of '*Reservation*' as ideologically build up by B R Ambedkar and Periyar Ramaswamy during the nationalist period was meant to create an educated intellectual group that emerges out of the historically oppressed castes. Right from the times of the Kautilya state and Manu's legal code, Brahmanism had denied the oppressed castes access to education and employment.

Sites of Colonial Contestations Phase I: Pre Independence

In colonial period, those who work in the field and produce the food of the soil were considered as socially low or backward communities and were not allowed to own any money land, wage ect. State land were settled with working class (Shudras, labouring and polluted caste at the bottom) and in return they had to pay one fourth of the produce to the state. The life of the low caste or the untouchables, backward communities who worked on the land became increasingly miserable. The poor peasants who were from the low castes faced huge problems and suffering because they were forced to produce surplus to pay high rents and often expressed their disturbance and disappointment through revolts. However, the revolts from their side are considered as the turning point for attaining their livelihood.

How do we trace the intellectual history of reservation policies in india, and what are its connections, resonance and intersections. Reservation system in india is deeply connected with caste hierarchy or society oriented actions. At the time when caste practices was gaining ground, colonial historical evidence had reached its peak in the subcontinent also. Ideas about the racial outlook is important for British rulers and foreigners. The 'Rule of colonial Difference' (Partha Chatterjee) in Reservation policies. Public Sphere dominated by European residents of the Country.

The Colonial kaleidoscope of reservation policies has been vogue for centuries, in the different way of convergence and divergence treatment of people in a same paradigm. Anyway, racial imprints of individual is one of the crucial factors for defined hierarchy in each society. Racial interpretation of caste were derived from European interpretation of Indian society beginning with William Jones in eighteenth century. Bayly point out that many pre independence ethnographers from Britain portrayed India as a composite social landscape in which only certain peoples, those of superior Aryan blood, had evolved historically in ways which left them 'shackled' by a hierarchical, Brahminically -defined ideology of caste. At the same time large numbers of other Indians -those identified in varying racial terms term's as Dravidians, as members of 'servile' classes. aborigines, wild tribes and those of so-called 'mixed -racial' origins were portrayed as being ethnologically distinct from this so called Aryan population, and were not all thought to belong to a ranked Brahmincal caste order (Kannabiran 2012 :150).

Obviously, Reservation policy had occurred in India in both the recent and distant past, but somehow the groups of the latter half of the 19th century were perceived Differently and hence represented differently.

The year 1600 is turning point for the history of india. It should be remembered that selection and recruitment are packages are part of a much larger policy. it comprises a series of governmentalization (Kothari 1970: 287), legislations, ameliorative steps and selection criteria in Indian society. The pre-British record and British East india company, after establishing their power in Bengal in 1765. In 1867-71 a nationwide census operation was undertaken for the first. The British regime in India was largely responsible for both positive and suspicious role in the making of rules and regulations regarding reservation. Government then assumed the role of promoter and protector of the interest of the disadvantaged groups or minorities (Government is protector of group rights).

In the late nineteenth century, after the British merge as a authoritative hold on substantial parts of subcontinent, their initial strategies was one of 'non-interference'. which meant recognition of established social order, but no conscious attempt to change it. (Galanter: 1984). The caste practices and continuous movements in colonial era witnessed the expansion of group quotas in government employment. Caste based reservation or inclusion of caste as an indicator of selection first introduced in 19th century to deal with the Brahmin predominance in the public services.

Christian missionaries recognized the problems of depressed classes. Accordingly, they provided welfare schemes for untouchables for their upliftment was considered as one of the most spectacular start up by the missionaries. This initiative influenced Hindu reformers inevitably the attention and assistance turned back to reformers like Jyothiba Phule of Maharashtra, who along with his wife Savithribai gave special attention on education for untouchables (Chitnis 94). Thus in 1880 s British government started scholarship, schools, and other programmes and policies according to their needs. These, initial steps contributed a grand deal towards awakening to disadvantaged groups and promoting the level of literacy. (Ibid).

The Hunter Commission was appointed in 1882.and the reports of the Commission highlights the fact that special measures were undertaken to uplift backward castes and bring on par with other sections of society. Mahatma Jyothirao Phule made a demand for free and compulsory education for all caste along with proportionate reservation or representation in government jobs.

Thus, the Government of India passed a resolution on the 4th December 1886 to appoint a Commission. Thus, the best statute during British period, the commission headed by Sir Charles Aitchison, Lt. Governor of the Punjab. The commission ,included number of Indian natives suffered the problems of statutory civil service. However the objective of the British rulers behind the appointments in bureaucracy was quite different. The commission was entrusted with the work to examine the causes of dissatisfaction of Indians with the statutory system and to examine the system under which natives of India.

Pre-independence period the positive discrimination favoring specific caste groups and other communities existed before independence in several areas of British India. The demands for reservation in education and employment had been made for example in 1882and 1891. Jyothirao Phule of Poona advocated adequate representation for members of all castes in the public services. His demand went unheeded till the 1880's when Shau Chatarapati, the king of princely state of Kolhapur introduced reservation in favor of Non-Brahmin and backward classes under the Montague Chelmsford Reforms (Sharma 1982: 2). Which came into force in 1902. He advocated free education to everyone and opened hostel fecilities. He also attempted to ensure that people thus educated were suitably employed and he appealed both for a caste free India and eradication of untouchability. His 1902 recommendation created 50 %reservation for backward communities.

In British India, the Punjab government start a pioneer step in the 1880s a policy of equilibrium in Hindu and Muslim numbers in the administration. In 1925, the Indian Government declared it would reserve a portion of civil service jobs for the redress of communal inequalities. Twenty five per cent of the posts to be filled by the direct recruitment of Indians were earmarked for Muslims and 8.3 per cent for other minority communities. In 1937 Governors of several British provinces were issued with directions under the Government of India Act of 1935, to secure a due proportion of appointments in our services to the several communities, but proportions were not specified. (Bajpai 2011: 36).

In Madras, a public Service Commission was established under the PSC Act of 1929 for the recruitment to the provincial and subordinate services or the province. The recruitment in PSC has evolved before over a long period of time, which was constituted in October 1926 at the centre. This initial start up was in resolution to the provision made in section 96(C) of the Government of India Act of 1919 and the proposal of Lea commission.

The initial steps of Simon Commission started in November 1927 as a component of the section 84 of the Government of India Act of 1919. However, the commission was created two years back under Sir John Simon. In the colonized space this report was a product of the legal and policy framework of colonial regime. It demarcated a separate electorates for minorities. Despite the protest by the Indians, the Simon Commission continued its work and submitted its Report in June 1930. The colonial response to this report perceived as a new debate in the Public realm.

The mid measure of reform introduced by the British and known as the Indian Council Act of 1909. Accordingly, the act overemphasize communal and special criteria for other classes for representation in the councils: landowners and Muslims. In 1933, seperate electorate for untouchables also were to be introduced. Ambedkar (1891-1956) standing as chief spokesman for the 'Depressed' was endorsed by the colonial authorities with his appointment as a delegate to the first Indo-British Round Table Conference, which are convened in 1930 to deliberate further constitutional change for India (Bayly 1999: 262). Dr. Ambedkar in his first statement to the Southborough committee in 1919 at the first reform in the government of india act of 1919. Again ten years later as serious step was made to revise the 1919 Act, though a serious Round Table Conferences. after that, Ambedkar submitted two statements to the Simon Commission in 29th May 1928. In 1932, Gandhi and Ambedkar agreed on a compromise constitutional development stategies, the so called Poona Pact. During the Round Table conferences from 1930 to 1932 he made various interventions through memorandums in the meetings of the conferences which ultimately led to acceptance of reservation policy in the central and state legislatures.

Site of Contestation Phase II: Post - Independence

India gained her independence from Great Britain in 1947, and became a Republic in 1950. The new Indian state's legal quality was a real replica on British lines - establishment of a parliamentary democracy with the President as the titular head of state, while the legal system was constituted according to common-law traditions (Nagarajan 2009: 490).

The history of reservation policy has been a flash point during Muslim League demand for separate electorate as for the reports of reserved seats in legislature for Muslims, Indian Christians, Scheduled Castes, and Tribes in proportion to the population of these communities for a period of ten years (Bajpai 2011: 118). Post-independent period is in transitional stage. Modern democracies provide citizens with superior social and political rights, a higher standard of living, more leisure and better educational and employment opportunities. The extension to these benefits to more and more citizens during the past hundred years or so has been described as the process of the growth of citizenship or 'basic human equality'. The fundamental rights due to individual by virtue of their membership in a state as the rights are so essential to the well-being of an individual.

The first and foremost spontaneity in history of reservation was it investigates the possibilities of institutional expressions in India. However, as a result of the dynamics of democratic polity developed several commissions with strong terms of reference are analyzed in broad context of revolutionary change in the politics of reservation policies. Policy of reservation is a 'reform measure' (Choudhary 1991: 105). If the democratic potential of the committees and commissions debated the question and significance in detail. The fact of the matter is that commissions were also indented to as machinery for canvassing people. Other Backward Classes credited a fresh debate on the merit of a caste-based reservation policy that was introduced first by the British colonial government in India and retained and re-figureised by the post-Independence nationalist elite as a policy of socio-economic upliftment of the different sections of the society.

The Constituent Assembly Debates in Parliament

The Indian democracy, in search of both formal and substantive equality, had to address on an urgent basis the cause of the historically disadvantaged groups. Whereas the requirements of formal equality meant the equal protection of law against discrimination on morally insidious grounds, the requirements of substantive equality meant recognizing the needs of the more disadvantaged. Both of these commitments run parallel in the constitution. In order to fulfill these requirements, the following provisions have been made in the Indian Constitution. The Constituent Assembly debates, it has been most appropriate technique for framing the framing of the constitution of India.

As the leader of the Congress Party in the Constituent Assembly of India, Jawahar Lal Nehru moved a historic resolution on the aims and objectives of the constitution. The resolution stated that: "Wherein shall be guranteed and secured to all the people of India, justice, social, economic, and political, equality, of status, and opportunity before the law, freedom of thought, expression, belief, faith, worship, vocation, association, and action, subject to law and public morality, and wherein adequate safeguards shall be provided for minorities, backward and tribal areas and depressed and other backward classes (CAD Vol. III: 696-697).

Andre Betelie has explained that the plea for giving all sections of society a fair chance rather than making merit the sole criterion was argued constituently in the Constituent Assembly debates on the equality provisions.

One of the Harijan member said, The Government can expect necessary qualification or personality from the Harijans, but not merit. If you take merit alone into account ,the Harijans cannot move forward other members spoke about the special 'needs' of Harijans as a whole and the various measures that might be adopted to meet them.

Nothing herein contained shall prevent the State from making provision for reservations in favour of classes who, in the opinion of the State, are not adequately represented in the public services. (CAD 29, April 1947: 47).

The vocabulary of constituent assembly primarily two fold opinions, i.e, Indian Nationalist, Majority vs. Minority opinions (Bajpai 2011: 71). The chain of events committees commissions centering around the name of reservation, In 1986 to 1990 (this period called as 'moment of crisis' Bajpai 2011: 173) saw a key changes in policies of group rights ad preferential policies in India. State Backward Class Commission Andra Pradesh, Bihar, Delhi, Gujarat, Haryana, Jammu and Kashmir, Karnataka, Kerala, Madhya Pradesh, Maharashtra, Manipur, Orrisa, Rjasthan, Thamil Nadu, and Utter Pradesh set up commissions and Committees for defining criteria for Social and educational backwardness and recommending measures for its removal.

Commissions and Committee: Analysis

The First Backward Class Commission

The backward classes are the largest groups in India including SC/ST/OBC. In pre-independent period Constitution does not define backward classes in India. However, in Article 340 of the Constitution, it is mentioned that a Commission can be appointed to investigate the conditions of backward classes, which could propose measures to be taken by Central or State Governments in order to improve their condition. Such a Commission was appointed on January 29th 1953 under the chairmanship of Kaka Saheb Kalelkar, and it submitted its report on March 30th 1955. The commission issued a set of 182 questions for identifying the position of state government and the general public on various aspects of its inquiry.

Some noteworthy recommendations of the commission were: (i) Undertaking caste-wise enumeration of population in the census of 1961. (ii) Relating social backwardness of the class to its low position in the traditional caste hierarchy of Hindu society. (iii) Treating all women as a class or backward. (iv) Minimum reservation of vacancies in all Government services and local bodies for other backward classes on the following scale:- 25% in class 133.3% in class II, 40% in class II and IV. (Report of First Backward Class Commission 1955: 1)

In fact, Kalelkar commission was established to assess the situation of the socially and educationally backward classes. The report was accepted as far as Scheduled Castes and Scheduled Tribes were concerned and schedules were amended accordingly. However, its recommendations for OBC's were rejected. Thus, the commission emancipates the unprivileged rather than privileged. Previously, position of negation of communities starts from here. This negated position of communities has gone deep into economic, social, polictical facets of the Indian society. Kakasaheb Kalelkar argued that, "I am definitely against reservation in Government Services for any community, for the simple reason that the services are not meant for the servants bit as it is for the society as a whole. Administration must have the service of the best men available in the land and these may be found in all communities. Reservation for posts for certain backward communities would be as strange as reservation of patients for particular doctors." (Vakil A.K 1985: 183).

Second Backward class Commission

The second Commission appointed under the chairmanship of B.P. Mandal submitted its report in 1980. This report, on the basis of 1931 census, identified 3743 castes as backward. Using a controversial toolkit of caste backwardness, it favoured proportional equality between those that it considered as backward and the rest that were fortunate enough to be forward.

The Mandal Commission in India was established in 1979 by the Janata Party government under Prime Minister Morarji Desai with a mandate to "identify the socially or educationally backward." It was headed by Indian parliamentarian Bindheshwari Prasad Mandal to consider the question of seat reservations and quotas for people to redress caste discrimination, and it used eleven social, economic, and educational indicators to determine "backwardness". In 1980, the commission's report affirmed the affirmative action practice under Indian law whereby members of lower castes (known as Other Backward Classes and Scheduled Castes and Tribes) were given exclusive access to a certain portion of government jobs and slots in public universities, and recommended changes to these quotas, increasing them by 27% to 49.5% but the creamy layer was excluded from the overview of reservations (Arkodayroy 2011).

The plan to set up the commission was taken by the Morarji Desai government in 1978 as per the mandate of the constitution of India under article 340[2] for the purpose of articles like 15 and 16 of the constitution of India. The decision was made official by the president on 1st January, 1979. The commission is popularly known as the Mandal Commission, its chairman being B.P. Mandal. The Commission, after going through a scientific investigation and with the help of experts from various disciplines worked out 11 indicators to determine social backwardness. These indicators are social, educational and economic, and as the major controversy resolves around the caste criteria allegedly adopted by the commission, it would be relevant to reproduce the actual criteria used by the Commission. The 11 indicators formulated by the commission are: (Report of the Backward Class Commission 1980 Vol. I, 2-4).

In pre-independence period the reservation was the mandatory one for SC/ST s. Even Odisha and West-Bengal do not seem to have any reservation for OBCs. In 1977-78 Mr. Karpoori Thakur, then the Chief Minister of Bihar, tried to introduce 30 percent reservation for the OBC s and the issues occupied after this recommendations and this provoked a violent outburst in which 118 people were reported to have died. The ambiguous nature of these commission is notable Instead, caste identity is fragmented and reformed under changing material and social conditions. Karpoori Thakur firstly farming the seeds of "Economic criteria" or class into practical lines. He mentioned caste and class are interwoven and do not collapse well into each other In 1985, Madhya Pradesh raised reservation from 28 percent to 82 percent provided violent riots and agitation and was forced to withdraw the order. Other Backward Classes (OBCs) as totality of groups entitled by preferential treatment on the basis of backwardness, different states have their own categorization of backward classes. In detail, Karnataka have used the scale of 'backward' and more backward, Bihar and Kerala have made backward and most backward such differences is considered as a inclusive strategies of reservation policies of state governments.

It is a fact that the bulk of those who are categorized as OBCs in the States belong to the rural poor. They are sharecroppers, small tenants or poor peasants with small holdings. Further, in the rural areas the OBCs are in occupations which are still based on the traditional caste hierarchy such as dhobis, barbers, cattlerearers and artisans. Their lowly caste status prevents their entry into education and new occupations. These are the facts confirmed by detailed studies conducted by the Havanur Commission in Karnataka (1975); the Backward Classes Commission in Tamil Nadu (1971); the Backward Classes Reservation Commission in Kerala (1971);

the Socially and Educationally Backward Classes Commission in Gujarat (1976) and the Backward Classes Commission in Andhra Pradesh (1970); that within OBCs there are many sub-castes which are educationally and economically backward judged by a number of socio-economic indicators.

Therefore, the scheduled castes and tribes have managed to fare better, thanks to reservations, whereas OBCs continue to lag behind them precisely because they do not get the benefits of protective discrimination. The picture in this case is however not exactly clear, since the degree of stratification that exists among these castes, now generically called OBCs, obscures the reality to a great extent. For even among these OBCs, whatever proportion of government jobs they occupy, the share of the really depressed among them is difficult to estimate. If this section of the well-to-do OBCs is separated, the figure should be really insignificant. For example, of the 128 OBCs identified by the Mungeri Lal Commission in Bihar (of which 94 were termed 'most depressed') barring four upper backward castes 'the lower backwards are no better than scheduled castes except that they are not untouchables' (lshwari Prasad 1986: 22).

Backward Class Movements and Reservation policy

System encompasses the potential for new rudiments as well as the reality of established ones. Such new elements often enter the political arena via a backward class movements. The latter term is a rubric for a wide variety of related but not identitical social experiences. Backward class movements become a vehicle by which policy makers are influenced directly, as well as indirectly through general social change.

In particular, the upshots of the general atmospheric changes caused by the movement will be more assumed than delineated. Instead the focus will be on the specific relationship. It is understood that while the same social conditions which create a social movements may have a direct effect on policy, it is when the people most strongly affected by changes in social conditions and consciousness are not already part of the policy making process that they must organize themselves for political action. Thus a social movements becomes the vehicles by which policy makers are influenced directly, as well as indirectly through general social change.

Post-Independence period, SC/ST and OBCs movements were primarily concerned about the relationship between movements and policy. Policy get shorter shift than movement in the case of scheduled Caste in India. In part because its development is more recent after 1990s and there is less to talk about and in part because the backward class movements for reservation is an extra ordinarily multifaceted phenomenon which simply requires more results for even an cursory appraisal. Even here it is an understood fact that there is a dynamic interrelationship which is still in process - Jats, Marathas, and the movements in Gujarat 2015. There is an absence of *spontaneous* generation theory of social movement formation in India.

The informative structures exerted mobilizing as well as restraining effect on individual participation in social movements because they formed a caste/class network that assisted in the rapid spread of new ideas. A Backward class movements is more likely to meet its early success among the more strongly integrated citizens. Firstly the branch of the movement in taking positions favoring the position of caste, the fundamental questions concerning the caste structure of society premised on colonial-feudal depth effects in Indian social-political-economic arenas.

Sites of Contestation Phase III: Emergence of Quota Politics

Quota is usually understood as a fixed number or amount of 'people' or 'things'. Justice and ethics of affirmative action and reservation quotas are relevant contexts." Quotas- a term which enables one in juxtapose the concept of substantive equality within the caste system through the shared belief in equality of results. Quotas and special scholarships for backward groups were first established in the 1920s. There are important differences substantive equality is based on recruitment, the caste system on birth, the similarity lies in that both operate on quotas and both are ultimately based on birth ascription for the quota, especially if the quota is based on sex or race which are based on birth.

What has gone wrong with our thinking on Other Backward Classess is that we have allowed the problem to be reduced largely to that of job reservation. The crucial situations of backward classes are too varied, too complex and too sharp to be job reservation alone. The quota system sets beside the Principle of merit, some other principle in the name of social justice (Beteille 1992: 77). Job quotas in public employment are by no means the best way of reducing social and economic disparities between caste and communities, and they have serious institutional costs that far outweigh the benefits they bring to some individual members of backward castes.

There has been much discourse recently of the relative importance of caste and class-Reservation following its practicality- a preference for applied ideas, support for policies that "work" it is an important norm with the discourse and practice of Indian politics. How to solve the problem of

'Quota within Quota'? and the problem of criteria and classification arose when state was permitted to contextualize the beneficiaries according to their preference or choice. The reservation policy has become materialized, politicized, and communalized to such an extent that even governments were made and unmade in recent past over the issue. However, the fundamental question of who is actually eligible for the privilege has not yet been finalized so far.

The history of reservation in post independence period was of a lightly mixed nature. History is always mixed history, its combination with state, institution and Non-state actors. The vocabulary of reservation changed policy tracing the antagonistic relation with political agendas. In the case of relative dimension state and its policy act as an apparatus of social control. The ideal typical model of Caste politics is the central proposition in Indian society., simply called caste as a societal Cliché in post independence period.. Reservation policies anchored different voices and politics in India- Mandal I and Mandal II ie., Mandalization of politics, identification of OBCs, Vote Bank Politics, License to increase quota.

These core historical debates in post Independence period never attracts "upper caste quota". One of the typical and omnipotent feature of Indian society is the division into castes. Caste in the narrower sense applies primarily to Hindus, who constitutes 85% of India's population. The principle argument of Partha Chatterjee is that, upto 10% reservation for economically weaker Sections of Upper Caste is a cynical fraud on the constitution (see The Wire by 30/12/2018). We can quote many such experts or intellectuals who maintain that reservation will perpetuate and maintain 'Dominant Caste hierarchy in India society. For example, the The reason behind the Non Brahmin Movement in Madras to obliterate the upper caste domination in public employment, as 80% of all elite position /jobs handled were handles by upper castes.

Now reservation strengthens the institutional tones with monarchical monologues and policy dynamics over ruling the state and non-state actors. In contemporary phase we have started thinking about where and how such policies are leading towards equality. The Constitution (124th Amendment) Act, 2019, deals with a classification called "economically weaker sections of citizens other than the classes" currently mentioned in Articles 15 and 16, i.e. Scheduled Castes, Scheduled Tribes and Other Backward Classes. Upper caste have acquired some political clout with the rightwing power structures in the country. After this EWS monologue, or policy initiative we can see silent negation of the year old legacy of backward class movements, leaders genealogies of texts, slogans, Leaders struggles against matrix of exploitation.

Galanter perceptively observes that, in India Reservation is a crude device that is inherently incapable of eliminating all the effects of unearned privilege and undeserved handicap...the policy of protective treatment for disadvantaged groups cannot be universalized to address all of the arbitrarinesses and unfairness of life. But generalizing protective treatment to all groups dissolves the original and distinctive national commitment to the core beneficiary groups, the Scheduled castes and tribes (Galanter 1991 xxi).

Contextualize the *'lawness'* on Reservation: Post-Independence

The Indian constitution has provided reservation to secure a judicial protection and socio economic justice to humiliated downtrodden and least advantaged peoples in India. Law is a rational (Weber), mode of enforcement and lawness of law is distinctively legal, as legal boundaries and reservation logarithms are live logics. In Logarithm its rules and the lines of distribution are constantly contested, negotiated and reproduced, justified- in ways that confront our understanding of 'How much Reserve quota? These reserve rules as neutral templates of interaction, Taylor writes, 'Rule is Practice" Rule and practice are two eyes in the same face, practice is continued 'interpretation and re-interpretation of what the rule pronounced really. Question about lawness in reservation policy, the historical tradition of the question of lawness of law can be reflected into question of nature of social order.

Post-Independence the constitutional bodies, public institutions and constitution makers deliberately analyzed the scale of distributive justice which involves distribution of resources, benefits and burdens in society according to needs, merit, and work. Art 15 (4) and 16(4) of the constitution of India express constitutional values of compensatory or protective discrimination for equalizing backward sections like Scheduled Castes (SCs) Scheduled Tribes (ST s) and other Backward Castes (OBCs). Are the benefits of reservation really reaching the targeted people or not is a serious question to be answered. Judicial handling and curiosity about reservation starts with the question of Whether the 50 percent rule or scale laid down by the Supreme court is relevant or not? Where, when, and why its exceeding in India? Whether judicial standpoints and cases towards the recognition of reservation policy is quite satisfactory or not?

Following these questions Supreme Court of India witnessed adjudicatory arguments and discussion on reservation, in the judgments of Champakam Dorairajan versus State of Madras (1951), Balaji versus State of Mysore (1964), and Indira Sawhney versus Union of India (1992).

The initial legal interpretation of reservation policy or rules as strengthening social justice principles through quota was noticed by the Supreme Court in the case of State of Madras versus Champakam Dorairajan. In Champakam Dorairajan v. State of Madras[3], the government of Madras had reserved seats in state medical and engineering colleges for different communities in certain proportions on the basis of religion, race and caste. This was challenged as unconstitutional. The government defended its order on the grounds of Article 46 of the Constitution, which permits the state to promote with special care the educational and economic interests of the weaker sections of the people and in particular Scheduled castes and Scheduled tribes to secure social justice. But the Supreme Court struck down the order as it was violation of equality principles in Indian Constitution ie., guaranteed under Article 15 (1) and observed that directive principles cannot override the guaranteed fundamental rights. As a result, the Parliament brought an amendment to Article 15 and inserted clause (4).[4]

In another verdict delivered on the same day on April 4, 1951 in the case of Venkatramana versus State of Madras, the same bench declared that the denial of the post of Munsiff to the petitioner on the basis of communal government order was unconstitutional .The court presents legal clarification as Article 16(4) makes provision for reservation of appointments in favour of any backward class citizens, who are not adequately represented in the services of the state, and reservation of appointment in favour of any backward class citizens. The court declared that Venkatramana was not recruited only because he happened to be a Brahmin, and ruled that the communal government order is repugnant to the provisions of Article 16 and as such void and illegal. (Singh 1996: 51).

As the Constitution has not fixed any limit for providing reservation, the Supreme Court in Balaji v. State of Madras, has held that the government order reserving 68% of the seats available for admission to the engineering, medical and other technical colleges is unconstitutional and ultra virus the equality provision. The Supreme Court interpretation is quite interesting in this case. The job reservation for OBCs in Mysore was challenged on the ground that the lists of backward classes were prepared only on caste grounds, that is unconstitutional. In this case court examined that a detailed analysis criteria was applied for preparing the lists of backward classes and it was proper and valid and its is the part and parcel of government machinery to show the criteria for determining backward classes only on caste basis. (*Ibid*).

In this case court observed that the 68% reservation fixed by the government was excessive and unreasonable as it affects the merit candidates. However, the court fixed the ceiling limit of 50% for reservation in educational institutions and in providing public employment. But it is unfortunate that the 45 year old 50% rule is still in trend though population of SCs and STs and OBCs has substantially changed and economic resource of the state has enormously increased.

In T. Devadasan v. Union of India the question, which came before the Supreme Court, was whether the 50% rule of reservation laid down, is applicable to those posts which were carried forward for next year also. In the present case, as a result of the application of carry forward rule, the reservation of vacancies went up to 64%. This was challenged as unconstitutional, as it would obliterate the right guaranteed under articles 16 (1) and 14 of the Constitution. The Supreme Court struck down the carry forward rule as unconstitutional and declared it invalid and observed.

"We would like to emphasize that the guarantee contained in Article 16 (1) is for ensuring equality of opportunity for all citizens relating to employment and to appointments to any office under the State. This means that on every occasion for recruitment, the State should see that all citizens are treated equally. The guarantee is to each individual citizen and therefore, every citizen who is seeking employment or appointment to an office under the State is entitled to be afforded an opportunity for seeking such employment or appointment whenever it is intended to be filled. In order to effectuate the guarantee, each year of recruitment will have to be considered by itself and reservation for backward communities should not be so excessive as to create a monopoly or to disturb unduly the legitimate claims of the other communities."[5]

In Chitralekha versus State of Mysore case[6] addressed two major points on backwardness firstly, the caste of a group of citizens may be a relevant circumstance in ascertaining their social backwardness and secondly, the relevant factor to determine the social backwardness of class of citizens, it cannot be the sole or dominant test in that behalf. The Supreme court briefly summarized that "While this court has not excluded caste from ascertaining the backwardness of a class of citizens, it has not made it one of the compelling circumstances affording the basis for the ascertainment of the backwardness of a class. To put in differently the authority concerned may take caste into consideration in ascertaining the backwardness as a group of persons, but if it does not, its order will not be bad on that account, if it can ascertain the backwardness of a group of persons on the basis of other relevant criteria (Singh 1996: 57).

There is at another judgmental clarification by Supreme Court. In K.S Jayasree versus state of Keralam (1976)[7] economic backwardness act as a carburettoring machinery for social backwardness and educational backwardness, and the case addressed the economically slandered or class positions of society. The Supreme Court opined that, caste cannot be made sole or dominant test in ascertaining social backwardness although it may not be irrelevant to consider it in ascertaining the same. However, it took the view that social backwardness is in the ultimate analysis the result of poverty to great extent, although it may be aggravated by consideration of caste.

But in N. M. Thomas v. State of Kerala,[8] the Supreme Court has shown the positive approach towards the members of the SCs/STs. In the instant case, the government through its Government Order exempted the members of the SCs/STs employees of registration department from passing the departmental test for promotion to higher posts. This exemption was given only for a period of 2 years. This was challenged as violation of article 16 of the Constitution. But the Supreme Court upheld the GO as valid, as the classification of employees belonging to the SC/ST for allowing them an extended period of 2 years for passing the departmental test for promotion is a just and reasonable classification having rational nexus to the object of providing equal opportunity for all the citizens in matter relating to public employment.

Indra Sawhney case or Mandal case was not an ordinary one. This case is regarded as a landmark in the struggle for reservation in public employment and although it was centrally concerned with Article 16, it addressed the naive meaningful questions in Article 15. The benchmark case discussion starts in V.P Singh Government on August 13, 1990. The recommendations of Mandal Commission proposed to extend 27 percent reservations to the SEBC s in government services. Reservation was to apply direct recruitment. OBC s recruited on merit in open competition were not to be counted in the 27 percent quota. OBCs were to compromise castes and communities common to state wise lists in the Mandal Commission report and state government lists.

But in Indra Sawhney v. Union of India[9] the Supreme Court upheld the 50% *rule of reservation* and observed that, at no point of time, the reservation shall go beyond the scale of 50% rule as laid down in Balaji's case[10]. The court also pointed out that if the reservation exceeds 50% through carry forward rule, the rule is invalid and volatizing article 16(4) of the Constitution. Importantly ,it rejected the rule-exception construction and article16(4)was read to be an 'instance of classification implicit in Article 16(1) (Khosla 2012: 100) For the rational of protecting the interests of SC/ ST and to extend the reservation even in promotion, Constitution was amended and clause 4 A was inserted to article 16 empowering the state to make provision for reservation in matter of promotion to any class or classes of posts in the services under the state in favour of SC/ST' s where they are not adequately represent.[11]

The central government which assumed office following the general election in the first half of 1991 was asked by a five member constitution bench to make legal clarity on the issue. The government indicated its intention to implement the memorandum of September 25 1991 with certain modifications and introduce the economic criterion in grant of reservation by giving preference to the poorer section of the SEBC s in the 27 th percent quota and secondly reserving another 10 percent of the vacancies in the civil services for other economically backward sections of not covered by any of the existing schemes of reservation, which was elaborated to extend to the poorest amongst the higher castes and other religious also. The economic criterion was to be specified separately.

After this landmark judgement, the OBCs of India achieved their long standing output on reserved posts in Central Government services. In March 1993, R.N. Prasad Committee determined the creamy layer or advanced sections of OBC s and in September 1993 reservation of 27 percent posts in central services become effective. (Singh 1996: 71). While the new dynamics are launched after the case that is, Supreme Court rightly excluded creamy layer from the list of OBCs. It also critically negated the policy of reservation regarding promotions. But it has not mentioned the side lining of advance backward castes from the beneficiaries of the policy of protective discrimination. In is noticed by relevant case i.e, Periakaruppan versus State of Tamil Nadu (1972).

Balaji also addressed the question of how many of a given number of openings in a university or branch of government service may be reserved for Scheduled Castes, Scheduled Tribes, and Other Backward Classes. After two decades of refinement, evolution, and confusion in subsequent cases,

State of Kerala v. Thomas significantly modified Balaji by broadening permissible means of selection. Though Thomas' contours and implications are still being revealed, initially it was widely viewed as opening Pandora's box. The most expansive view of Thomas would accord a claim of hardship to army veterans and disabled children of diplomats so as to entitle them to preferences. Galanter vehemently criticize the India caste system. Galanter puts it, "embrace the ancient notion that there is an ordering in society of communities from highest to lowest." Professor Galanter finds that "overall the courts have been harsh critics of governmental arrangements for compensatory discrimination." 3' Of the eighty-one cases dealing with compensatory discrimination between 1950 and 1977, 32 high courts ruled against the state in twenty-four of the fifty-seven cases concerning preferential treatment. according to Professor Galanter, have been "preventing communal quotas, inhibiting runaway expansion of the category of Other Backward Classes and gross over-inclusion without tangible criteria, encouraging flexibility while confining the quantum of preferences."

Ours is a "compartmental society" (Galanter), "Divided society" (Beteille 1992: 74) with extremes of inequality between caste and communities inherited from the past that are pausing societal cliché in India. Caste mobilization that challenged this hierarchically compartmentalized society began with subaltern movements promising a new equality beyond caste and even class (Heredia 2012: 67) Any discussion of affirmative action for the backward classes must keep in view two important distinctions. The first is the distinction among the various spheres of public life: the case for reserved seats in bodies such as parliament and assemblies to which members are elected in different from the case for reserved posts in bodies such as the civil service to which persons are appointed. The second is the distinction between the Scheduled Castes and the Scheduled Tribes on the one hand and the Other Backward Classes on the other; the moral basis of the claims for special treatment of Harijans and Adivasis is quite different from the moral basis of the claims made by the various castes and communities which seek inclusion among the Other Backward Classes.

Conclusion

The overall picture of Post -independence phase shows that state and central Government way of operation of reservation policies is more unique because all selected appropriate tools are over-directed and over-regulated by constitutional norms and social justice principles. In the realm of public policies social justice is still a nascent enterprise. Historically, the provision of reservation is akin to a temporary crutch. The Indian constitution envisages to protect the downtrodden and powerless sections of the society through its enumeration of constitutional laws and reservation policies for their protection. However in post-independence era the institutions and laws in place have not at all failed in ensuring the social justice to its citizens.

The nature and impact of protective discrimination processes was thus adequately 'represented' through commissions and committee – through narrating the majority vs. minority experiences and stories in Indian society. Only by combining the understanding of the nature and experience of exclusionary processes, historical injustice from past are rectified to make the way for effectiveness in policy and action.

In addition, policies are neither emerging out of these reports and recommendations. Recently, there is a considerable uncertainty with regard to understanding the eclipse of reservation phenomena Thus reservation policy making in central as well as state is a dynamic process occurring in a 'networking' society, rather than within one with hierarchies. There have been substantial stratification of society over the years. Implementation of common criteria for all society is a questionable fact in the Indian context. I have argued that, this Graded autonomy in public educational institutions and employment opportunities, has been obvious with serious dangers of social justice as it creates an under-representation dilemma in Indian society over reservation policy.

The filtration process of reservation has not been thorough or uniform for all states in India. The examination of efforts to transform the reservation policies in state and centre, State cannot simply be assumed to be monolithic agent like narrative 'Chowkidar', (Watchman or gate keeper) for the name sake. Perhaps, we know that the recent reservation policy for Economically weaker sections (EWS) is deviating from the principles of social justice.

In the end, we can say that the vision of the Indian Constitution was to establish an egalitarian social order. For that, the Constitution has provided the legal and institutional safeguards to secure both formal and substantive socio-economic equality. Secondly, the biggest challenge is how to move away from a easiest identity to an Indian Identity. Over time, it has been observed that Reservation has helped the backward classes for nearly several decades and is still continuing with decreasing possibilities. After analyzing how the basic conjunctures of reservation programme of preferential treatment to the backward castes is against equality among individuals, it may be stated that reservation based on caste divide societies even though our ultimate goal is to develop a casteless stateless society.

References

Primary

Government of India (1980): Backward Class Commission Report First Part (Volumes I & II)

Government of India (1980): Backward Class Commission Report First Part (Volumes III to VII)

Constituent Assembly Debates, Vol. III.

Seetharaman S. Potty (2001): The Handbook on Reservation in Public Services & Educational Concessions in Kerala for Scheduled Castes, Sheduled Tribes & Other Backward Classes Vol. I, Kerala Public Service, Thiruvanathapuram.

Seetharaman S. Potty (2001): The Handbook on Reservation in Public Services & Educational Concessions in Kerala for Scheduled Castes, Sheduled Tribes & Other Backward Classes Vol. II, Kerala Public Service, Thiruvanathapuram.

Books

Anirudh, Prasad (1991): Reservation Policy and Practice in India: A Means to an End, New Delhi: Deep and Deep.

Engineer, A. A. (1991). Mandal Commission Controversy. New Delhi: Ajantha.

Engineer, A. A. (1991). Mandal Commission Controversy. New Delhi: Ajanta.

K.C, Y. (1994). India's Unequal Citizens: A Study of Other Backward Classes. New Delhi: Manohar.

Khosla, M. (2014). Indian Constitution Oxford Indian Short Introduction. New Delhi: Oxford University Press.

M.L, M. (2004). Encyclopedia of Backward Castes. Reservation Vol. 1. New Delhi: Kalpaz.

M.L, M. (2004). Encyclopedia of Backward Castes. Reservation Vol. 2. New Delhi: Kalpaz.

M.L, M. (2004). Encyclopedia of Backward Castes. Reservation Vol. 3. New Delhi: Kalpaz.

M.L, M. (2004). Encyclopedia of Backward Castes. Reservation Vol. 4. New Delhi: Kalpaz.

Nadeem Hasnain and H.S Verma. (2006). Stagnation, Restrograde change or positive progress? Virnettes from the journey of the OBC Communities in the process of change in India. New Delhi: Serials.

Prasad, A. (1991). Reservation policy and Practice in India: A means to End. New Delhi: Deep & Deep.

Sharma, S. R. (2002). Protective Discrimination :Other Backward Classes in India. New Delhi: Raj.

Singh, S. (1966). Reservation Policy for Backward Classes. Jaipur: Rawat.

Panandikar, Pai. (1997): The Politics of Backwardness: Reservation Policy in India. New Delhi: Konark.

Vakil, A.K (1985): Reservation Policy Scheduled Caste in India. New Delhi: Ashish Publishing House. .(Chapter1 Evolution of Reservation Policy 1-28)

Articles

Basavaraju (2009): "Reservation Under the Constitution of India :Issues and Perspective", Journal of the Indian Law Institute, Vol. 51, No. 2 (APRIL-JUNE 2009), pp. 267-274 Published by: Indian Law Institute Stable URL: https://www.jstor.org/stable/43953443 Accessed: 27-02-2019 05:08 UTC.

Baghvan Das (2000): "Moments in a History of Reservations," Economic and Political Weekly October 28, 3831-3834.

Balagopal, K. (1990): "This Anti-Mandal Mania," Economic and Political Weekly, 25(40), October 2231-2234.

Baxi, Upendra (1985): "Caste, Class and Reservations," Economic and Political Weekly, 20(10): 426-428.

Das, Bhagwan (2000): "Moments in a History of Reservations," Economic and Political Weekly, 35(43/44), October: 3831-3834. at http://www.jstor.org/stable/4409890.

Choudhary, Kameshwar (1990): "Reservation for OBCs: Hardly an Abrupt Decision", Economic and Political Weekly,Vol. 25(35), September 1-8, 19291935.

Datar, Abhay (2017): "Defining Backwardness: Debates in Bombay," Economic and Political weekly, December 23, 2017 Vol. 1-II no. 51.

Dick Kooiman (1995):"Communalism and Indian Princely States: A Comparison with British India Economic and Political Weekly, Vol. 30, No. 34 (Aug. 26),2123-2133, URL: http://www.jstor.org/stable/4403135 Accessed: 21-04-2018 05:54 UTC.

Galanter, Mare (1978): "Who Are the Other Backward Classes?: An Introduction to a Constitutional Puzzles, Economic and Political Weekly, 3(No. 43/44), October: 1812-1828.

Hebsur, R.K. (1981): "The Havanur Commission on Backward Classes: An Analysis, "The Indian Journal of Political Science," 42(4), October - December: 14-29. http://www.jstor.org/stable /41855107.

Nagarajan, Karthik (2009): "Compensatory Discrimination in India Sixty Years After Independence: A Vehicle of Progress or a Tool of Partisan Politics?",Washington Lee Journel of Civil Rights and Social Justice Spring 3-1,Vol 15(2).486-516.

Nigam, Aditya(1990): "Mandal Commission and the Left", Economic and Political Weekly Vol. 25,18 December, 48-49.

Radhakrishnan P (1989): "Ambasankar Commission and Backward Classes", Economic and Political Weekly, Vol. 24, No. 23 (Jun. 10,). 1265+1267-1268 URL: https://www.jstor.org/stable/4394921 Accessed: 15-02-2019 12:06 UTC.

Radhakrishnan, P (1990): "Karnataka Backward Classes," Economic and Political Weekly, 25(32).

Rochana Bajpai (2000): "Constituent Assembly Debates and Minority Rights", Economic and Political Weekly, May 27, 1837-1845.

Yadav, Nomitha (2002): "Other Backward Classes: Then and Now", Economic and Political Weekly November 2-9, 4495-4500.

Website

Chatterjee, Partha (2019): The 10% Reservation Is a Cynical Fraud on the Constitution https://thewire.in/government/the-10-reservation-is-a-cynical-fraud-on-the-constitution

Notes

1. Ph.D Scholar ,University of Hyderabad, Department of Political Science, School of Social Science, email:rnreshmarn@gmail.com.
2. Mathur M.L 2004, P. 54, Article 340 of part XVI regards the socially and educationally backward classes, "OBC" The only special provision for them.
3. AIR 1951 SC 226.
4. The Constitution of India (First - Amendment) Act, 1951.
5. AIR 1964 SC 179: (1964) 4 SCR 680.
6. AIR 1964 S.C. 1823 (Report of the Backward Classes Commission: 20)
7. AIR 1976. S.C. 2381.
8. AIR 1976 SC. 490.
9. AIR 1993 SC 477.
10. Basavaraju C (2009) The 50% rule of reservation laid down by the Supreme Court in Balaji's case and which continues to be in vogue has to be modified and Parliament itself should make an amendment to the Constitution regulate the percentage of reservation to 65. This is due to the growth of the backward classes population since 1963.
11. The Constitution (Seventy-Seventh Amendment Act 1955.

Chapter - 18

Reservations in India: Mapping the Caste, Class Debates

Prof. Naidu Ashok & Dr. Rajesh Kota

Abstract

The subject of reservation has figured prominently in public debates ever since the implementation of the Mandal Commission recommendations report which advocated that 27% of the jobs under the Central government and public sector undertakings should be reserved for Other Backward Classes (OBCs). From the debates generated by the Mandal Commission recommendations, we examine criticisms and the underlying principles for caste-based reservations. *The continuing debate on the reservations issue is beginning to reveal a pernicious split among the pro-reservationists on the question of economic versus caste-based criteria for identifying backwardness. Left and democratic people must reflect on the significance of demanding economic criteria.*

Introduction

The arguments of those who advocate economic criteria seem to be the following class is more 'primary' than caste. By implication, class oppression comes before caste oppression; in fact the latter derives from the former. The economic base is the determining factor for analysis, not the superstructure, and caste belongs to the latter; only BC and SC/ST elites benefit from caste-based reservations; caste-based reservations 'reinforce' caste difference, and lead to casteism.

It is an impoverished and inflexible Marxist model indeed which cannot question the neat division between base and superstructure.[1] This division; discredited at the conceptual level, breaks down even more dramatically when faced with the specific problems of societies like India where caste-relations are part of the so-called base, part of the relations of production and economic organisation. Caste is not merely a 'social' problem separate from the economic. Innumerable surveys have shown that 'caste-ranking is strongly and positively correlated with poverty'. We cannot gain access to the pure category of class in isolation from how caste has operated in our context. Even a cursory glance at modern Indian history will reveal that caste and class struggles seldom oppose one another but are closely interlinked, making it difficult for us to view them as completely separate entities or even categories of analysis

The NDA-led government has passed a gazette notification securing reservations for 10% of the economically weaker sections.[2] The debate over what the basis of reservations should be has been a particularly polarising point in the discourse. The government's latest notification has sparked this debate once again by offering reservations based on economic status. Ever since the formation of Indian constitution, there has been continuous debates over the reservation issue particularly whether reservation shall be provided on economic ground or social inequality. These debates were intensified during the 90's with response to Mandal Committee recommendations. Even now it is unresolved issue in the political as well as academic arenas. Hence, this paper is going to map the arguments and will try to provide logical conclusions based on Indian socio-economic realities.

A Longer History of Reservations in India

The idea of caste-based reservations has always been vociferously resisted by the dominant social forces in the country, right from colonial times. It was suggested that reservations were a British machination to "divide and rule" India. In his article, discussing the history of reservations in India, Prof.Kanche Ilaiah highlighted the importance of English being instituted as the official language which served to further insulate Dalits and backward castes from employment and educational opportunities.[3]

With the Poona Pact, 1932, the disprivilege faced by Dalits was accentuated once again as their identity was subsumed under the Hindu fold. "The Poona Pact had far-reaching effects and obstructed their progress in other fields also. The government issued orders regarding reservation in services vide resolution No F 14/17-B 33 dated July 4, 1934 (Gazette of India, part I, July 7, 1934).[4] Reservation in public services was provided for all minorities excepting the depressed classes.

In regard to the depressed classes, it is common ground that all reasonable steps should be taken to secure for them a fair degree of representation in the public services. The intention of the caste Hindus in this respect was formally stated in the Poona Agreement of 1932[5] and His Majesty's government in accepting that agreement took due note of this point. In the present state of general education in these classes the government of India considers that no useful purpose will be served by reserving for them a definite percentage of vacancies out of the number available for Hindus as a whole, but they hope to ensure that duly qualified candidates from the depressed classes are not deprived of their opportunities of appointment merely because they cannot succeed in open competition."

Debate on Reservations in Writing the Constitution

The distinction between castes and classes is blurred anyway. So even if the Constitution does not provide for caste-based reservation, it is desirable. Since caste is still a dominant factor in our social behaviour, its existence should be admitted for identifying the unprivileged groups.

Because backwards have been deprived for ages on the basis of their caste, now they should be provided facilities on the same basis. Says Lok Dal MP Ram Avdhesh Singh: "Even the rich backwards are not given social status, which poor forwards enjoy.

That is why we need representation in the Government on caste basis, where wealth and respect go hand in hand. These reservations are not for the economic good, but to link backwards with the state."

Some opponents of reservation argued against the choice of reservations as a remedy for social disadvantage, but not the category of beneficiaries. HC Mookherjee, the chair of the Sub-Committee on Minorities, opined that the appropriate remedy for backward groups was economic but not political safeguards. ZH Lari, an elected member of the United Provinces Legislative Assembly from the Muslim League, argued that the representation of religious minorities and Scheduled Castes ought to be secured through the system of proportionate representation—by counting cumulative votes in multi-member constituencies—and not through reservation.

There were two voices opposed to the classification of beneficiaries on the basis of caste. Mahavir Tyagi, an elected member from the United Provinces, and Jerome D'Souza, a professor and theologian from Madras, suggested using other markers of social disadvantage. Tyagi, a vocal proponent of class-based reservations, argued that minorities should be categorised on economic criteria, based on "jobs" that do not earn enough to make a living. "I do not believe in the minorities on community basis, but minorities must exist on economic basis, on political basis and on an ideological basis and those minorities must have protection," Tyagi said. "I would suggest that in the place of the Scheduled Caste, the landless labourers, the cobblers or those persons who do similar jobs and who do not get enough to live, should be given special reservations ... Let cobblers, washermen and similar other classes send their representatives through reservations because they are the ones who do not really get any representation." [6]Tyagi's case for economic reservations differs from the 103rd Constitutional Amendment, because he did not rely on income or wealth as indicators of disadvantage. He was focused on occupational communities and classes of labourers.

D'Souza argued that a person's caste or religion should not be the exclusive basis for reservations. Instead, he stated, reservation ought to be provided based on "individual deficiencies and need, bearing, no doubt in mind the social background." D'Souza added, "A man is to be assisted because he is poor, because his birth and upbringing have not given him the opportunity to make progress, socially, politically and educationally."

The house's final vote was in favour of reservations based on the social disadvantage of caste. In January 1950, the constitution was adopted, permitting the government to make reservations for Scheduled Castes and Tribes, and socially backward classes of people who were inadequately represented in the services of the state. The State was also required to reserve seats in the Lok Sabha and state legislatures, for candidates from SCs or STs, proportionate to the population of SCs or STs residing in that particular state. The outlook of the Indian constitution was that reservation would be a tool to ensure representation of political minorities—SCs, STs, as well as other classes of citizens setback by structural, social disadvantage.

The next year, the question of using economic criteria as a marker for backwardness resurfaced. In May 1951, the constitution was amended to give the state the power to make "special provisions for the advancement of any socially and educationally backward classes of citizens, or for the Scheduled Castes and the Scheduled Tribes." In line with the constituent assembly's focus on remedying social disadvantage, the former prime minister Jawaharlal Nehru argued that the amendment served the need "to put an end to all those infinite divisions that have grown up in our social life or in our social structures ... We may call them by any name you like, the caste system or religious divisions."

KT Shah, an advocate and an economist who had been a member of the Advisory Committee, critiqued the proposed amendment's reliance on social and educational—and not economic—criteria to determine backwardness. Shah also questioned categorising "classes of citizens" and not individual citizens as beneficiaries. He noted that provisions for the advancement of socially and educationally backward classes of citizens would be of no use to India's impoverished citizens, who had seen little progress to "a normal reasonable standard of living and working" since the promulgation of the constitution.

In response, Nehru proclaimed that the social disadvantage to be remedied was a result of cumulative factors including economic considerations. To specifically list "economic" disadvantage would "not make it a kind of cumulative thing but would say that a person who is lacking in any of these things should be helped." In these debates, it became clear that only structural disadvantage, which comprised social, educational and economic disadvantage cumulatively, would be remedied by constitutional provisions. In contrast to the social disadvantage experienced collectively by groups of people, disadvantage that varies from one individual to another, manifesting as solely economic disadvantage, was not to be constitutionally remedied by special provisions or reservations.

The 1951 amendment went on to be the basis for reservations, fee waivers or concessions for persons from Scheduled Castes and Scheduled Tribes in educational institutions run or aided by the state. The thinking underlying such measures was that representation of political minorities in the services and legislatures could only be realised if the same logic of representation also governs access to educational institutions.

In 1953, Rajendra Prasad, who was the president of India at the time, appointed the first backward classes commission, under the chairmanship of Kaka Kalelkar, a member of the Rajya Sabha and prolific Gujarati literary figure, to determine the criteria for classifying citizens as "socially and educationally backward." The commission's 1955 report laid down the following criteria: "low social position in the traditional caste hierarchy"; "lack of general educational advancement among the major section of a caste or community"; "inadequate or no representation in government service"; and "inadequate representation in the field of trade, commerce and industry."

Caste can be a basis for discrimination only in special cases. After two years of intense debate in the Constituent Assembly and at public platforms, the framers of the Constitution decided to extend state patronage to

Scheduled Castes because they were out of the social system on account of their "untouchability" and the Scheduled Tribes because of their social isolation due to geographical reasons.

The Mandal Commission's Recommendations

In 1990, the VP Singh government announced that it would implement the Mandal Commission report for the castes and communities that are common to both the Mandal Commission report's list and the state governments' lists. It issued an office memorandum stipulating reservations in the services of the union government to the extent of 27 percent for "socially and educationally backward classes," or OBCs[7]. In 1991, the PV Narasimha Rao government amended the memorandum to reserve 10 percent of seats and posts in the services of the central government for "other economically backward sections of the people who are not covered by any of the existing schemes of reservation." Since, SCs, STs, and "socially and educationally backward classes" were already covered by the existing provisions for reservation, these other "economically backward sections" would be identified from among the upper castes. Criteria for determining these other sections were to be issued separately, according to the memorandum.

The memorandum was challenged in writ petitions before the Supreme Court in the period between 1990 and 1991. In a landmark judgment in the case of Indra Sawhney *vs Union of India,*[8] nine judges of the Supreme Court held that sections of citizens cannot be classified as "backward classes" solely on economic criteria, if they experience no structural or social disadvantage. The court affirmed that social backwardness leads to educational and economic backwardness, as the Mandal Commission had found. Accordingly, the Supreme Court struck down the 10 percent reservation for "economically backward sections," for being incompatible with the constitution.

The 1991 office memorandum is the only precedent to the 103rd constitutional amendment's provision for upper-caste reservations in independent India. The two differ only in terms of the issuing authority. The 1991 memorandum amendment was issued by a bureaucrat on the assumption that the government had the power to make such reservations, while the present amendment alters the constitution to explicitly empower the government to make such reservations. Since the constitution itself has now been amended to permit what *Sawhney* disallowed, the judgment in *Sawhney* cannot be used to challenge the amendment. Constitutional amendments can be struck down by the Supreme Court only if they damage or destroy the "basic structure" of the constitution. It remains to be seen whether any aspect of *Sawhney* will be considered a part of the basic structure of the Indian Constitution by the Supreme Court.

Time and again, the purpose of reservations has been reaffirmed as being a political safeguard to secure representation for socially marginalised groups in social and political spaces. When viewed through this lens, there is little in the history of independent India to support reservations for upper-castes based solely on individual economic criteria that lack a genesis in social structures.

Disputing Principles

One of the primary criticism against reservations has been that they should not be caste-based, and should be based on economic status instead. Dipankar Gupta makes an argument about socially valuable assets being the basis for reservations and argues that OBC reservations were not justified on the grounds that they were dominant agrarian castes who were not entirely alienated from assets.

"Reservations for the ex-untouchables and tribes were instituted because of the fact that they lacked those assets which a market-oriented liberal society values. They had neither wealth, nor land, nor education. To romanticise the labours of hereditary cobblers, scavengers, agrestic serfs, and other menials is certainly a view taken safely from the outside. Why else is it that it is nobody's ambitions to be a scavenger or an agrestic serf? Regardless of the intrinsic worth or dignity of such labours the moot point is that such skills that the historically disprivileged possess are not acknowledged as social assets worth acquiring. Only an apologist of the caste system and of the estates order can argue otherwise. It cannot, however, be said that the OBCs are without socially valuable assets as their initial point of departure. Large sections of the OBCs are made up of castes and caste clusters of the rural rich.[9]

Meritocracy

One of the primary criticisms that caste-based reservations faced, even from liberal quarters, was that it would lead to an inefficient bureaucracy. During the Mandal Commission debates, it was impossible for critics to separate caste from party-politics and it was often seen as a populist measure that would not yield any benefits for the nation.

"The most popular argument against reservation is that it would encourage inefficiency which already is high in our system. Irrespective of how the states with and without reservations for other backward classes (OBC) have performed with regard to their levels of efficiency in public management, it must be granted that any reservation based on social or historical criteria affects efficiency adversely. However, this is a cost our society must pay for a few years, perhaps a few decades if it has to have any pretence of undoing the effects of social and economic exploitation of the masses by a handful minority for over thousands of years. Unless one believes in a genetic theory of inefficiency and corruption linking these. to the backward classes only, there is no reason, why our society should not be able to get over this transitionary problem."[10]

The base of reservation is not economic but socially, educationally backwardness. It clears the structure of hierarchy in the society which is so ridge that it can't be easily break even through economic status. So the purpose is clear to equalize the society.

Second, you can't compare two unequal things with the same parameters. So before for fair competition equal merit should be there and these merits or talent also require some amount of cultural capital which comes through an inheritance. So economic status can' t be appropriate parameter until this huge gap is not fulfilled.

It is not an overtake of 'meritorious' student, if they are really 'meritorious' they would be surely selected. Equality should be based on equal parameters, not one sided.[11]

Anti –National Argument

"The Mandal Commission is being condemned by the intelligentsia, above all, for what is being called its divisive role. It is in keeping with the current elite thinking that distrusts all anti-national identities as indicated by the contemptuous sense in which terms like regionalism, communalism, casteism and tribalism are used. In practice, sub-national identities are becoming more and more assertive and all those who are in the business of politics recognise and cultivate them. Even in the advanced democracies of the west, parties make conscious efforts to carve out their respective constituencies among different ethnic groups. This practice is sanctioned by what are called post-modern theories of politics which recognise ethnic identity as a basic human urge."[12]

Logic behind Caste based Reservations

Despite the flood of resistance from several quarters, what could be the logic behind caste-based reservations? Gail Omvedt argues that the objective of caste-based reservations is to remove caste-monopoly in access to social resources. She suggests that the discourse of reservation is forcibly turned towards economic criteria because upper-castes want to "avoid dealing with caste". Furthermore, she lays out the specific outcome that can be expected from caste-based reservations.

"Caste-based reservations cannot remove poverty, cannot end economic exploitation; they cannot "uplift the poor". They can only make some of the poor, non-poor. (It has to be stressed that this is also true for reservations based on economic criteria, which is why the class organisations of the poor have never demanded them). What they can do is end the caste-monopoly of organised sector jobs, especially of the public sector.

This is a caste monopoly of the twice-born, most predominantly Brahmans, and as many have pointed out, including S S Gill, secretary of the Mandal Commission, it is a caste monopoly that has arisen out of a heritage of thousands of years of caste reservation in India in which Shudras and ati-Shudras were forbidden access to power, wealth and status. Destroying or lessening this caste-monopoly helps to create a middle class section among castes that are largely poor - a fact that is sometimes used as a charge against caste reservations, but in fact it is inevitable and progressive to the extent that it breaks up the correlation of 'caste and class'. This itself will not end casteism but it may be a necessary condition for doing so."

K. Balagopal (Published in EPW on 6th October, 1990)

"...Caste is very much a living reality. Caste was one of the principal determinants of the distribution of resources and power in medieval India, and the principal theoretical justification of exploitation; today it continues to play both the roles, in spite of a certain amount of capital penetration and political democratisation, the principal difference being that it is today juridically displaced from the high place it had in the age of the dharmasastras. Caste is juridically dead, but very much alive politically and ideologically. If it is in general a theoretical fallacy to confuse the juridical form with the real content, one must be particularly careful in wishing away things which do not exist juridically, in a country like India whose ruling classes do not possess the requisite measure of progressive potential to be able to afford even an ideologically camouflaged reflection of all real political and economic relations in juridical forms. The inability to see this point is one of the main reasons why Marxist analysis of caste in contemporary India has generally been very unsatisfactory..."

Merit and efficiency are never the monopoly of the forward classes. If equal opportunity is given to the backward castes and tribes including OBC community there is definitely no doubt that most of them would excel the esteemed upper class meritocracy. Merit and efficiency is the product of the system and therefore not the preserve of one differentiated social group or community. The so-called forward classes who had been occupying most of the top position of the country's administration are steadily reducing the country into shambles. Aren't we under the administration of the so-called merit and efficient hand? Crude and barbaric forms of protest like committing suicide, self-immolation and destroying public utility, etc, has, if anything, slurred the image of merit and of the efficient Indian. It is a sheer madness grown out of the impulse of self-preservation. For decades most of the fruits of freedom and progress has been enjoyed by a few upper strata of the society. It is high time they saw reason and got rid of the feeling of undue jealousy and grudge against their, fellow brethren who were still caught in the deep mire of all-round backwardness.

Conclusion

In a nutshell, the Indian Constitution is a social document and the reservation policy has been conceived as a key to social reconciliation and power sharing. Keeping this in view, the nation is to be governed with absolute commitment, positive thinking, judicious planning, optimum effort, harmonizing initiatives and relentless determination, or to sum it up, a perfectly proactive and sensitized inclusive governance, to lead the nation to an era of development where the ideal of development would not need a contradistinctive term as inclusive growth, but growth itself would come to mean a natural, homogeneous and integral inclusive growth. There is a crucial need for the sensitization of every citizen of the country towards his or her individual role in creating, developing and maintaining the inclusive and sustainable development. This would include propagation of the express need of the nation and responsibility of all to preserve national resources and assets natural, physical as well as human. Mass awareness drives, creating in all a sense of responsibility and ethics towards the participation of all in the development of the nation, need to be constantly reinforced.

Many are debating from the perspective that 10% reservations are given to the upper caste. Though it might be basically true, the important premise of this reservations happen to be based on economic criteria. Rather than the point that it is given to the upper castes, the more important point that should be focussed on is that it is primarily based on economic criteria. Social justice has been the only basis on which reservations have been implemented until now. Economic basis had not been considered a criterion before. Social status and discrimination based on birth have affected all spaces such as society, politics, economics and culture. As a result of which many communities have been affected and thus have been identified. The basis for the principle of social justice is to ensure justice to them. That reservation should be ensured to these effected people in the fields of education, occupation, and politics so as to empower them in all fields is ideology behind social justice.

That reservation should be given to economically backward people has been a constant demand for so many years. This demand has been debated since the times when Jawaharlal Nehru was the Prime Minister. It was in the very same period, Ambedkar, the revolutionary, held the position of a cabinet minister. An extensive debate was held back then regarding whether economic status should be considered the basis to give reservations or not. The then leaders, such as Nehru and Ambedkar and their contemporary leaders the activists who had worked beyond the political spectrum and intellectuals had held an extensive, deep debate regarding this. Yet, they all finally came to the conclusion that economic status should not be considered as criteria, and that the true democratic way was to considered social status as the only criterion. That is how reservations have been guaranteed in the constitution.

References

Bagwan Das, 'Moments in a History of Reservations', Economic and Political Weekly, Vol. 35, No. 43/44 Oct. 21 - Nov. 3, 2000, pp. 3831-3834.

Constituent Assembly of India, Volume, X, October 14, 1949.

Dipankar Guptha, 'Positive Discrimination A question of Fraternity-Contrasting Ambedkar and Mandal on Reservations', Economic and Political Weekly, Vol 32, Issue No.31, August 2, 1997, pp. 1971-1978.

Gazette of India, Part 1, July 7, 1934.

Indra Sawhney V. Union of India (1992) 3S.C.C. 217.

Kanche Ilaiah Shepherd, 'Dalits and OBCs losing out because of limited access to English education', published article on *Hindustan Times* editorial page, 30th May 2020.

K.Balagopal, This Anti-Mandal Mania, Economic and Political Weekly, Vol. 25, Issue No. 40, Oct 6,1990, pp. 2232-2234.

Krishnadas Rajgopal, It is up to States to Provide 10% EWS Reservations, Published in *The Hindu* News Editorial page, Jan 7, 2020.

Report of the Second Back Ward Classes Commission (Mandal Commission), 1980

Sudhir Krishnaswamy, *Democracy and Constitutionalism In India: A study of Basic Structure*, Oxford University Press, New Delhi, 2009.

Sukhadeo Thorat, Nitin Tagade and Ajaya K Naik, "Prejudice against Reservation Policies: How and Why?", *Economic & Political Weekly*, Vol. 51, Issue No. 8: Feb, 2016.

Tejaswani Niranjana, 'Class, Caste and Reservations', Economic and Political Weekly, Vol. 25, No. 46, 1990, pp. 2514-15.

Notes

1. Tejaswani Niranjana, 'Class, Caste and Reservations', Economic and Political Weekly, Vol. 25, No. 46, 1990, pp. 2514-15.
2. Krishnadas Rajgopal, It is up to States to Provide 10% EWS Reservations, Published in *The Hindu* News Editorial page, Jan 7, 2020.
3. Kanche Ilaiah Shepherd, 'Dalits and OBCs losing out because of limited access to English education', published article on *Hindustan Times* editorial page, 30th May 2020.
4. See Gazette of India, Part 1, July 7, 1934.
5. Bagwan Das, 'Moments in a History of Reservations', Economic and Political Weekly, Vol. 35, No. 43/44 Oct. 21 - Nov. 3, 2000, pp. 3831-3834.
6. Constituent Assembly of India, Volume, X, October 14, 1949.
7. Report of the Second Back Ward Classes Commission (Mandal Commission), 1980
8. Indra Sawhney V. Union of India (1992) 3S.C.C. 217.

   See also Sudhir Krishnaswamy, *Democracy and Constitutionalism In India: A study of Basic Structure*, Oxford University Press, New Delhi, 2009.
9. Dipankar Guptha, 'Positive Discrimination A question of Fraternity-Contrasting Ambedkar and Mandal on Reservations', Economic and Political Weekly, Vol. 32, Issue No. 31, August 2, 1997, pp. 1971-1978.
10. K. Balagopal, This Anti-Mandal Mania, Economic and Political Weekly, Vol. 25, Issue No. 40, Oct 6, 1990, pp. 2232-2234.
11. Sukhadeo Thorat, Nitin Tagade and Ajaya K Naik, "Prejudice against Reservation Policies: How and Why?", *Economic & Political Weekly*, Vol. 51, Issue No. 8: Feb, 2016.
12. K. Balagopal, "The anti-Mandal Mania", Vol. 25. Issue No. 40.06 Oct, 1990.

Index

A

Aakrosh Rally, 61
Adi-Andhra, 104, 139
Adi-Andhra Mahasabha, 73
Adi-Kannada, 139
Adjustment Against Unreserved Vacancies, 222
Administrative Reforms Committee, 166
Advanced agricultural societies, 114
African Americans, 155
Akhand Bharat, 59
All India Services, 190
All India survey of higher education, 127
Alladi Kuppu Swamy Iyyar, 22
Allahabad Court judgment, 57
Allahabad High Court, 56, 60
Ambedkar insisted, 119
Ambedkar University, 61
Anagarina Kulala Ikya Dandora, 150
Anantaraman Commission Report, 172
Anantharaman Commission, 167
Ananthsayanam Ayyangar Committee, 168
Ancient History, 57
Andhra and Malabar, 72
Andhra Pradesh, 99, 128, 136, 138, 167, 169, 191
Andhra Pradesh and Telangana, 137
Andhra Pradesh Madiga Sangam, 141
Anglo-Indians, 96
Anti –National Argument, 268
Anti-Congress agenda, 19
Anti-Mandal agitation, 56
Apex court, 40
Aristotle, 155
Arjun Singh, 121, 190
Arun Jaitley, 186
Arundhatiyars, 140
Arya Samaj, 73
Asia development bank, 217
Assistant Professors, 58
Atal Bihari Vajpayee, 101
Australia, 81

B

B P Mandal, 62
B. R. Ambedkar, 195
B.S. Munje, 19
Babu Jagjeevan Ram, 142
Backward Castes, 46
Backward Class Delegation, 100
Backward class reservation, 143
Backward Classes, 84
Backward Classes among Muslims, 180
Backward Classes Commission, 183, 200
Backward Classes Commissions, 91
Backward Classes List, 167
Backward Classes movement, 200
Backward Classes Welfare Organization, 197
Bahujan Azad Party, 125
Bahujan Sahitya Sangh, 61
Bahujan Samaj, 196

Bahujana Samaj Party, 195
Bahujana Vigyana Vedika, 144
Balmikis, 104
Banaras Hindu University, 61
Benefits of reservation, 228
Bengal Presidency, 167
Bengluru, 48
Bhangi, 104, 139
Bharatiya Janata Party, 88
Bhaskar Rao Jadav, 19
Bhim Army, 61
Bhopal, 48
Bihar, 62
Bihar Government, 139
Bindheshwari Prasad Mandal, 210
BPL Ration card, 220
Brahma, 73
Brahma Samaj, 73
Brahmin caste, 75
Brahminical domination, 74
Brazil, 81
British East india company, 241
British Empire, 164
British Government, 20, 96
British India, 124, 164, 182, 242
British period, 183
British policies, 116
British rule broke, 115
British rule in India, 44
Buddhism, 159

C

C.P. Ramaswamy, 119
Calcutta, 48
Canada, 81
Canada and Australia, 155
Caste and Reservation, 33
Caste based Reservations, 268
Central Universities of Punjab, 57
Central University of Tamil Nadu, 58
Chamar, 139, 104
Chatrapati Sahuji Maharaj, 96, 181
Chelmsford Reforms, 242
Chhatrapati Shahu Ji Maraharaj, 118
China, 81
Chittoor district, 143
Chola kings, 113
Christian Kammas, 159
Christian Madigas, 159
Christian Malas, 159
Christian missionaries, 117, 241
Christian philosopher Saint Augustine, 98
Christian Reddies, 159
Christianity, 159
Cicero, 98
Colonial Power, 26, 114
Colonial Presidencies, 81
Congress Party, 244
Constitution and Reservations, 35
Constitution Fundamental Rights, 23
Constitution of Free India, 96
Constitutional limit to reservations, 89
Constitutional Perspective, 33
Constitutional Provisions, 54
Cooperative societies, 82
Cow protection, 20
Creamy layer, 89
Criminal tribes, 24
Criminal Tribes Act, 167, 168
Criteria for Income & Assets, 221

D

Dalit communities, 159
Dalit Jatiya Sangh, 138
Dalit leadership, 145
Dalit Mahasabha, 138
Dalit movement, 102
Dalit Panthers manifesto, 138
Dalit Sarsvat Parishat, 138
Dalit-bahujan movement, 78
Dalits and Adivasis, 103

Dandi March, 143
Dandora movement, 137, 146, 150
Defence, 103
Delhi Teachers Initiative, 61
Delhi University, 60
Delhi University Teachers Association, 61
Demands for Liberty, 103
Denofited Tribes, 174
Denotified Communities, 168
Denotified Tribes, 167, 170, 171, 172
Depressed Class issue, 19
Depressed Classes, 19, 20, 21, 23, 81, 137, 138
Dhangar in Maharashtra, 173
Difficulties in getting caste certificate, 89
Discrimination and Destitution, 125
Distinguishing Untouchables, 45
Distributive justice, 155
Diwan Nanjappa, 116
Diwanship of Col. Munroe, 116
Dominant castes demand, 90
Dr. B. R. Ambedkar Resigned, 99
Dr. B.R. Ambedkar, 18, 96
Dr. Manmohan Singh, 102
Dr. Rajendra Prasad, 99

E

Economic criteria for quotas, 33
Economic Inequality, 45
Economic Reservation, 170
Economically Weaker Sections, 60, 93, 170, 172, 175, 220, 224
Education Commission, 83
Education Committee, 83
Educationally Backward Classes, 82, 83
Edumudi Madiga, 141
Election Manifesto, 100
Emancipation of slaves, 116
Emergence of Quota Politics, 249
Equal Opportunities, 201
Equality and Fraternity, 103
Equality and Reservation, 211
European History, 57
Evolution of Reservation Policy, 43
Exemption from Reservation, 221
Exterior Classes, 137
Ezhavas of Kerala, 19

F

Fiji, 81
Finance Minister, 102
First Backward Class Commission, 245
First Backward Classes Commission, 166
First Constitutional Amendment, 46
First Round Table Conference, 96, 97
Food Security Card, 220
Fundamental Right, 204

G

Globalisation, 106
Governor-General's Executive Council, 124
Govind Vallabh Panth, 25
Great Britain, 243
Greater Hyderabad Municipal Corporation, 232
Green Revolution, 91
Gujarat, 169
Gujarat Central University, 61
Gujars in Rajasthan, 128
Gujjars in Gujarat, 191

H

Habitual Offenders Act, 167, 168
Harijan Sevak Sangh, 19, 73
Haryana, 82, 136, 169
Hidden Language of Caste, 121
Hindu communities, 183
Hindu cosmology, 111
Hindu fesivals, 160
Hindu Mahasabha, 19, 21

Hindu society, 137
Historical background of Reservations, 216
History of Reservations, 96
Holayas, 139
Holeya, 104
Hunter Commission, 95, 164, 241
Hyderabad, 99
Hyderabad Central University, 61

I

Imperial Civil Service, 164
Implementation challenges, 33
Implementation of reservations, 38
Inclusion and exclusion, 90
Income and Asset Certificate, 222
Indian Christians, 96, 243
Indian Civil Servants, 164
Indian Civil Service, 164
Indian National Congress, 69
Indira Gandhi, 101
Indira Sawhney, 32, 254
Indra Sawhney Case, 36, 38
Intellectual history of reservation, 240
Interlinking Philosophy of Reservation, 50
Intervention and Structural Changes, 114
Islam and Christianity, 218
Israel, 81
Iyothe Thass Panditar, 53

J

Jai Bheem, 62
Jai Prakash Narayan, 120
Janata Dal government, 197
Jatavs, 104
Jawaharlal Nehru, 22, 123, 124, 195, 244, 264, 271
Jotirao Phule, 96
Journalistic writing of dalit, 73
Judicial objection, 39
Judiciary, 103
Justice Party, 73, 78
Justice Ramachandra Raju Commission, 146
Justice Sri Krishna Commission, 201
Justice Venkatachaliah commission, 24
Justice VR Krishna Iyer, 39
Jyotiba Phule, 187
Jyotirao Phule, 155, 164

K

K.N. Panikkar, 155
Kaka Kalelkar, 25, 183
Kaka Kalelkar Commission, 46
Kaka Kalelkar Commission Report, 168
Kakasaheb Kalelkar, 99
Kakasaheb Kalelkar Commission Report, 101
Kalelkar Commission, 100
Kancha Illaiah, 60
Kanshiram, 195, 198
Kapus, 191
Karamchedu Dalit movement, 150
Karem Shivaji, 144
Karnataka, 72, 136
Karpoori Thakur, 120, 247
Kelkar Observation Reports, 171
Kesavananda Bharati case, 32
Khori, 104
King of Mysore, 96
King of Travancore, 117
Kohlapur Presidency, 96
Krishna Madiga, 141, 142
Krupakar Madiga, 142
Kurmis in Bihar, 191

L

L.C. Guruswamy, 140
Laloo Prasad Yadav, 101, 121
Land reforms, 120
Laxmi Narasu, 74

Legislative Assemblies, 54
Liberalisation, 106
Logic behind Article, 36
Lokur Committee, 168
Lost Generations Trapped, 105
Lucknow, 48

M

M. Radhakrishna Sharma, 98
M.C. Rajah, 20
M.G. Ramachandran government, 47
M.N. Srinivas, 123
Madhava Rao, 140
Madhya Pradesh, 61, 62
Madhya Pradesh States, 172
Madiga, 104, 139
Madiga Employees, 140, 142
Madiga rank, 146
Madiga Reservation Porata Samiti, 135
Madiga subgroups, 136
Madigas, 139
Madigas (Karnataka), 139
Madras High Court, 46, 101
Madras Presidency, 72, 83, 96, 167, 199
Mahadalits, 104
Mahapadayatra, 143
Mahar, 104, 139
Maharaja of Kolhapur, 181
Maharaja of Mysore, 44
Maharashtra, 139, 165
Mahars of Maharashtra, 19
Mahatma Joti Rao Phule, 187
Mala community, 145
Mala Dasaries, 146
Mala hierarchy, 146
Mala Jangam, 146
Mala leaders, 137
Mala Mahanadu, 136
Malamahanadu activities, 145
Malaysia and Indonesia, 81
Mandal Commission, 88, 100, 101, 184, 185, 188, 197, 209, 212, 246, 254, 266, 269
Mandi House, 61
Mang, 104
Mangs' movement in Maharashtra, 136
Manmad (Maharashtra, 104
Maratha community, 171, 224
Marathas, 82
Marathi-speaking circles, 103
Marriage of Hindu widows, 117
Marxist model, 261
Mathangs, 139
Media, 103
Media, Education, 103
Meghalaya, 154
Miller Committee, 96
Minimum reservation of vacancies, 245
Ministry of Home Affairs, 166
Mitha Ayyalwar, 146
Mizoram Christians, 154
Morarji Desai, 100
Morley-Minto Reform, 165
Most Backward Classes, 200
Most Backward Classes List, 167
Mother Teresa, 142
Moulana Abdul Kalam Azad, 22
MR Balaji, 32
MRPS (Dandora) Movement, 140
Mudiraj community, 173
Mulayam Singh, 121
Mumbai, 48
Muralidhar Rao Commission, 200
Muslim community in government jobs, 173
Muslim Corporators, 233
Muslim League, 20, 21, 263
Muslim Women Corporators, 233, 234
Muslims and Indian Christians, 160

N

Nadars of Tamilnadu, 19
Namasudras of Bengal, 19
Nandalal Bose, 17
Naravarepally, 143
Narayana Guru, 187
National Commission for Scheduled Castes, 55
National Democratic Government, 50
National Front Government, 101
National Judicial Appointments Commission, 226
National politics, 20
National Sample Survey, 182, 186
Nawabs, 115
New Dalit Movement, 150
New Economic Policy, 102, 104
New Economic Reforms, 102
New Zealand, 81
Nineteenth century India, 70
Nitish Kumar, 121
Nizam period, 138
Nomadic and Denotified tribes, 168
Nomadic Communities, 174
Nomadic Tribes, 170, 171, 172, 173
Non Brahmin Movement, 250
Non-Brahmin identity, 74
Non-Brahmin ideologues, 74
Non-brahmin movement, 74
Non-Brahmins in South India, 19
Non-Cooperation Movement, 19
Non-Hindu communities, 183
Non-Party Conference, 21

O

Osmania University, 234
Other Backward Classes, 17, 68, 82, 83, 86, 99, 100, 104, 181, 182, 183, 225, 244, 247, 249
Other Backward Classes list, 90

P

P.V. Narsimha Rao's regime, 102
P.V. Narasimha Rao, 121
Pakistan, 81
Pallars, 139
Pandita Ramabai, 53
Parayas, 139
Pareeksha Pe Charcha, 59
Partha Chatterjee, 250
Pashwans, 104
Periyar, 187
Policy of Reservations, 98
Political Reservation, 99
Poona Agreement, 263
Poona Pact, 73, 119, 262
Post Colonial Period, 46
Post-Independence era, 196
Post-independent period, 81
Pre-Independence era, 196
Pre-independent period, 238
Prime Minister Morarji Desai, 209, 246
Princely State of Kolhapur, 165
Princely State of Mysore, 43
Princely states, 81
Privatisation, 106
Provincial elections in December, 22
Public Service Commission, 242
Punjab, 136, 139, 140
Punjab Balmiki Depressed Classes League, 20

Q

Quantum of Reservation, 221
Question of women reservation, 110
Quota-based restrictions, 213

R

R.K. Mukerjee, 122
R.N. Prasad Committee, 255
Rajasthan, 62, 82, 169, 191
Rajendra Prasad, 22, 265

Rajyanga Parirakshana Committee, 144
Ram Manohar Lohia, 120
Ram Singh, 32
Ram Vilas Paswan, 121
Ramachandra Raju Commission, 142
Ramachandran Pillai, 166
Ramaswami Naickar, 19, 66
Rashtriya Janata Dal, 195, 196
Rath Yatra, 101
Ravi Dasis, 104
Religious position of Dalits, 156
Representation and Segregation, 111
Reservation and History, 118
Reservation and sub-classification, 39
Reservation in Ancient period, 238
Reservation Movements in Telangana, 175
Reservation Policy, 47
Reservation policy, 103
Reservation Quota, 189
Reservation System in India, 208
Reservations for Other Backward Classes, 219
Reservations in India, 196
Reservations in private institutions, 219
Revenue collection, 115
Right to Equality, 84
Rohit Vemulas, 62, 129
Roman political thinker, 98
Roster Movement, 60
Round Table Conference, 96, 243
Rural handicrafts, 22

S

Sahuji Maharaj of Kolhapur, 45
Samajwadi Party, 195
Sansad Marg, 61
Sarat Chandra Bose, 20
Sardar Patel, 22
Sathanathan committee, 47
Savitribai Phule, 53, 62
Scheduled Caste, 20
Scheduled Caste certificates, 161
Scheduled Tribe Status, 159
Scholarships for backward classes, 119
Second Backward Classes Commission, 87, 189, 246
Self Respect Movement, 67, 73, 197
Self-Respect Association, 78
Semi-Nomadic Tribe, 172, 173
Shahu Maharaj, 165
Shepherd Community, 171
Sikhism, 158
Simon Commission, 96, 97, 242
Sir Charles Aitchison, 241
Sir Leslie Miller, 118
Slavery was abolished in Travancore, 116
Small scale works, 117
Social Justice, 84, 98
South Asia Books, 36
Soviet Union, 81
Special Backward Class, 170
Special Scheduled Caste Political Conference, 20
Sri lanka, 81
State of Cochin, 116
State of Madras, 101
State Reorganization Commission, 172
State Reservation Act, 170
States of Karnataka, 169
Strong Disapproval, 49
Struggle for Social Justice, 140
Struggle for Survival, 105
Subhas Chandra Bose, 20
Supreme Court judgment, 27

T

T.N. Madan, 122
Tamil Country, 19
Tamil Nadu, 58, 72, 104, 140
Techno-economic power, 117
Tej Bahdur Sapru, 21

Telangana, 169, 200
Telangana Movement, 201
Telugu Desam Party, 200
Telugu Madiga, 140
Temple entry movement, 20
Territorial constituencies, 26
The fifty percent limit, 35
The Roster Movement, 62
Tiruchirappalli, 159
Tirunelveli district, 113
Touchable Hindus, 45
Traditional folklorist community, 173

U

Uma Chakravarti, 56
Union Cabinet, 172
Union Public Service Commission, 190
United Against Hate, 61
United Kingdom, 164
United Progressive Alliance, 153
United States, 23, 155, 212
Unraveling Modinomics, 59
Untouchable castes, 96
Untouchables, 112
Urban Local Government, 232
Uttar Pradesh, 62, 120, 183, 191

V

V.P. Singh, 56, 121
Vaddera community, 173
Valmiki, 139
Valmiki Samaj, 190
Valmikis, 104, 140
Valmikis movement, 136
Vanjari communities, 171
Vedic civilization, 122
Vernacular press, 73
Vice-Chancellors, 127
Victor Premasagar, 155
Vijay Nambiar, 160
Viluvandi journey, 66
Vishwanath Pratap Singh., 186
Vokkaligas and Lingayats, 185
Vote Bank Politics, 197, 198

W

Ward Development Plan, 234
Weak disapproval, 49
Western India, 44
Western Uttar Pradesh, 82
Widow burning, 117
Woman reservation bill, 110
World Bank, 217